Collaborative Language Learning and Teaching

Edited by

David Nunan

CAMBRIDGE
UNIVERSITY PRESS

Published by the Press Syndicate of the University of Cambridge
The Pitt Building, Trumpington Street, Cambridge CB2 1RP
40 West 20th Street, New York, NY 10011–4211, USA
10 Stamford Road, Oakleigh, Melbourne 3166, Australia

© Cambridge University Press 1992

First published 1992
Reprinted 1993

Printed in Great Britain by Bell & Bain Ltd, Glasgow

Library of Congress catalogue card number: 91-35573

A catalogue record for this book is available from the British Library

ISBN 0 521 41687 6 hardback
ISBN 0 521 42701 0 paperback

Collaborative Language Learning and Teaching

6

CAMBRIDGE LANGUAGE TEACHING LIBRARY
A series of authoritative books on the subjects of central importance for all language teachers.

In this series:

Teaching and Learning Languages *by Earl W. Stevick*

Communicating Naturally in a Second Language – Theory and practice in language teaching *by Wilga M. Rivers*

Speaking in Many Tongues – Essays in foreign language teaching *by Wilga M. Rivers*

Teaching the Spoken Language – An approach based on the analysis of conversational English *by Gillian Brown and George Yule*

A Foundation Course for Language Teachers *by Tom McArthur*

Foreign and Second Language Learning – Language-acquisition research and its implications for the classroom *by William Littlewood*

Communicative Methodology in Language Teaching – The roles of fluency and accuracy *by Christopher Brumfit*

The Context of Language Teaching *by Jack C. Richards*

English for Science and Technology – A discourse approach *by Louis Trimble*

Approaches and Methods in Language Teaching – A description and analysis *by Jack C. Richards and Theodore S. Rodgers*

Images and Options in the Language Classroom *by Earl W. Stevick*

Culture Bound – Bridging the cultural gap in language teaching *edited by Joyce Merrill Valdes*

Interactive Language Teaching *edited by Wilga M. Rivers*

Designing Tasks for the Communicative Classroom *by David Nunan*

Second Language Teacher Education *edited by Jack C. Richards and David Nunan*

The Language Teaching Matrix *by Jack C. Richards*

Discourse Analysis for Language Teachers *by Michael McCarthy*

Discourse and Language Education *by Evelyn Hatch*

Research Methods in Language Learning *by David Nunan*

Collaborative Language Learning and Teaching *edited by David Nunan*

Contents

Contents

Acknowledgements

The contributors and publishers would like to thank the following for permission to reproduce copyright material:

Cassell plc for T. Wragg (1984) 'Education for the twenty-first century' p. 19; *Language Teaching* for M. Breen (1987) 'Contemporary paradigms in syllabus design' pp. 208–9; National Centre for English Language Teaching and Research (Sydney) for D. Nunan (1989) *New Arrivals: Initial-Elementary Proficiency. A Curriculum Framework for Adult Second Language Learners* pp. 245–53; Prentice Hall for D. A. Kolb (1984) *Experiential Learning* pp. 2, 14, 16, 17.

Contributors

Kathleen M. Bailey, Monterey Institute of International Studies, California

Roger Budd, Overseas Education Unit, School of Education, University of Leeds

Ted Dale, Monterey Institute of International Studies, California

Donald Freeman, Master of Arts in Teaching Program, School for International Training, Brattleboro, Vermont

Jerry G. Gebhard, Indiana University of Pennsylvania, Indiana, Pennsylvania

Shirley Brice Heath, Stanford University, Stanford, California

Viljo Kohonen, University of Tampere, Finland

Bonnie Meath-Lang, National Technical Institute for the Deaf, Rochester, New York

Bernard Mohan, University of British Columbia, Vancouver, British Columbia

Denise E. Murray, San Jose State University, San Jose, California

David Nunan, National Centre for English Language Teaching and Research, Macquarie University, Sydney, New South Wales

Rafael Ramirez, University of California at Berkeley, California

Nora B. Shannon, National Technical Institute for the Deaf, Rochester, New York

Sandra R. Schecter, Center for the Study of Writing, University of California at Berkeley, California

Sondra Marshall Smith, University of British Columbia, Vancouver, British Columbia

Benjamin Squire, Monterey Institute of International Studies, California

Peter Sturman, British Council, Tokyo

Akiko Ueda-Motonaga, Tokyu Seminar BE, Tokyo

Tony Wright, International Education Centre, College of St Mark and St John, Plymouth

Introduction

David Nunan

The purpose of this introductory chapter is to provide a context for the collection as a whole, as well as to situate collaborative language learning, teaching and research within the sphere of second and foreign language education. While drawing on traditions reaching back to the turn of the century, collaborative teaching and learning have emerged over the last ten years as significant concepts within the field of language education. In doing so, they bring together a number of disparate philosophical perspectives and research traditions. These include humanistic education, experiential learning, systemic-functional linguistics, and psycholinguistically motivated classroom-oriented research. In the rest of this chapter, I shall briefly outline the theoretical and empirical bases which provide a rationale for collaborative teaching and learning. In the first part, I shall examine the effect of collaboration on the learning process, pointing out links between contributions to the volume and related work on psychology and education. In the second section, links will be drawn between the chapters in this book which deal primarily with teaching, and relevant research in the educational literature. The chapter concludes with a series of key questions relating to collaborative research, learning and teaching, along with an indication of where the reader might look for answers.

In language education, teachers, learners, researchers and curriculum specialists can collaborate for a number of reasons. They may wish to experiment with alternative ways of organising teaching and learning; they may be concerned with promoting a philosophy of cooperation rather than competition; they may wish to create an environment in which learners, teachers and researchers are teaching and learning from each other in an equitable way (a trend which is enhanced by the growing interest in action research); or they may wish to experiment with ways of incorporating principles of learner-centredness into their programs. All of these motives are reflected in one way or another in the chapters in this collection, each of which deals with some aspect of collaborative learning, teaching, research, teacher education or curriculum development in second and foreign language education.

The chapters are grouped into two principal sections. The first of these focusses on the learner, while the second focusses on the teacher. I have organised the collection in this way as much for convenience as anything else, and readers will note that in most chapters discussion is not confined solely to the principal point of focus. Thus contributions to the section on learning must of necessity deal with teaching, and indeed with research, while chapters in the section on teaching deal also with learning and research. All contributions contain implications for teacher education and curriculum development.

The learning process

Humanistic psychology has had an influence on language education in a number of respects. It provides a rationale for several of the more prominent methods such as Community Language Learning, the Silent Way and Suggestopedia (although it could be argued that as they are practised, some of these methods are anything but humane!). It has also influenced curriculum theorising, particularly learner-oriented approaches to curriculum development. The influence of humanism on experiential learning is also traced by Kohonen in this collection who argues (see page 14) that: 'In experiential learning, immediate personal experience is seen as the focal point for learning, giving "life, texture, and subjective personal meaning to abstract concepts and at the same time providing a concrete, publicly shared reference point for testing the implications and validity of ideas created during the learning process" (Kolb 1984: 21).'

In empirical investigations of the subjective meaning brought by learners to the learning process, researchers have found that learners are different and learn in different ways (Willing 1988). It has been argued that these differences should be reflected at the level of methodology in the selection of learning experiences. At each stage in the curriculum process, be it planning, implementation or evaluation, information about learners (and, where feasible, from learners) will be used to guide the selection of content, learning experiences and the means of assessing outcomes.

> [A learner-centred] curriculum will contain similar elements to those contained in traditional curriculum development, that is, planning (including needs analysis, goal and objective setting), implementation (including methodology and materials development) and evaluation (see, for example, Hunkins 1980). However, the key difference between learner-centred and traditional curriculum development is that, in the former, the curriculum is a collaborative effort between teachers and learners, since learners are closely involved in the decision-making process regarding the content of the curriculum and how it is taught.

> This change in orientation has major practical implications for the entire curriculum process, since a negotiated curriculum cannot be introduced and managed in the same way as one which is prescribed by the teacher or teaching institutions. In particular, it places the burden for all aspects of curriculum development on the teacher.
>
> (Nunan 1988: 2)

In this collection, the chapter by Budd and Wright provides a case study of what happens when a group of learners are involved collaboratively in programme planning and implementation. Nunan describes a large-scale curriculum renewal project involving the collaborative efforts of teachers, learners and curriculum specialists. Despite the problems and difficulties involved it was found that collaboration encouraged learners:

- to learn about learning, to learn better and
- to increase their awareness about language, and about self, and hence about learning;
- to develop, as a result, metacommunicative as well as communicative skills;
- to confront, and come to terms with, the conflicts between individual needs and group needs, both in social, procedural terms as well as linguistic, content terms;
- to realise that content and method are inextricably linked, and
- to recognise the decision-making tasks themselves as genuine communicative activities.

In practical terms, collaborative learning entails students working together to achieve common learning goals (see Slavin 1983; Sharan *et al.* 1984). It stands in contrast with competitive learning. (Although, of course, collaboration and competition can coexist in the same classroom; for example, when learners work collaboratively with some learners in a small group, but competitively against other learners in other groups.) Recent empirical work in literacy instruction has supported the theoretically motivated arguments in favour of cooperative learning. In two investigations into the efficacy of cooperative approaches to reading and writing instruction in third- and fourth-grade classrooms, as opposed to traditional instruction, Stevens, Madden, Slavin and Farnish (1987) found that students working in cooperative groups significantly outperformed those receiving traditional instruction on standardised measures of reading comprehension, reading vocabulary, language mechanics, language expression and spelling. They also performed better on writing sample and oral reading measures (see also Stevens, Slavin and Farnish 1991). In foreign language instruction, Bejarano (1987) assessed the effects of two small-group cooperative techniques and a whole-class method on the academic achievement of 665 seventh-grade pupils. It was found that students in both small-group methods significantly outperformed students in the whole-class method. The researcher concludes from the investigation that the findings 'support the link between the communicative approach to foreign language instruction and cooperative learning in small groups. The study demonstrates how to forge a link between the content and the process of instruction' (Bejarano 1987: 483).

Cooperative learning is also supported by recent research inspired by process-oriented models of second language acquisition. This research has focussed on the question: what patterns of classroom organisation and types of classroom tasks are most beneficial for language acquisition? It has been argued that those tasks in which learners are required to negotiate meaning among themselves in the course of completing an interactive task are particularly suited to language development (for a review of this research, see Larsen-Freeman and Long 1991; Long 1981; Nunan 1989a).

The need to augment this research agenda with studies informed by a social view of language development forms the point of departure for the study by Mohan and Smith in this volume. Their research complements recent work by Bassano and Christison (1988), among others, who see the development of cooperative learning techniques in ESL classrooms as an important element in successful classroom management. Bassano and Christison point out that there are at least three areas in which cooperative learning can figure. These are: '(1) classroom environment and social tasks; (2) process tasks such as peer tutoring and goal setting; and (3) progress monitoring and evaluative tasks.' They make several practical suggestions for increasing the amount of cooperative learning in each of these areas. In their view, classroom environment and social tasks are perhaps the areas which lend themselves most readily to cooperation. They suggest that learners can take partial or full responsibility for the following: arranging classroom furniture before class; keeping attendance records; decorating bulletin boards and the classroom; carrying out classroom maintenance, setting up equipment for films; handing out and replacing materials; collecting money for coffee-break supplies; generating advice on disciplinary matters; making announcements and signalling when breaks are over; welcoming and greeting new students and introducing them to class routines. Students can also be involved in curriculum work such as the selection of tasks, goal setting, and materials development. Monitoring and evaluation is the last area where learners can be encouraged to collaborate through tasks such as self-assessment and progress monitoring charts.

The research on collaborative as opposed to competitive learning has generally been positive. According to Good and Brophy (1987) 41 studies are reported in the literature. Of these, 26 found significantly greater learning in classes using cooperative methods, 14 were not significant, and only one found significantly greater learning in a control group. It would seem from the studies that it is the reward structure rather than the task structure which accounts for these findings. Good and Brophy go on to suggest that:

> There is no evidence that group competition offers advantages over other cooperative learning methods so long as arrangements are made to provide specific group rewards based on the cumulative performance of individual group members. . . . although the effects of cooperative learning on achievement appear to be basically motivational, the key is not motivation to win competitions against other teams but motivation to assist one's teammates to meet their individual goals and thus insure that the team as a whole will do well.

(Good and Brophy 1987: 437–8)

The theoretical, empirical and practical advantages of cooperative learning have been aptly summarised by Slavin in the following manner:

> . . . the research done up to the present has shown enough positive effects of cooperative learning, on a variety of outcomes, to force us to re-examine traditional instructional practices. We can no longer ignore the potential power of the peer group, perhaps the one remaining free resource for improving schools. We can no longer see the class as 30 or more individuals whose only instructionally useful interactions are with the teacher, where peer interactions are unstructured or off-task. On the other hand, at least for achievement, we now know that simply allowing students to work together is unlikely to capture the power of the peer group to motivate students to perform.

(Slavin 1983: 128)

The teaching process

Although collaborative and team approaches to teaching have been around for many years, there is comparatively little literature on the subject. Most of what one hears remains anecdotal. Some years ago, in a large-scale investigation of the curriculum practices of some 800 teachers (reported in Nunan 1988), teachers nominated team teaching as a highly favoured option in their professional practice. However, when it came to documenting the collaborative practices of the teachers, very few of them had anything to report. In a major review of team teaching and academic achievement, Armstrong (1977), lists the following five strengths of collaborative teaching approaches to pedagogy (see also W. L. Rutherford 1975):

1. Team teaching permits team members to take advantage of individual teacher strengths in planning for instruction and in working with learners.
2. Team teaching spurs creativity because teachers know they must teach for their colleagues as well as for their learners.
3. Team teaching facilitates individualized instruction because it is possible to provide learning environments involving close personal contact between teacher and learner.
4. Team teaching provides for better sequencing and pacing of increments of instruction because perceptions of an individual teacher must be verified by at least one other team member.
5. Team teaching builds program continuity over time. Team teaching programs abide. Specific teachers within a team do not.

(Armstrong 1977: 60)

There have been numerous studies carried out to evaluate the effectiveness of collaborative teaching, and the results make interesting reading. In primary/elementary classrooms, reading and language skills were significantly enhanced by team teaching in four out of six instances. Ten studies reported no significant differences. In secondary classrooms, five studies reported significant differences for collaborative approaches. There are no reported instances of single-teacher instruction resulting in significantly better test scores. In general, then, the studies favour collaborative classrooms, although, like most empirical research, the implications are not particularly clear-cut, and some of the outcomes are open to question. Most of the studies are small-scale and conducted over a limited period of time. In addition, the criterion measure is generally success on a standardised achievement measure. Not all teachers would agree that such scores should be the only or even the most important measure of educational success. (For a review of this and other research, see Armstrong 1977; Good and Brophy 1987.)

The most important implication of this research is that for collaborative teaching to be effective, teachers need appropriate training and support. It is insufficient simply to throw teachers together without giving them opportunities for developing the skills they need for success. They also need adequate time to plan their programs as well as opportunities to review their teaching. There is sufficient evidence, both in the existing literature and in the studies in this volume to suggest that, as a pedagogical innovation, collaborative teaching can only hope to succeed if:

- teachers possess or are given skills appropriate to the innovation;
- teachers are given time to implement the innovation;
- appropriate administrative and managerial arrangements and mechanisms are developed in tandem with the pedagogical innovation.

An important characteristic of this volume is that all of the chapters apart from Kohonen's, are data based. Further, the research has resulted from projects which have been conjointly carried out by teachers and learners as well as researchers. As such, they provide a model and an exemplification of the philosophy pervading the collection. Of particular note is the involvement of the practitioner in research. Such collaboration can help bridge the gap between theory and practice, and increases the likelihood that research outcomes will actually find some sort of realisation in the classroom itself (Kemmis and McTaggart 1987; Nunan 1989b). In calling for a greater role for teachers Beasley and Riordan observe that:

> ... the gulf between research bodies and the teaching profession has ensured that many research programmes are not related to professional concerns and interests of teachers and students. Priorities for research too often reflect the interests of academic researchers or central office administrators not school people. Teachers and students in the classroom are rarely actively engaged in the research. Within the experimental framework the researcher protects his or her independence for the sake of 'objectivity'. The tacit knowledge of teachers is devalued. Many of the findings are recorded in a form and style which is accessible to the trained researcher but fails to communicate to teachers, school administrators, parents or advisory people. The primary audience for research has been the research community not the practising teacher. Not surprisingly, we the practising teachers have come to distrust and reject theoretical research and the researcher who takes but does not give.

(Beasley and Riordan 1981: 60)

Insofar as they stimulate teachers to observe and reflect on their professional practice, the sorts of collaborative engagements by teachers with learners, colleagues, researchers and curriculum developers described in this volume represent a valuable form of professional development. It also reflects a philosophical shift as we move 'from a period of "teacher training," characterised by approaches which view teacher preparation as familiarising student teachers with techniques and skills to apply in the classroom, to "teacher education," characterised by approaches that involve teachers in developing theories of teaching, understanding the nature of teacher decision making, and strategies for critical self-awareness and self-evaluation' (Richards and Nunan 1990). This view of professional development as a matter of developing internal rather than external criteria for judging the worth of what we do as teachers entails different roles for the teacher educator and for teacher education. The collaborative rather than directive nature of teacher education is captured by Freeman (1989):

> Through development, the collaborator works to trigger the teacher's awareness of what the latter is doing. By asking questions, by making observations in a detached way, by sharing personal teaching experience, the collaborator endeavors to start the teacher on a process of reflection, critique, and refinement of the teacher's classroom practice . . . development is a far less predictable or directed strategy than training. It is highly dependent on the individual teacher, the collaborator and their interaction. Because the collaborator's role is to trigger change through the teacher's awareness, rather than to intervene directly as in training, the changes that result from development cannot be foreseen or expected within a designated time period.
>
> (Freeman 1989: 40–1)

Discussion

In this Introduction, I have provided a rationale for collaborative learning and teaching. I have described the philosophical and ideological antecedents to the movement, as well as sketching out some of the more significant research outcomes to be found in the educational and language teaching literature. The main aim of the Introduction is to provide signposts for what is to come, and the various themes and issues canvassed here are taken up and elaborated in the chapters which follow. I should like to conclude by indicating the central questions and issues which emerge in the course of the book.

In relation to research

- What are the central characteristics of a collaborative approach to classroom research, and in what ways do the different contributions of teachers, learners and researchers provide us with insights which would be difficult to obtain in any other way? (The issue of the differential contributions of teacher, learner and researcher are central to the chapters by Heath, Freeman, Mohan and Smith, Budd and Wright, and Nunan.)

- What are appropriate theoretical models of language and learning for informing collaborative research? (Not surprisingly, linguistic models, such as that provided by Halliday (1985), which incorporate a social dimension or which integrate social and psychological approaches to language and learning are favoured by the authors in the collection. Such models are referred to explicitly by Kohonen, Heath, Freeman, Mohan and Smith, and Murray. Kohonen, Heath, and Freeman also point out the complex interplay between the social/interpersonal and cognitive/intrapersonal dimensions of language learning and use.)
- What are appropriate research methods, tools and techniques for collaborative investigations? (All of the contributions to the collection provide rich descriptive and interpretive accounts of language learning and teaching. The range of research techniques reported include participant observation, lesson transcripts and protocols (written records of learner language), ethnographic narratives, case studies, diaries and journals, questionnaires and interviews.)

In relation to learning

- What classroom tasks and patterns of organisation facilitate cooperative learning? (Numerous practical suggestions and ideas are outlined by Kohonen, Heath, Mohan and Smith, and Murray.)
- In what way is context an important element in language learning? (Contextualised learning, teaching and research underlies most of the contributions to this book, and is dealt with at some length by Heath, Mohan and Smith, and Murray.)

In relation to teaching

- What are the advantages and disadvantages of team teaching? (For case studies of team teaching, see Shannon and Meath-Lang, Sturman, and Bailey, Dale and Squire.)
- What organisational patterns underlie successful collaborative teaching? (This question is dealt with by Shannon and Meath-Lang, and Bailey, Dale and Squire.)
- How can the notion of the extended professional be realised through a collaborative approach to teacher education? (The use of action research (i.e. the process of teachers identifying problems, formulating these as research questions, collecting relevant data, and interpreting and acting on them) is described by Kohonen, Schecter and Ramirez, and Nunan. Gebhard and Ueda-Motonaga argue for a collaborative approach to teacher supervision.)

Conclusion

From the studies in this collection, the following conclusions emerge:

1. Cooperative learning provides a viable, and in many contexts, a more effective alternative to the competitive ethic which dominates much educational thinking today.
2. Learning, teaching and research can be enhanced by an extension and redefinition of the role relationships of learners, teachers and researchers. In particular, teachers can be researchers and learners can embrace the roles of researcher and teacher.
3. Team teaching is a difficult, but not impossible, mode of organising teaching and learning, even in cultural contexts where such modes are largely unknown, and the benefits for teachers and learners far outweigh the extra effort involved.
4. In order to understand and appreciate the complexities of the language classroom, it is important to study processes of teaching and learning where they actually occur, that is, in the classroom itself.
5. Teachers, learners, researchers and teacher educators all have different voices. It is important for modes of teaching, learning, and research to evolve in which all of these voices can be heard.

In this chapter, I have made numerous references to teaching and research in content classrooms. By making reference to collaborative research in classrooms where subjects other than language are taught, I hope that I have situated language learning within the broader context of the educational mainstream. There is a great deal of theory, research and practice within this mainstream which speaks directly to the concerns of the language teacher, researcher, curriculum developer and teacher educator and it is vitally important that this work guide and inform what happens in the language classroom.

Part I   Focus on learning

The chapters in this section of the collection all focus primarily on the learner, although there are extensive cross-references to teachers and researchers.

The initial chapter, by Kohonen, is an important position statement on experiential learning. A central notion in this theory is learner education, which emphasises the importance of helping learners to develop an awareness of their learning in terms of three types of knowledge: (1) their self-concept and view of their role as a learner; (2) the process of learning; and (3) the learning task. It thus belongs within the philosophy of learner-centred instruction which advocates a twin focus on the language content and the learning process. Focussing on the learning process through awareness-raising tasks can empower learners by helping them to identify their own preferred ways of learning, and also assisting them to monitor their own learning. Cooperative learning in mixed-ability teams provides a major pedagogical structure for working toward such goals. This orientation entails a paradigmatic shift from the transmission model of teaching to a process-oriented, participatory model, seeing learners as active agents in their learning and teachers as researchers of their work.

The study by Heath picks up and extends some of the themes and issues articulated by Kohonen. In particular, it illustrates the enormous potential which is released in teachers, students and researchers when they work together toward a common goal. The body of the chapter is devoted to two case studies which show how the combined talents of teacher, student and researcher redefine our notions of literacy. Jerome Bruner reminds us that 'Learning is most often figuring out how to use what you already know in order to go beyond what you currently think' (1983a: 183). In this study, students, teachers and researchers working together play out Bruner's insight into learning. The author argues that the attempt to reduce students' uncertainties about language should not come through teacher imposition of rules of grammar and occasions for practised drills of decontextualised and depersonalised tasks. Instead, together, students, teacher, and researcher can focus on what students already know to accomplish a joint reduction of the uncertainties of language. With such collaborative work, we can all better appreciate that a single piece of evidence of language use touches a world of

11

antecedents and assumptions; if we follow these beginnings, they will lead us to the centres of social and cognitive worlds about which we can best learn together.

The chapter by Freeman is a valuable addition to the language teaching literature because it represents a genuine process study of a classroom in action, and such studies of learning processes, rather than outcomes, are difficult to find. Freeman began with the question: 'How does the teacher define what can or cannot go on in her teaching – how are the boundaries of possibility constructed and negotiated through the talk and activity of the teacher's work?' During the course of the investigation the focus shifted, and the question became: 'How are authority and control distributed, through pedagogy and interaction, to build a shared understanding of the target language?' This shift in focus reflected the interaction of data and analysis, and is not untypical of qualitative research (Kirk and Miller 1986). Through his interpretive analysis of the data, which consist of lesson transcripts, field notes and interviews with teachers and learners, Freeman is able to demonstrate how collaboration and self-regulation are important constructs in building an understanding of the ways in which learners come to control the target language. In keeping with most of the papers in this volume, Freeman's study highlights those social and interpersonal aspects of language learning which are often randomised out of the language learning equation in psychometric research. In addition, it provides an excellent model of the collaborative relationship between teacher and researcher, and demonstrates how, through the provision of multiple perspectives on the teaching/learning process, the teacher's and learners' voices can be added to that of the researcher.

Mohan and Smith investigate how a group of Chinese students manage to succeed in a graduate education program, despite the fact that their language proficiency is below the required level. Like the study by Freeman, this investigation shows the importance of 'language socialisation' to language development, and underlines the inadequacy of language models which fail to incorporate a social dimension. It also provides an alternative conceptualisation of 'task' to that normally provided within the second language acquisition literature. In keeping with the central theme of this volume, the study demonstrates the way in which the cooperative interaction between instructor and learners enables the learners to 'outperform their competence'.

In the final contribution to this section, Murray looks at collaborative writing as a literacy event. The chapter is based on a descriptive and interpretive account of a group of ESL professionals going about the task of producing texts about their professional work. This provides a basis, and a rationale, for the teaching of second language writing. In particular, Murray questions the notion that learning to write must necessarily be an isolated, individual process, and proposes an alternative strategy in which learners are required to collaborate, in the same way as the native speaker model, in order for the writing task to be completed successfully. The chapter concludes with suggestions for implementing real collaborative writing in the ESL classroom. These include group report writing, jigsaw writing, teacher-mediated joint-text construction, and collaborative writing conferences.

Despite their diverse contexts and concerns, a number of common themes emerge quite strongly from these chapters. In particular, the studies reported in this section show that:

- learners are an important resource for their own collective learning, and this resource can be accessed through collaboration, cooperation and experiential learning;
- learning is a social as well as a psychological process;
- interpretive, ethnographic accounts provide rich data on language learning and teaching;
- collaborative learning can help learners use what they already know to go beyond what they currently think.

1 Experiential language learning: second language learning as cooperative learner education

Viljo Kohonen

> Motto: Anything that a child should do and
> can do, and we do for them takes away an
> opportunity to learn responsibility.
>
> **Gene Bedley**

The purpose of this chapter is to provide a theoretical and empirical justification for experiential language learning, and to justify the incorporation of cooperative learner education into language programs. In the first part of the chapter a theory of experiential learning is presented. This is followed by a detailed justification for the adoption of an experiential approach to language learning. The chapter then deals with learner training, and its incorporation into language programs. In the final part, principles of cooperative learning are set out and discussed.

An outline of the theory of experiential learning

What is experiential learning?

The foundations of experiential learning can be traced back to Dewey's progressive approach, Lewin's social psychology, Jean Piaget's work on developmental cognitive psychology, Kelly's cognitive theory of personality, and to humanistic psychology, notably the work of Maslow and Rogers.

In experiential learning, immediate personal experience is seen as the focal point for learning, giving 'life, texture, and subjective personal meaning to abstract concepts and at the same time providing a concrete, publicly shared reference point for testing the implications and validity of ideas created during the learning process' (Kolb 1984: 21). But experience also needs to be processed consciously by reflecting on it. Learning is thus seen as a cyclic process integrating immediate experience, reflection, abstract conceptualization and action.

A good starting point for the discussion of experiential learning is provided by Kelly's theory of personal constructs (1955). Kelly's basic

This chapter is based on an earlier publication (Kohonen 1989).

14

assumption is that individuals make sense of the world through constructs which they have developed for themselves over a long period of time. People function in terms of their expectations about future events, making plans on the basis of expected outcomes. They are active and responsible participants, not passive responders, making choices based on reality as they perceive it. Personal constructs thus suggest a proactive rather than a reactive system.

The importance of personal experiences for the growth of personality is similarly prominent in humanistic psychology. Thus Rogers (1975) argues that the individual's self-concept is a social product that is shaped gradually through interaction with the environment. It is an organized, integrated pattern of self-related perceptions, which become increasingly differentiated and complex. The development of a healthy self-concept is promoted by a positive self-regard and an unconditional acceptance by the 'significant others'. In an environment of unconditional positive self-regard, the individual can progress towards becoming a fully functioning person. This process of change is characterized by a widening range of human experience: an awareness of one's own feelings, an openness to new experiences, tolerance, a basic trust in others, and an ability to listen to them empathically and perceive their feelings.

Rogers argues, like Kelly, that one responds to events in accordance with how one perceives and interprets them. This thinking entails what have been called 'self-fulfilling prophecies' (cf. Rosenthal and Jacobson 1968; Rosenthal and Rubin 1978): anticipations of future events will affect one's choices and may thereby lead to anticipated outcomes. In order to break a negative chain of anticipations, one needs help to enhance one's self-concept and thereby change one's perceptions of the future.

In the light of this discussion, the importance for personal growth of learning experiences in school deserves serious attention. Emphasis on the learning process is not, of course, a novelty in education. Good teachers have probably always realized the importance of the process for the product. Experiential learning theory, however, invites conscious attention to the importance of the learners' subjective experiences, attitudes and feelings about their own learning. As learners undertake learning tasks, they compare their task performance with the projected outcome. Such comparisons yield learning experiences, which may be positive or negative. The learning experiences gained in the process of learning will have a cumulative effect on the development of the learners' cognitive and affective characteristics, their views of themselves as learners. If we can help learners to improve their views of themselves as learners they may become better learners, able to utilize their learning potential more fully.

A model of experiential learning

Kolb (1984: 42) advances a general theoretical model of experiential learning as follows:

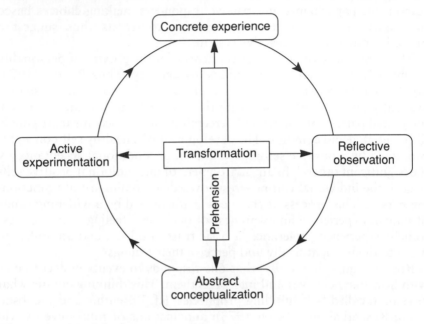

Figure 1   Model of experiential learning

According to this model, learning is essentially seen as a process of resolution of conflicts between two dialectically opposed dimensions, called the *prehension* and *transformation* dimensions.

1. The *prehension* dimension refers to the way in which the individual grasps experience. This dimension can be seen as two modes of knowing, ranging from what Kolb calls grasping via 'apprehension' to what he calls grasping via 'comprehension'. Apprehension is instant, intuitive knowledge without a need for rational inquiry or analytical confirmation. The other end of the dimension, grasping via comprehension, on the other hand, emphasizes the role of conscious learning, whereby comprehension introduces order and predictability to the flow of unconscious sensations. This dimension is thus concerned with the ways of grasping reality through varying degrees of emphasis on unconscious and conscious learning.

2. The *transformation* dimension, on the other hand, refers to the transformation of experience by an orientation towards reflective observation as against action and active experimentation. An indi-

vidual with an active orientation is ready to take risks, attempting to maximize success and showing little concern for errors or failure. An individual with an excessive reflective orientation, on the other hand, may be willing to sacrifice successful performance in order to avoid errors, preferring to transform experiences through reflective observation.

(Kolb 1984: 42–60)

The polar ends of the two dimensions will thus yield four orientations to learning:

1. *Concrete experience*, with an involvement in personal experiences and an emphasis on feeling over thinking. This is an 'artistic' orientation relying on intuitive decision-making.
2. *Abstract conceptualisation*, using logic and a systematic approach to problem-solving, with an emphasis on thinking, manipulation of abstract symbols and a tendency to neat and precise conceptual systems.
3. *Reflective observation*, focussing on understanding the meaning of ideas and situations by careful observation, being concerned with how things happen by attempting to see them from different perspectives and relying on one's own thoughts, feelings and judgement.
4. *Active experimentation*, with an emphasis on practical applications and getting things done, influencing people and changing situations, and taking risks in order to accomplish things.

(Kolb 1984: 68–9)

Experiential learning is seen as a four-stage cycle combining all of these orientations. Thus simple everyday experience is not sufficient for learning. It must also be observed and analyzed consciously. Only experience that is reflected upon seriously will yield its full measure of learning, and reflection must in turn be followed by testing new hypotheses in order to obtain further experience. It can be argued, in fact, that theoretical concepts will not become part of the individual's frame of reference until they have been experienced meaningfully on a subjective emotional level. Reflection plays an important role in this process by providing a bridge, as it were, between experience and theoretical conceptualization. The process of learning is seen as the recycling of experience at deeper levels of understanding and interpretation. This view entails the idea of lifelong learning.

Self-directed learning

An important notion in experiential learning is that of intrinsic motivation and self-directed learning. Learners are encouraged to see themselves as increasingly competent and self-determined and to assume more and more responsibility for their own learning. Intrinsic motivation:

1. satisfies needs such as belonging, acceptance, satisfaction from work, self-actualization, power and self-control;
2. manifests itself primarily in the form of feelings, e.g. feelings of success and competence;
3. is connected with work, involving feelings of relevance of work, satisfaction derived from work, feelings of progress and achievement, and feelings of growth as a person.

By designing learning experiences that can promote such feelings it is possible, at least to some extent, to enhance learners' feelings of self-direction.

Accordingly, learners will find school motivating to the extent that it satisfies their needs. Satisfying work gives them feelings of belonging, sharing, power, importance and freedom regarding what to do, and it is also fun. If they feel no sense of belonging to their school and no sense of commitment, caring and concern, they lose their interest in learning. Glasser (1986) notes that discipline problems are less likely to occur in classes in which learners' needs are satisfied and where they have a sense of importance allowing them to feel accepted and significant. This suggests that school learning might be structured in a way that is conducive to learner commitment and is need-fulfilling for them. As a pedagogical solution he suggests the use of cooperative learning techniques, or learning teams as he calls them. A well-functioning team is a need-fulfilling structure that leads to successful learning.

Why experiential learning?

The justification for experiential learning can be based on the following arguments: (1) it facilitates personal growth; (2) it helps learners adapt to social change; (3) it takes account of differences in learning ability; and (4) it responds to learner needs and practical pedagogical considerations. These arguments are examined briefly in this section.

AN AID TO PERSONAL GROWTH

Becoming a person entails an increasing capacity to assume responsibility for what one does. Personal awareness and responsibility are also necessary for the development of self-directed, autonomous learning. Autonomy can be defined as a willingness and ability to make up one's mind about what is right or wrong, independent of external authority, but it does not mean individualism and a neglect of the social context.

Personal decisions are necessarily made with respect to social and moral norms, traditions and expectations. Autonomy thus includes the notion of interdependence, that is, being responsible for one's conduct in the social context: being able to cooperate with others and solve conflicts in constructive ways. Its development can be seen as an open-ended dimension involving both personal, social and moral education. The task of education is to facilitate the developme... of the learner towards being a 'fuller' person with the capacity to reason, to feel and to act responsibly. The capacity to understand others and relate to them in meaningful ways is an integral part of personal growth (cf. Pring 1984: 72–5).

ADAPTING TO SOCIAL CHANGE

As education is also future-oriented it is important for educators to have a vision of the demands of social developments on school education. It is advisable to ask what kinds of skills and knowledge the school might aim to give learners during their obligatory education in order to prepare them to live in a society about which we can only make some predictions at the moment. What we do know is that Western society has undergone a rapid social and technological change during the past few decades, and the process is likely to continue.

The implications of change for school education have been outlined in the following manner by Wragg (1984):

- While we cannot know everything, we must know something. This implies an idea of a core of knowledge.
- With regard to knowledge expansion and the possibility of multi-media libraries, it will be important to be able to utilize existing information services and discover things independently. This emphasizes the importance of being able to use information by making critical choices and fostering a spirit of inquiry and independence.
- People must learn to work in teams and pool their expertise for common benefit. If a great deal of human endeavor involves collaboration, we might make sure that children learn to help each other in group work and share out the work and responsibility fairly, learning to get along with their fellows.
- Increasing leisure time will necessitate new demands for personal creativity, imagination and inventive thinking. This means an emphasis on developing one's personality in the spirit of lifelong education and using leisure time in humanly valuable ways.

Consequently, social, interpersonal and learning skills and attitudes will become increasingly important. To serve such needs, Wragg suggests a multi-dimensional view of the curriculum which will foster:

- – creativity: capacity for imaginative and inventive thinking;
- – social and interpersonal skills: ability for cooperative work;
- – learning skills: capacity for autonomous learning.

It is thus interesting to note that the educational values and attitudes that seem to be conducive to a healthy personal growth also seem to be appropriate to the new developments in society.

DIFFERENCES IN LEARNING ABILITY

It is a commonplace that children without any severe learning impediments will become functionally competent in any second language, given sufficient exposure to it in a naturalistic environment in which it is used as a medium of communication. They can thus become bilingual without formal school instruction. In classroom-learning situations, however, there appear to be great differences in the talent for second (or foreign) language learning: some learn languages quite easily and rapidly, while others need more time, and some seem to have little ability even if they make a serious effort.

Since the mid-1970s, with the advent of cognitive psychology, there has been a shift of attention away from seeing individual differences as relatively stable genetic differences to seeing them largely as differences in information processing. Cognitive psychology is concerned with the mental processes that contribute to cognitive task performance: information processing in memory, how knowledge is stored and retrieved, what strategies are employed when solving problems, and how such strategies can be learned and monitored consciously.

Comprehension is regarded as an active process of constructing mental representations of meanings by anticipating message contents. The models of communicative competence generally include the notion of strategic competence, referring to the ability to process language data in real time and under the constraints of a limited short-term memory. An important way of saving time is to anticipate what will come next in discourse by making quick meaning-based predictions. Such predictions are based on schemata, which can be understood as configurations of interrelated features that define concepts, and which provide a generalized framework to which new information can be integrated. Schemata consist of more situation-specific scripts that contain knowledge of goals, participants and procedures in various real-life situations (e.g. expected ways of behaving in school, home, supermarket, restaurant, etc.).

Fluent language use requires the ability to identify and select suitable schemata and scripts in communication. The learner is seen as an active organizer of incoming information with a limited processing capacity. He or she imposes cognitive schemata on the data in an effort to organize it. But the development of fluency also requires that low-level language processes (such as recognition of graphic and phonological patterns, some syntactic aspects) are automatized, thereby freeing portions of working memory to deal with new learning associations. In an important sense, second language development is also a matter of a gradual automatization of sub-skills to release processing capacity for more demanding tasks. (Cf. Sternberg 1985; McLaughlin 1987; O'Malley and Chamot 1990.)

If some learners, then, can process second language data more quickly than others, there is a need to release learners from the necessity to work all at the same rate, as has been the case in traditional teacher-centered, frontal instruction. This suggests the need for more flexible learning arrangements whereby fast learners are encouraged to take on more demanding learning tasks than slow learners and work for both accurate and fluent communication skills. They can thus aim at both quantitatively and qualitatively higher standards of language use than slow learners. But this does not need to imply permanent ability grouping of learners. Such differing aims can also be accommodated within a basically heterogeneous, mixed-ability class using cooperative learning techniques and individual learning contracts negotiated between teacher and learners.

PRACTICAL REASONS

For adult learners in particular, more practical arguments for self-directed learning include greater flexibility for people who may not be able to attend classes for various reasons (work, disability, distance from institutions, unavailability of tuition). The skills, initiative and courage to work independently to learn on one's own and in suitable small groups is thus highly beneficial for adult learners. The school would seem to do a good service to young learners by helping them to learn the necessary skills of planning, monitoring and assessing their own learning while still in school (cf. Dickinson 1987).

Towards second language learning as learner education[1]

The above discussion suggests three areas of knowledge and awareness in experiential learning which supplement each other: (1) personal growth; (2) the learning process; and (3) the learning task (knowledge, skills, etc.). These areas can be seen as the three angles of a triangle that constitutes the notion of language learning as learner education. Experiential learning can be seen as the mode of learning within the triangle, emphasizing the need to reconcile intuitive experience with various ways of conceptualizing it. This can be presented by the following diagram:

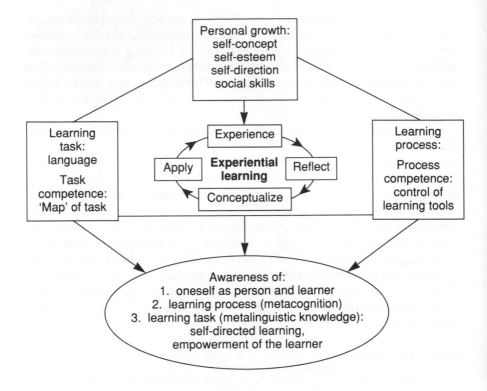

Figure 2   Second language learning as learner education

As the figure suggests, developing the learner's awareness of all of these aspects of learning is seen as a way of empowering the learner to be a more competent person and learner.

Language learning and personal growth

The influence of affective personality factors on language learning is difficult to isolate for valid and reliable measurement, but there is consistent evidence to suggest that learning attitude and motivation are important predictors of achievement. As noted above, intrinsic motivation is an important element in experiential learning. It can be seen as a general drive towards competence, self-direction and self-determination. It contains three primary dimensions:

– a desire for challenge;
– a desire for independent mastery;
– curiosity or interest.

If people's perceptions and feelings of competence are enhanced, their intrinsic motivation will be increased. Language learners need positive experiences of what (and how much, in fact, even at the elementary stages) they *can* do with their language communicatively. Such feelings of success will increase their self-confidence. In an important sense it can thus be argued that competence develops through confidence. The development of competence also entails an internalization of the criteria for success. This is fostered by teaching that encourages the learner's self-assessment of his or her own learning, both alone and with peers in cooperative learning groups.

The learners' view of themselves as language learners and their self-concept and self-esteem are thus important characteristics that correlate with successful second language learning. Language learning requires the ability and courage to cope with the unknown, to tolerate ambiguity and, in a sense, to appear childish and make a fool of oneself when making mistakes. A person with a reasonably balanced self-concept can cope with these demands better. This point is emphasized by Stern (1983: 380), who suggests that a person who is ready to accept with tolerance and patience the frustrations of ambiguity is in a better position to cope with them than a student who feels frustrated in ambiguous situations.

Such tolerance is particularly necessary in the early stage of second language learning, which is bound to involve unpredictability, novelty and insolubility because of the new linguistic system. New learning and understanding are always potentially threatening. Learners with high self-esteem are less likely to feel threatened. Confident persons have the advantage of not fearing unfamiliar situations or rejection as much as those with high anxiety levels, and are therefore more likely to take risks and try new and unpredictable experiences. Cognitive factors are thus not the only ones that matter in second language learning. As Stern (1983: 386) points out, the affective component contributes at least as much as and often more to language learning than the cognitive skills represented by aptitude assessment.

Self-direction and knowledge of the learning process

Self-direction describes an attitude to learning, where the learner assumes increasing responsibility for the decisions concerning his or her learning but does not necessarily undertake the implementation of all of those decisions alone.[2] There are various degrees of self-direction depending on the learner's attitude and ability to organize and manage his or her learning. There is thus a continuum between other-directed and self-directed learning involving a range of possibilities between the extremes. To the extent that the learner is able to undertake learning tasks without direct teacher control he or she displays various degrees of autonomy. A fully autonomous learner is totally responsible for making the decisions, implementing them and assessing the outcomes without any teacher involvement. The development of such independence is a question of enabling learners to manage their own learning. They need to gain an understanding of language learning in order to be able to develop their skills consciously and to organize their learning tasks. Learners need not see themselves as consumers of language courses; they can also become producers of their own learning (Holec 1987).

Raising the awareness of one's own learning and gaining an understanding of the processes involved is thus an important key for the development of autonomous learning. Conscious reflection on learning experiences and the sharing of such reflections with other learners in cooperative groups makes it possible to increase one's awareness of learning. The teacher's task is to provide learners with the necessary information and support at suitable points. Such learner guidance involves knowledge about learning strategies and, at a higher level of abstraction, metacognitive knowledge about learning.

Learner strategies are language learning behaviors learners actually engage in to learn and regulate the learning of a second language (Wenden 1987: 6–7). Strategies are problem-oriented, that is, learners utilize them to respond to a learning need. They are techniques of memory management used by learners in order to facilitate the acquisition, storage, retrieval or use of information. Strategies develop over time as a result of learning how to deal with problems. They can become automatized and function without conscious control. But they can also be brought to conscious observation and awareness and can be modified as a result of conscious effort. To the extent that learners have 'strategic knowledge' about learning strategies it seems possible for them to develop their strategies by learning new techniques of memory management. They can become more effective language learners (cf. Chamot 1987). Cognitive strategies such as keyword techniques for learning vocabulary, visualization strategies, and physical response techniques (see, for example, Asher 1982), have proved effective in language teaching.

In contrast to such task-specific cognitive strategies, general learning skills have a wider application in terms of helping the learner to gain a control of the whole process of language learning by reflecting on the nature of learning. Understanding of the various ways of using memory in language learning will give learners options and help them to make informed choices, finding out ways that work for them. As noted by O'Malley (1987: 133; cf. also O'Malley and Chamot 1990), there is evidence to suggest that good language learners can use a variety of strategies to assist them in gaining command over the new language skills. This implies that less competent learners might benefit from the training on strategies evidenced among more successful language learners.

In terms of experiential learning theory, an essential part of such learner training is that it includes the cyclic process of having 'hands-on' experience of learning strategies and megacognitive knowledge, reflecting on such experience and conceptualizing it, thereby gaining a conscious understanding of the knowledge.

Heterogeneous cooperative teams would seem to provide a good environment for such discussions, enabling learners to compare and contrast each others' preferred or habitual ways of learning and gain a deeper understanding of the processes in so doing. Thus reflecting on and talking about learning is beneficial for learning. To complete the cycle, learners are given opportunities to experiment with different ways of using their memory, to gain new experiential data for reflection. For instance, to learn about vocabulary learning strategies, learners might be given various vocabulary lists in L2, which they learn using different types of mnemonic techniques. Explanations of the rationale behind the different techniques will help them to understand why they work and to make personal choices depending on what seems to work best for them.

Such learning will result in what Wenden calls pedagogic autonomy, that is, acquisition of the skills and knowledge necessary to learn to manage one's learning and learn on one's own. Learners can become competent as learners of the new language, learning to deal with the learning task in rational and informed ways. Learning about learning may, in fact, help to demystify the processes involved and thus increase the learners' feelings of confidence and competence. As O'Malley and Chamot (1990) point out, learners without metacognitive knowledge are essentially learners without direction and ability to review their progress. Learners are not 'blank slates' that absorb the new language; they can learn in purposeful ways.

Knowledge of the learning task

The learner's knowledge of the language learning task can be seen as a map of the task. To use a familiar metaphor from orienteering, this knowledge can be compared to the topographic map of the terrain. To be able to use the map one has to possess a sufficient knowledge of the topographic symbols and be able to match the map with the surrounding terrain. Equipped with such a map, the necessary literacy and a compass, it is safe to explore and enjoy an unknown terrain and find one's way properly.

Similarly, it is helpful for language learners to know the 'terrain' of the

B

second or foreign language: what elements there are, how they are inter-connected and patterned, what combinations are possible and likely to occur, which ones occur frequently, and what similarities and differences exist between their native languages and the target language. Such infor-mation will create order out of the seemingly chaotic primary data that the learner has to confront when dealing with the new language. Order and structure, in turn, will create predictability and thereby facilitate the processing task as learners can make heuristic guesses of the message form and content. An awareness of the task functions as a framework to which they can integrate new learning experiences and thus feel safer when confronting new language elements. They can feel able to master, to some extent, the unknown terrain that they are about to enter.

It is also beneficial for language learners to know how human communication can be understood, how the relevant properties of language can be analyzed consciously in the target language, and what elements the new language contains. This awareness, called meta-linguistic knowledge, can exist at various levels of linguistic sophisti-cation. It is also important for learners to be aware of the notion of risk-taking in language use. A risk-taking situation may be defined as an occasion where an individual has to make decisions involving an uncertainty of the outcome and a possibility of failure (Beebe 1983: 39). This implies that risk-taking develops in situations in which learners are exposed to challenging tasks and the possibility of failure. Communi-cative approaches suggest taking risks in the spirit of the old saying: 'Nothing ventured, nothing gained', as Beebe points out (1983: 63).

In actual language use, learners will obviously face situations and tasks where their linguistic skills are not adequate either for compre-hending messages or producing their intended meanings at a desired level of sophistication. They will thus encounter mismatches between their communicative skills and intentions. To deal with problems due to an insufficient knowledge of language, learners will adopt different kinds of communication strategies, which can be seen as 'potentially conscious plans for solving what to an individual presents itself as a problem in reaching a particular communicative goal' (Færch and Kasper 1983: 36).

The learner's involvement in the task, as well as knowledge about it, is necessary for effective learning. Materials and tasks do not as such guarantee anything; the essential question is what the learner does with them. It is important that the learner does something to the input so that the output has a personal meaning, no matter how modest such modifi-cations or productions are in the beginning. An input which is not worked on by the learner has not much subjective meaning for him or her. It does not turn into a real output. It could be rather described as 'throughput' – an output which is nothing but the unmodified input and does not touch the learner inside. From the communicative point of view, experiential learning implies encouraging authentic language use which involves the learner. The learner is brought in touch with real-life language use, involving some reason for reading a text or listening to somebody. In spoken language use, interactions usually involve a small number of speakers, in which conversational roles and meanings are constantly negotiated. The roles of the speaker and listener may change rapidly, and the dialogues are not so 'tidy' as suggested by textbook dialogues: people hesitate and misunderstand each other, ask for clarification and check their interpretations, interrupt and get distracted by other people and events.

The foregoing discussion raises the issue of the role of grammatical instruction in language learning. There is a tension between a conscious, explicit knowledge of the rules, and the use of language in communication without consciously reflecting on the rules. The former type of knowledge can be called declarative knowledge ('know-that'), while automatized skill performance involves what is called procedural knowledge ('know-how'). The traditional learning sequence progressed from the presentation of the rules to practice and application, aiming at automatization, i.e. from declarative to procedural knowledge. This position was challenged by Krashen's (1982) well-known claim that the formal teaching of rules should be reduced to the minimum, with a shift of emphasis away from conscious learning to unconscious acquisition. This distinction, however, seems artificial as new learning is always a more or less conscious process at the initial stage. New learning associations are controlled processes requiring a conscious effort of learning. Controlled processes place demands on short-term memory, and their automatization is a gradual integration of initially conscious sub-skills. A conscious learning of rules is thus seen as a precursor to an automatic skill execution. (Cf. McLaughlin 1987; Nunan 1988; O'Malley and Chamot 1990.)

Rather than assuming that declarative and procedural knowledge about language are separate, it seems to make more sense to assume that they constitute a continuum. Færch (1986: 126) suggests the following stages on such a continuum from implicit to explicit rules:

1. the learner uses the rule but does not reflect on it;
2. the learner can decide whether a given item of language use is in accordance with the rule;
3. the learner can describe the rule in his own words;
4. the learner can describe the rule in metalinguistic terms.

A communicative use of language results in implicit knowledge, while presentation of rules yields explicit knowledge. But the latter type of knowledge can become implicit through automatization, just as implicit knowledge can become explicit through consciousness-raising.

Viljo Kohonen

Experiential learning suggests that the learning of rules might be seen as a recycling process gradually leading to their internalization. When this proceeds from procedural to declarative learning, learners are first provided with experiences of language data through the meaningful use of language in natural contexts. At this stage, the structural rules are not presented or explained formally, only their meanings are provided in the mother tongue. Rules are thus approached as lexical units in the first place, thereby simulating the first language acquisition (e.g. *go* and *went* are learned separately). Learners make observations and reflect on them, becoming vaguely aware of the systemic connections between different linguistic forms and possibly making some implicit rules and generalizations of their own (e.g. *go* → *goed* as the past tense form). They may check the rules' applicability by asking the teacher. A formal presentation of the system will follow only after learners have had a reasonable amount of experience of the rules by being exposed to meaningful language in relevant contexts of use. Explicit comprehension of the rules will enable learners to control them consciously. To secure automatization, the rules are used in new contexts to obtain further experiential data. The experiential learning cycle can thus be presented as follows, in accordance with Kolb's model.

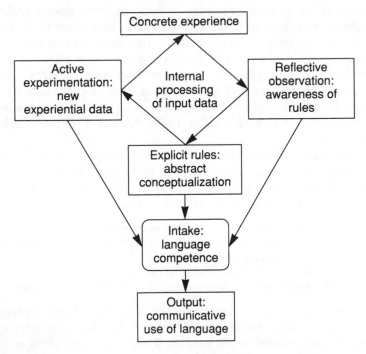

Figure 3   Experiential second language learning: a model

28

According to the model, learning requires a continuous recycling of experience, reflection, conceptualization and active experimentation. Just as rules without a sufficient experiential element remain shallow learning, experiences that are not reflected upon and conceptualized will not yield controlled learning; and reflections must in turn aim at testing the newly refined understanding of the system by further experience (e.g. *go* → *went* as part of a systemic understanding of the past tense). Language learning is thus a continuous process of recycling the input data, aiming at a more sophisticated understanding and incremental automatization of the system. If the meaningful learning process continues, the learner's second language competence will expand and he or she will be able to deal with increasingly complex language data. In the opposite case, that of language attrition (and possibly eventual loss), the once-acquired competence will decrease as a result of lack of opportunities and motivation for meaningful language use.

In summary, then, experiential learning theory suggests that effective second language learning might involve:

1. abundant, comprehended input in the target language with an emphasis on understanding the content of the texts and thereby using language as a vehicle of learning about the subject matter rather than as an end in itself;
2. learner reflection on language structure and an explicit teaching of the systemic structure of the target language, aiming at a conscious control of the language;
3. comprehensible output, emphasizing the importance of the learner's productive use of the target language in interactive communication, in an attempt to be increasingly comprehensible by taking communicative risks and thereby stretching the learner's skills (cf. Swain 1985);
4. corrective feedback by the teacher and peers, i.e. information about the development of the competence in the target language, aiming at an internalization of the criteria of acceptable and accurate language use through self-assessment and reflection in cooperative learning teams.

Learning is thus seen as a continuous process aiming at an incrementally fine-tuned understanding of the system and an increasingly automatized use of it in meaningful communication with plenty of opportunities for practice.

Viljo Kohonen

Experiential language learning as cooperative learning

Two models of teaching

When the total context of education changes substantially, as a result of developments in society and educational theory, it may become necessary for educators to examine their assumptions and review their educational practices in the light of new developments. Such a critical examination may now be expedient, as current pedagogical thinking seems to be shifting away from the traditional behavioristic model of teaching as transmission of knowledge towards an experiential model whereby teaching is seen as transformation of existing or partly understood knowledge, based on constructivist views of learning. What is involved is nothing less than a major paradigmatic shift in educational theory, and the need for change is further motivated by ongoing developments in society.

The paradigmatic shift can be analyzed by juxtaposing the polar ends of some pedagogically relevant dimensions as in Table 1 (cf. Brandes and Ginnis 1986; Miller 1988). However, doing so does not imply any criticism of the earlier paradigm: it is not justifiable to criticize one paradigm on the basis of the premises of another paradigm. Any pedagogical decisions have to be evaluated within the relevant theoretical framework and the current socio-cultural and educational context. The comparison can suggest a range of options for educators which may help them to clarify their own positions and examine the extent to which their choices are consistent within the broad paradigmatic framework that they have adopted. If educators make a conscious decision to move towards the experiential model, this means shifting the emphasis towards the right-hand side of Table 1 opposite.

The transmission model of teaching assumes that the teacher is the person in authority in the class whose job is to impart knowledge and skills to the learners. Knowledge is seen as definable in terms of right and wrong answers. Students tend to see their role as relatively passive recipients of the knowledge, expecting the teacher to be in charge of their learning (cf. Salmon 1988; Nunan 1988).

Glasser (1986) gives as an example of this model the traditional structure of secondary schools with the teacher at the front of the room facing thirty to forty learners. The underlying behavioristic model involves various rewards and sanctions to ensure learning. But there are limits to what we can pressure students to learn if they do not experience satisfaction in their work. Sanctions will cause discipline problems and underlying tensions in the class in which the teacher has the final word and the power to reward, punish and evaluate. Students learn as individuals, and the cooperation between them is limited by competition for grades.

30

TABLE 1. TRADITIONAL AND EXPERIENTIAL MODELS OF EDUCATION:
A COMPARISON

Dimension	Traditional model: behaviorism	Experiential model: constructivism
1. View of learning	Transmission of knowledge	Transformation of knowledge
2. Power relation	Emphasis on teacher's authority	Teacher as a 'learner among learners'
3. Teacher's role	Providing mainly frontal instruction; professionalism as individual autonomy	Facilitating learning (largely in small groups); collaborative professionalism
4. Learner's role	Relatively passive recipient of information; mainly individual work	Active participation, largely in cooperative small groups
5. View of knowledge	Presented as 'certain'; application, problem-solving	Construction of personal knowledge; identification of problems
6. View of curriculum	Static; hierarchical grading of subject matter, predefined contents	Dynamic; looser organization of subject matter, including open parts and integration
7. Learning experiences	Knowledge of facts, concepts and skills; focus on content and product	Emphasis on process: learning skills, self-inquiry, social and communication skills
8. Control of process	Mainly teacher-structured learning	Emphasis on learner: self-directed learning
9. Motivation	Mainly extrinsic	Mainly intrinsic
10. Evaluation	Product-oriented: achievement testing; criterion-referencing (and norm-referencing)	Process-oriented: reflection on process, self-assessment; criterion-referencing

The experiential model, on the other hand, would seem to offer potential for a learning atmosphere of shared partnership, a common purpose and a joint management of learning. Class behavior is owned by the whole group, of which the teacher is one member. As the rules of conduct are agreed upon jointly, all share the responsibility for decisions and discipline. Such rules are called ground rules. An essential feature of ground rules is that they are based on mutual trust and respect; they are agreed upon jointly, and they apply to all. The rules are there to remind the participants of their joint responsibilities. Knowledge is seen as open to negotiation and redefining by challenging existing constructions of meaning. Learning can become a discovery of new understandings. As there are fewer underlying tensions, energy can be channeled into more creative pursuits (cf. Brandes and Ginnis 1986; Salmon 1988).

The degree of self-directed (as against other-directed) learning can be clarified by examining the degree of learner involvement at the different stages of the instructional process. This can be done by asking the following questions (Riley 1984: 127–30):

- who analyses the needs?
- who defines the objectives?
- who decides where and how often learning takes place?
- who chooses the materials?
- who chooses the work techniques?
- who decides on levels and criteria of acceptable outcomes?
- who monitors the learning program and process?
- who evaluates the results of learning?

The more learners are responsible for taking these decisions, the greater is their degree of self-direction. The extent to which the decisions are taken together reflects a shared management of learning, with the teacher functioning as a guide and expert consultant of learning. Various combinations of sharing the decisions are possible at different stages of learning, reflecting various degrees of learner autonomy.

At a deeper level, a learner-centered approach involves a basic trust in the learner's willingness and ability to cope with the various learning tasks, and a respect for his or her person and choices. On the basis of such a relationship, learners can be given increasing amounts of initiative in undertaking the task, choosing the contents and assessing their work. In this way they will develop a feeling of ownership and responsibility for their own learning. If the teacher is 'in charge' most of the time, the learner's responsibility cannot develop. Aiming towards autonomous learning thus means shifting emphasis onto the learner and allowing more and more room for the development of responsibility.

In this view, making schools more effective means ensuring that learners' basic needs for love, belongingness, power, freedom and fun are satisfied from their early classes onwards. As Glasser (1986: 54) points out, there is no sense in telling learners how valuable classes are and how much they need them unless we can structure classes so that they are more satisfying to them. Cooperative learning seems to provide a classroom environment in which such needs can be met in a way that is beneficial for both academic achievement and the development of the learners' social and learning skills (D. W. Johnson *et al.* 1988, 1990; Slavin 1987; Kagan 1989).

Ways of structuring classroom learning

Classroom work is goal-oriented, aiming to achieve certain learning goals, and it is conducted under some goal structure. A learning goal can be defined as a desired future state of competence or mastery in the subject area being studied, such as foreign language proficiency. The work to achieve learning goals can be structured so as to promote individual learning, competition between students or cooperation among them. The goal structure thus specifies the type of interdependence among students as they work to accomplish their learning goals. The way in which the teacher structures interdependence among students will determine how they interact with each other and the teacher during the instructional session. The differences between the individualistic, competitive and cooperative goal structures can be summarized as follows (D. W. Johnson and R. T. Johnson 1987: 2–7; cf. also D. W. Johnson and R. T. Johnson 1989; D. W. Johnson *et al.* 1990):

- in individual work, learners work on their own at their own pace and in their own space to achieve a pre-set criterion of learning;
- in competitive work, learners compete with each other to see who is best;
- in collaborative work, learners work together in small groups, aiming towards a common goal.

In individualistic tasks students work alone on their own sets of materials and at their own speed. Their achievements are usually evaluated on a criterion-referenced basis. Their goal achievements are thus independent of each other: students perceive that the achievement of their learning goals is unrelated to what other students do.

In competitive learning situations students compete to achieve their individual goals. If achievement is graded on a norm-referenced basis, students' test scores are rank-ordered to determine the individual grades. This tends to create a negative interdependence in the class: students perceive that they can obtain good grades when other students do worse. In such a learning environment there is thus little motivation to work together. While competition encourages some students to work hard to do better, there are other students who are labelled as being failures in school. There is also a number of students who give up because they do not believe that they have a chance to do well in the competition.

In cooperative learning situations learners work together to accomplish shared goals. Their achievements are evaluated on a criterion-referenced basis. However, since all group members now share a common goal, they are motivated to work together for mutual benefit in order to maximize their own and each others' learning. This creates a positive interdependence among the learners: they perceive that they can reach their goals best when the others in the same learning group also do as well as possible.

Obviously, each of these goal structures has its place in classroom work and they can all be used flexibly during instructional sessions. Learners need to know how to work on their own, how to collaborate with others, and how to compete, for fun and enjoyment. But the pedagogically interesting question is: what might be an integrated balance between the different options? When is it desirable to use frontal instruction, individual work (alone or in competition), or various grouping combinations? In the long run, the cumulative effects of the different goal structures will gain importance because they affect both the cognitive and affective outcomes of instruction: the way learners interact with each other determines how they process information and what kinds of learning experiences they get. The teacher might thus consider what goal structure to use and when, depending on the nature of the learning task and the instructional aims.

In the light of this discussion, cooperative learning would seem to deserve more attention from educators than it has received so far. This is because it can foster learner growth both in terms of academic achievement, personal growth and the development of social and learning skills. We might therefore consider shifting attention to some extent away from an emphasis on competitive and individualistic learning towards promoting learner collaboration in the classroom.

Cooperative learning: possibilities and challenges

The work in cooperative learning teams is structured so that there is positive interdependence among the members in the group: the learners feel that they work together for mutual benefit. Positive interdependence needs to be structured carefully in order to encourage all group members to work to their full capacity. In a well-functioning cooperative group there is a sense of joint responsibility where learners care about and get committed to each others' success as well as their own; a sense of 'sinking or swimming together'. A team environment where learners celebrate each others' successes and provide assistance to each other is likely to promote more positive peer relationships, social support, and, partly for that reason, higher self-esteem and academic achievement. Social support is especially beneficial for learning complex materials more thoroughly. The following five factors are necessary for successful cooperative learning (cf. D. W. Johnson and R. T. Johnson 1987, 1989; D. W. Johnson *et al.* 1990; Brandt 1987):

1. positive interdependence, a sense of working together for a common goal and caring about each other's learning;
2. individual accountability, whereby every team member feels in charge of their own and their teammates' learning and makes an active contribution to the group. Thus there is no 'hitchhiking' or 'freeloading' for anyone in a team – everyone pulls their weight;
3. abundant verbal, face-to-face interaction, where learners explain, argue, elaborate and link current material with what they have learned previously;
4. sufficient social skills, involving an explicit teaching of appropriate leadership, communication, trust and conflict resolution skills so that the team can function effectively;
5. team reflection, whereby the teams periodically assess what they have learned, how well they are working together and how they might do better as a learning team.

Cooperative learning teams provide an effective context for the development of new understandings. Learner talk can be harnessed to the exploration of dawning understandings and new learnings, producing at its best something quite different from traditional classroom discourse. In an affirming and encouraging small group, learners feel free to talk in provisional, exploratory ways. They speak tentatively, trying out their ideas on each other. As there is no need to defend opinions or pretend certainties that are not felt, the mode of learner talk can be one of 'perhaps', of voicing uncertainties and trying out rudimentary ideas, as pointed out by Salmon (1988: 81).

Cooperative learning teams are deliberately heterogeneous and consist of two to four members. In bigger groups, there is a high achiever, one or two average achievers and a low achiever. The groups are chosen by the teacher after careful consideration. The teams are responsible for learning the tasks together, helping each other. Learners are encouraged to explain ideas or skills to one another, each member being an active participant and an important resource person for the whole team. Such discussions can be beneficial to all: faster learners will consolidate their own understanding of issues at hand when explaining them to slower learners, thus engaging in cognitive elaboration that enhances their own understanding. Similarly, slower learners will benefit from peer tutoring by their teammates who are wrestling with the same question. Sometimes learners seem to be more able to translate the teacher's explanations into a 'kid language' which is easier for their teammates to understand, being involved in the same experience and having just passed the stage of understanding themselves (cf. Slavin 1987).

An important advantage of heterogeneous learning teams is that they can be facilitated to work independently to a large extent, with learners helping each other. Thus valuable teacher time is released for individual or group consulting functions, and for observing learning in action and thereby gathering information about how individual learners and groups are doing. In an important sense teaching is also a matter of observing student learning, 'kid-watching', collecting and analyzing information about learners and using this information as a basis for planning further instructional actions.

How long might cooperative teams stay together? There is no definite answer to this question; everything depends on the aims and scope of the work in hand. Teams can work together for a few minutes, a lesson or several lessons. Teams can be used for various purposes: to identify and solve problems, to master jointly the material introduced by the teacher, to work on agreed projects, and so on. It is thus possible to use flexible learner groupings to introduce variety, carry out projects and cater for learner interests. Team work can also involve contracts between the teacher and individuals and independent projects carried out at least partly alone. Teams can also be formed on the basis of learner interests and wishes, e.g. project groups for a given purpose. While teams are usually heterogeneous, it can at times be expedient to use homogeneous ability groups. This makes it possible to give more challenging tasks to fast learners and less demanding ones to slow learners.

To encourage long-term caring and commitment in the class it is also possible to use more permanent cooperative base groups. These groups can work together for the whole academic year and even longer, for several years. They meet at regular intervals to plan and review the learning of the members, but the members are simultaneously also working in other short-term cooperative teams. Such groups can increase learners' psychological health by providing a nurturing environment. It is important that the school also provides permanent personal relationships in a small group. Receiving social support and being accountable for appropriate behavior by peers who have a long-term commitment for each others' success and well-being is an important aspect of growth and progress through school.

Discussion

Experiential learning theory provides the basic philosophical view of learning as part of personal growth. The goal is to enable the learner to become increasingly self-directed and responsible for his or her own learning. This process means a gradual shift of the initiative to the learner, encouraging him or her to bring in personal contributions and experiences. Instead of the teacher setting the tasks and standards of acceptable performance, the learner is increasingly in charge of his or her own learning.

It is worth considering how far such goals can be reached in school alone. School is only one setting for learning relevant knowledge, skills and attitudes, and a large portion of significant learning and learner growth will take place outside school, in families and extra-curricular activities and as part of natural maturation. But the big question for the school is, nevertheless: how could school learning be organized so as to support such academic and educational goals by conscious pedagogical design? How far can the goals of self-directed, autonomous learning be reached in educational settings in which the teacher assumes the main responsibility of defining the objectives, and planning, monitoring and evaluating student learning? What might thus be a suitable balance between teacher control and learner initiative? What could be a balanced combination of the different goal structures? And how might it develop over years as a result of learner (and teacher) growth?

Cooperative learning can provide a means of working towards such goals, with a significant part of learning taking place in small, mixed-ability teams consisting of two to four learners. The work in the teams is structured so that there is positive interdependence and individual accountability among the learners, with each participant contributing to the team product and the team being in charge of helping its teammates to learn.

However, it is still necessary to reflect on how 'learner-centered' work is in cooperative teams in the light of the notion of self-directed learning. If the teacher sets the task for the teams, defines the contents of the work to be done, determines how and when it is to be done and reported and how it is evaluated, it can be argued that much of such cooperative work is still, in fact, teacher-centered. In the spirit of learner-centred thinking, careful pedagogical thinking needs to be attached to the learner's role in the whole process of learning. To gain new experiences and reflect on them, the learner needs to be both an actor and an observer of his or her own learning. Language learning is seen both as a process of reconstructing the linguistic system from comprehended input through internal processing and as conscious learning through explicit instruction aimed at raising the learner's awareness of the grammatical categories and concepts of learning.

When languages are taught to the whole of the age group, the range of learner differences is bound to be large. Having the class proceed at the same pace under the teacher's control can be undesirable for both slow and fast learners: while the progress tends to be too demanding for the former, it is usually too easy for the latter. For fast learners, frontal teaching may even impede learning in the sense that they are not offered incentives to work hard enough, having to wait for slower learners to catch up. Reducing frontal teaching and increasing learner-initiated independent work alone and in small cooperative learning teams offers pedagogically more effective ways of organizing the learner's work.

This orientation entails a paradigmatic shift in pedagogical thinking from the teacher-centered transmission model of teaching to the experiential model of teaching. In this process-oriented model evaluation is understood in a wide sense, ranging from informal classroom observation to formally administered summative tests. A distinction can be made between process and product evaluation. It seems that more attention needs to be paid to process evaluation. For the teacher, process evaluation is necessary for making pedagogical decisions: guiding the learners' progress and giving them relevant feedback about the development of their competence. From the learners' point of view, process evaluation is necessary for the development of an awareness of their learning skills and the learning task. As evaluation is always a time-consuming process, it needs to be geared to improving learning and education. And to improve education we need to know more about what takes place in the classroom and in the learner's mind. In a broad sense, evaluation turns into classroom research, the purpose of which is to help learners to be better learners and teachers to develop as professionals.

The notion of the teacher as a researcher thus constitutes an important element in experiential learning. Being a researcher of one's work entails a reflective awareness of and a deeper involvement in it. Teaching involves making decisions regarding the learner, and to be able to make informed decisions the teacher needs information about the learner's situation. Learner-centered learning does not mean leaving the learner alone and without support. The teacher's role is, in an important sense, even more significant than in teacher-centered instruction.

An essential element in reflective teaching is mutual support and cooperation among teachers. Professional growth is facilitated in an atmosphere of support and trust whereby teachers see their colleagues as resources for each other. In-service teacher education programs thus need to emphasize the importance of mutual support for professional development. This aim can be achieved in school-based staff development projects that involve the whole staff, or at least most of the staff members. Such staff development programs might be as follows:

- they are school-based, to ensure lots of face-to-face interaction and cooperation among the teachers;
- they extend over several years (2–5 years);
- they are initiated by the participating teachers and based on the needs identified by the teachers themselves, rather than being imposed by external authorities;
- the teachers are in charge of planning their training, thereby developing an ownership of their own learning;

- outside consultants are learners among the teacher-learners, facilitating the process;
- the general empirical framework is that of action research and experiential learning, involving a cyclic approach to the developmental projects: plan → act → observe → reflect → revise plans (cf. Kolb 1984; Carr and Kemmis 1986);
- they contain theoretical instruction, practical demonstrations, individual study, guided practice and feedback on it, and peer coaching. Teachers visit each others' classes to provide companionship and support in solving problems as new skills are integrated with the existing pedagogical repertoire. Coaching is strictly confidential and supportive, not evaluative, with teachers helping each other to grow professionally.

This approach involves a clear change of school culture from traditional teacher isolation to support and cooperation. (Cf. Kohonen 1987, 1989; Nunan 1987, 1989b; Slavin 1987; Zeichner 1987; Joyce and Showers 1988; Grimmett and Erickson (eds.) 1988; Legutke 1988; Brandt 1989; Joyce (ed.) 1990.)

It is important for teachers to clarify their basic educational philosophy and relate this to the nationally and locally defined educational goals and instructional aims. This provides a fundamental orientation to their work and criteria for their choices of instructional content and classroom techniques. It can perhaps be said that the most important pedagogical innovation is the teacher, with his or her pedagogical thinking and personal qualities. Teaching can be a profession which is both academically challenging and personally rewarding and empowering. Experiential learning attempts to meet such challenges and provide a framework accommodating various alternatives, promoting a holistic view of foreign language learning as learner education.

Endnotes

1 I am indebted to Anita Wenden for clarifying my thinking on the issues of learner education. Her manuscripts 'A curricular framework for promoting learner autonomy' and 'Metacognition: an expanded view on the cognitive abilities of L2 learners' have been instrumental for writing this section.

2 Dickinson (1987) offers a good example to illustrate this concept. Parents are responsible for their children's health, but this does not mean that they must undertake the diagnosis and treatment of their children's illnesses; they cannot do this (unless they are also medical experts). But they are responsible for making decisions about when to seek expert help, and what kind of help to seek. Similarly, they want to know what the diagnosis is and what treatment is proposed, how it is to be done, and what the prognosis is. A good doctor welcomes the parents' concern and provides the information. As the parents get more experienced in raising their children they are likely to assume some functions of the medical expert in terms of managing their children's illnesses.

2 Literacy skills or literate skills? Considerations for ESL/EFL learners

Shirley Brice Heath

The task I have given myself in this chapter is to argue that we are not in a crisis of literacy skills, but instead a crisis of literate skills. I want to argue that becoming literate is not the same thing as learning to read and write; it is learning to talk reading and writing. I want to argue that those who can solve this literate crisis are teachers, students, and researchers working together, and I mean here literally working together, not each independently toward a similar goal.

Teachers and teacher-educators may despair at this idea, since they could react with the view that they are being asked once again to add to their already overflowing task assignments. In addition to dealing with individualized teaching, mastery learning (learning programs designed to ensure that all students succeed), different languages and learning styles, and endless other innovations in education, they are being asked to take on responsibility for solving another crisis – another task is laid out for teachers at the same time that many societal and economic forces demean their role as professionals, and diminish their hope of receiving a living wage. Teachers may well ask if we can expect them to take on this additional task.

I am afraid the answer is yes, and I can offer no easy solutions. It is at once both the joy and the despair of human life that it is far too complicated for those of us in either the pure or social sciences to reduce it to simple solutions or explanations. But as a long-time teacher, I have an initial confession which is the assumption underlying all I have to say here. It is the expectation that a majority of those of us in teaching – regardless of the age of our students – believe in the infinite improvability of human beings. Any evidence we grasp that the potential of those we teach is being fulfilled is our reward for the long hours, lack of gratitude from the public, and demeaning tasks we are asked to do. Therefore, my suggestions here rest on the continued good will of teachers, but more importantly, on the ultimate professional army of talent that waits to be released in teachers, students, and researchers as they work together.

From *On TESOL '84* by P. Larsen, E. Judd and D. Messerschmidt (eds.), Washington D.C.: TESOL. Copyright 1984 by Teachers of English to Speakers of Other Languages. Adapted by permission.

I illustrate here in two cases how the combination of these talents redefined literate skills for students in a Basic English classroom of Black dialect speakers in an Alabama high school and for a group of limited English speakers in an ESL classroom in South Texas. Two themes run through these cases: the first of these is the 'tie-in' theme; the second is the 'tie-back' theme. Both themes remind us of ways to link the language of the classroom both to the home context of students and to their future uses of language. The tie-in theme refers to the ties across forms of communication, from joke or story in the oral channel, for example, to news article or explanatory essay in the written channel. The tie-back theme encompasses our efforts to tie back what we are trying to do in the classroom to the first language socialization of the students we are teaching and to better understanding of our own first language learning. Both of the teacher–researcher–student linkages described here were part of a loose network of such triads linked through letter-writing; this pattern of linking was originally the idea of Amanda Branscombe, a former teacher in Alabama who had studied the teaching of writing with James Britton, Dixie Goswami, Ken Macrorie, and Nancy Martin at the Bread Loaf School of English.

In Alabama

In 1981–82, Branscombe was the teacher of a ninth-grade Basic English class of eighteen students (fourteen black, four white), all but three of whom had previously been in special education classes designed for students judged mentally inferior and as having an intelligence quotient on the Stanford Binet Intelligence Test between 75 and 85. In a brief meeting with her during the summer of 1981, I heard Branscombe talk about her methods of teaching writing in which she used a letter exchange between her ninth graders and her college-bound third- and fourth-year high school students. I asked her to take field notes on this process for one class during 1981–82, to correspond with me throughout the year, and to share with me the writings of her students. I agreed to write letters to the students, asking them to focus on their own language learning and to become associate ethnographers with me as they collected data on language uses in their communities. Throughout the first semester the ninth graders wrote to Branscombe's high school students weekly, exchanging information on their respective social worlds. During the semester Branscombe read portions of ethnographies to the ninth graders, showed films describing the work of ethnographers, and prepared the class for their role during the second semester as my correspondents. In January, when the ninth graders no longer had the high school students as correspondents, I began writing to the class, asking them to collect data on their uses of oral and written language. I asked them to work together as a community of ethnographers, collecting, interpreting, and building a data bank of information about language in their worlds. They had access to knowledge I wanted, and the only way I could get that knowledge was for them to write to me. They collected field notes, wrote interpretations of patterns they discovered as they discussed their field notes, and they answered the questions I raised about their data collection and their interpretations. They agreed also to take responsibility for seeing through any research write-up which might result from their fieldwork; they were to read drafts of my research reports and offer comments, corrections, and additions (Heath and Thomas 1984).

I wrote my five- to ten-page single-spaced letters just as I would write to a university-level colleague, with one exception. In my first few letters, I spoke personally to the students, addressing individuals by name and inserting them into the text by asking questions, such as 'You may want to know why this information is important.' In subsequent letters, I wrote of general principles, depersonalizing the actions they were to take and decontextualizing interpretations of patterns I was beginning to draw from their data. In their field notes and letters, they described the contexts, speakers, and purposes of oral and written language which surrounded them in their homes, work settings, and classroom. Branscombe supplemented these requests by asking them to discuss in groups in her classroom their findings and to challenge interpretations of pattern development. She took field notes on these discussions, audio-taped some small-group work, and wrote accounts of her own assessments of the classroom as a learning environment.

Results of the year's work for individual students in the class are reported elsewhere (Heath and Thomas 1984, Heath with Branscombe 1985, 1986), and only general points applicable to the class as a whole will be mentioned here. First, the students learned that communication is negotiation. Nearly every student who took the task of associate ethnographer seriously had a crisis of understanding with me, the distant other with whom they could communicate only in writing. I challenged points they made in their letters and interpretive essays, asked for evidence of their conclusions, pointed out contradictions I found in their field notes, and critiqued their strategies in their oral interviews with informants. They initially responded emotionally to these challenges, countering with their own doubts about my aims. One student wrote:

> I would like to know why you are doing this what are you going to gain by doing this and the way things are going I believe you have changed your mind about coming and don't want us to know and I don't believe you are coming if you are not coming you are wasting our time.

Later they argued their points, asserting themselves as the experts they were over the knowledge they had collected, recorded, and interpreted. They turned the responsibility for careful reading back to me, asserting that I had not paid attention to their texts, or that they had written the information I said I lacked in an earlier letter. After an initial period of blaming the reader, they accepted responsibility as writers. They garnered evidence, admitted they sometimes saw the gaps I pointed out, and returned to collect more information, refine interpretations, or compare data collected at one point in time with those collected later.

In addition to learning that communication is negotiation, the students began to realize they could preplay their interpretations with either their classmates or themselves, listening for the arguments which had no data for support, identifying the gaps in knowledge which might keep readers from accepting their interpretation, and correcting their conclusions before they mailed them to me. Through the dyadic writing – first with the high school students and then with me – the ninth graders had learned to play the role of writer and reader, to anticipate and hypothesize the kind of information the reader will bring to the text and the questions the reader will raise. They had learned to listen – to truly listen – to their own arguments, comparisons and contrasts, and persuasions, and to hypothesize another listener who did not bring their knowledge and background to their writings.

If the students learned that communication is negotiation and that they must play reader and writer roles in response to their own tests, what did the teacher and researcher learn? Branscombe and I gradually recognized that the best way to assess students' progress was to ask them to analyze their own written work. They had recorded, described, and interpreted patterns of oral and written language in their homes and the work settings of their parents, as well as in their own classroom. Why couldn't they look at their early letters and compare them with later letters? Branscombe helped the students focus on the features of their letters through which they might measure their growth: length, use of formal features (such as salutations, closings, paragraphing, etc.), and introduction and follow-up of topics of interest to them. The evaluative process, usually imposed by the teacher, became one in which students helped determine how one letter might be 'better' than another, and how far they had come between September and May in their writing. Furthermore, they could listen to themselves in small-group discussions audiotaped early in the year and compare their arguments then with their assertion of thesis, evidence, and implications later in the year. Thus teacher and researcher learned that evaluating could be added to the process of collecting, recording, interpreting, and comparing information on oral and written language.

In addition, teacher and researcher learned that the more the students talked about their research, the better their oral arguments became. Moreover, as they talked more, they wrote more, and as they surrounded their writing with more talk, they could more efficiently and effectively make their points on paper. Talking out their ideas in an atmosphere in which all students were focussed on a similar task – the study of language – and in an interactive situation in which they knew a distant *other* would challenge their ideas empowered them to anticipate problems in their writing. As a result of their talk in class, they solved with each other many of the miscommunication problems which had arisen in their early writing, as the result of their failure to state clearly their topic, provide supporting evidence, and clarify the critical features (such as age, sex, situation, and audience) of samples of language they had recorded.

At the end of the year, all of the students moved out of Basic English into 'regular' English classes, and two moved into 'honors' English. Accomplishments were real and meaningful for these students. The teacher had, throughout the year, had a support system – a distant researcher with whom to share her students' work and her own ideas about curriculum, practice, and philosophy. The researcher had benefited from being called to task by informants and by having an opportunity to attach research to practical outcomes measurable not only in quantitative terms but also in changes in the quality of classroom experience for students and teacher. The cooperation with teacher and students had allowed the researcher to put ethnography into the hands of those who could use it to improve both their knowledge of what was happening in their learning and their skills in oral and written language.

In South Texas

In 1983–84, Evelyn Hanssen, a graduate student in the reading program at the University of Indiana, and Mark Ash, an ESL teacher in a South Texas high school, worked as researcher and teacher partners, studying the learning of English by the limited English speakers in two of Ash's classrooms. I had met Hanssen briefly at a conference where I talked about Branscombe's students; Ash was a teacher I met at the Bread Loaf School of English in the summer of 1983. He and Hanssen had never met, but through my written introductions, they agreed to begin a letter exchange in which Hanssen asked Ash's students to record for her their uses of oral and written language.

In early September, Hanssen wrote to Ash's classes:

> I . . . am interested in learning about how language is used in
> different parts of the country. Since I can't travel all around the

United States, I would like you to be the researchers in your area. This means that I will ask you to set up or observe different situations, record the results, and report back to me. In this way I hope we'll all learn a little more about language.

Luisa, a student who rarely spoke out in class, wrote to Hanssen:

> Hi my name is Luisa here you fine me writting to you this letter. I hope you are fine. I am fine thank you. I will tell you about me. I am 14 year old. I go 9 grader. I hope you writte to me soon as pasable to now more about you. I want a teacher can't now spansh, for our class can't talk spansh. For English. I hope when you take a picture to now more about you. Please seen me a picture. I don't now who [how] to make letter to a frande [friend]. Please i now you want under stande my latter. I want to now about you and i hope you tell me. Who [how] old are you. Miss or Mrs Evelyn Hanssen. Please Miss or Mrs pleas take care. I hope one day you come.

Hanssen wrote back to Luisa and all the other students with a long single-spaced letter in which she commented on the common points of interest in the students' letters and responded to their queries about her. She then asked them to join her in their first investigation focussing on their uses of reading and writing. She wrote:

> I'm interested in knowing how teenagers use reading in their everyday lives. Everyone from the age of three to eighty-three reads everyday and most people write daily. But if we can identify the kinds of reading and writing that teenagers do, this could help high school teachers plan lessons to better help their students.

She asked each class to split themselves into two groups; one half of the class kept track of everything they read, and the other recorded all they wrote each day. She suggested some of the items they might read (signs, cereal boxes, information on the blackboard, textbooks, the TV guide, etc.) as well as items they might write daily (notes to friends, telephone numbers, school assignments, etc.). She further suggested how they might work in groups to organize their 'data', a term she defined for the students. The groups could categorize types of reading and writing, talk about what the categories meant, identify different purposes for reading and writing, and consider how topics differed between their reading and their writing. Once the groups had drawn up categories and talked about these questions, they could count the number of times students in each group did reading or writing that fitted into one or other of the categories they had developed. She asked the classes to reflect after their group discussions on what their data meant and to answer some specific questions she posed for them:

- Do teenagers read or write more?
- Why do you think this is?
- What types of reading and writing do teenagers do most often?
- Why are some kinds of reading and writing more important than others?

The students responded with lists of types of reading and writing, notes answering specific questions, and reports of issues that had been raised in their discussion groups. They did not present a coherent picture of their views of reading and writing. Mary, a Spanish-English bilingual, wrote:

> We really enjoyed the work you gave us it was hard but fun not hard but hard to remember when you forgot to write it down.
> Yes a lot of teenagers read but they don't take it serious. I think they don't take it serious cause they well I have many more years to learn or thats the way I use to think. The most they do is writing cause theyre always writing to their girlfriends or boyfriends and reading to because they need to know how to read to be able to read the letters.

Mary argued that teenagers knew reading could benefit their learning, but they did not identify an immediate need to learn through reading for they had 'many more years to learn'. Writing, however, met a much more immediate need – communicating privately with members of the opposite sex in the public world of the high school.

Mary's classmates varied greatly in their individual interpretations of their data. Some focussed on comparisons of the amount of writing and reading different homework assignments required, refusing to recognize any other kinds of reading and writing as valid for analysis. Others, such as Jesus, commented on the way in which Hanssen presented the project and her involvement as inspiration for him: 'Thanks for all of your letters. They were so warm and friendly that I became even more excited about our working together.' Still others took her questions about reading and writing to be a subtle reminder of their need to prepare for tests; one student wrote: 'I think if I do my work and try hard I may have a good chince [chance] to pass the CTBS test.' Still others suggested there were other questions which could be raised about the data. Luis wrote:

> I fould your letter very interesting. I did the assignment you asked for and it wasn't very easy. I would like to know what kind of writing do students like best? What kind of reading do students also like? My general reactions to this project are that I enjoyed it very much and I found it very interesting. I had never done nothing so intresting before.

Yet another student wrote in Spanish, saying she could not yet write in English and she was having a hard time understanding, but she believed that being at school in the United States would be good for her because she would learn to speak English.

Hanssen responded by telling them she would need more information on these questions; they would have to pretend they were writing to a 'real dummy'. She promised to analyze their data and send another letter asking them to follow up. Meanwhile, she asked them to do interviews about language, practicing first with members of their class, and then with members of their family and community. The interviews were to focus on the uses of reading. She gave the students tips on interviewing she had picked up from practicing an interview: 'Don't be bothered by silence; wait and give the other person plenty of time to answer; don't suggest answers, just help them remember.' She reminded them that after the interview they would have to write down all they could remember from the interview in terms as specific as possible. The students responded by telling Hanssen about the person they interviewed and their ways of conducting the interview, as well as their results. For example, Esmeralda wrote:

> I interviewed Guadalupe. I had a little troble because she speaks Spanish and the troble I had was to write everything in English. I tryed very hard to do the best I could on writing it in English . . . Know what I have to write is what I learn about Guadalupe. Well in ways she is like me. The only thing different is that she speaks Spanish all the time and me I do speak Spanish but I speak English better and more than Spanish.

Other students assessed the project as 'too easy', 'not as hard as last time'; several asked for the next assignment. Still others used their letter to provide an update on the previous project; Juan wrote:

> . . . we're improving our writing. the first thing we do in class is write for ten minutes to our partner. Then write back to them. We're also writing letters to some other people in Alaska, Maine, South Dakota, and other places. We sometimes write to any students in our school.

The form of the interview results ranged from narratives within letters to listings of points made in the interview. Several students listed their questions and their partner's answers on separate pages; others tried to write down as best they could remember their partner's answers, and commented on the inadequacy of their recall. Letters to Hanssen were sprinkled with comments such as 'I hope you like the project', 'I think I need more practice on this', 'I hope you can send us more work similar to the one you gave us.'

In her subsequent letter, Hanssen turned the students' attention back to their first collection of the types of reading and writing in teenagers' lives, just as she had promised she would. She provided her own analysis of their data and raised questions she hoped they could answer. She noted that some students drew conclusions, others raised questions, and most must have grossly undercounted their instances of reading each day. She explained how she had looked at the data of the two groups:

> . . . both lists of reading had about the same number of instances of reading. One writing list, however, had three times as many instances of writing recorded as the other list. Here it is in chart form.

Number of instances of reading and writing

Reading	108	101
Writing	180	64

> I'm not sure what all this means. Is that really *all* the reading you did? A little arithmetic tells me that each of you keeping track of your reading averaged 14 instances of reading for the whole day. I bet you really did more reading than that before you even got to school, but you weren't aware of it. There are a lot of things we read that we don't even think about. Because we do it so naturally, we don't notice it.

Hanssen raised other questions, showing the students the figures she had developed from their writing and the questions she wanted them to consider as they collected more data. She pointed out that their data showed that they had as many different types of writing as they had of reading. She closed her letter by asking 'Do you think this would still be true if you remembered to record all the different types of reading you were doing that you didn't even notice?' Through the entire year, Hanssen responded to the students' data with analysis, questions of interpretation, and new, but related, research tasks.

The end of the tale of Mark Ash's students' adventures in their study of reading and writing has not come yet. Hanssen will analyze their writings and report the results (Hanssen with Mangiola, forthcoming). During the entire term, she kept a journal recording her thoughts about the project and her reasons for stressing certain questions at certain points during the year. The teacher had a very full year, filled with an increasing number of professional demands which came when others heard about his innovative project with his ESL students. Asked to travel about his region to tell other teachers about innovative approaches to teaching writing, he often had to leave his class to substitute teachers, who were not able to facilitate the discussions about the reading and writing research as the teacher himself could have. Family illness and resulting additional parenting responsibilities for Ash further eroded his time and energy in the classroom. At year's end, he positively evaluated the role the distant researcher Hanssen had played in sustaining reading and writing activities for his ESL students and in providing professional support, patience, and innovative ideas for him. The teacher–researcher–students collaboration had helped support a teacher during a year in which he had been hit by extraordinary personal and professional demands.

What had the results been for the researcher? As a former teacher, Hanssen wanted to explore ways to make her research directly helpful to teachers; she wanted to keep in touch with elementary or secondary classrooms. Through her involvement with Ash's classes, she had come to new understandings of research as teacher support. The data from students had raised questions relevant to the design of any research and to teacher education research specifically. Hanssen's work during the year had been both a pilot project and a curricular contribution. She had recognized how 'problems' for teachers and students can become data for researchers, and how important it is to link a teacher's language model with a teaching model.

What about the students? Why did students who presumably lacked basic skills in English not spend their time with obvious instruction on grammar, spelling, and pronunciation? Through their field notes, counts, brief reports, and letters, the students as a group learned to focus on language as an object of study; moreover, they received practice in a variety of oral language uses (interviews, deliberation over data, group interpretation of Hanssen's letters, etc.). Their teacher wanted his students to know that there are many ways of presenting information, and speakers and writers must learn to anticipate what their audience knows. Through their focus on a topic they knew well – themselves speaking, reading, and writing in their daily lives – the students could see themselves as experts, capable of explaining any questions or confusions which arose about the data they had collected. The interest of a distant researcher in work they generated gave them a real audience, purpose, and motivation for collecting, reporting, and interpreting their data. In their letters throughout the year, those students who had begun the year with little writing experience in English, dropped their formulaic phrases which were direct translations from traditional openings of letters in Spanish; they wrote longer letters, sustained discussion on more topics in each letter, mixed types of utterances (from questions to exclamations), and introduced new topics with sufficient background to enable Hanssen to understand their messages. Hanssen's curiosity about their different types of language uses generated talking, reading, and writing which focussed on language uses, forms, and content. Their focus on kinds of writing and reading in different types of occasions gave these skills a saliency they had not previously had and heightened students' awareness of the prevalence of reading and writing across types of jobs in their community. Some began to consider reading and writing not only in their current daily lives, but in terms of future scenarios in which they would like to place themselves. Their teacher had the goal of improving their reading and writing skills in English, to be sure, but he believed that these skills must be built on a solid base of understanding how language has to work differently on various occasions and for varying purposes. Since these students' experiences with individuals who have no knowledge about life in their South Texan town was rare, writing to Hanssen forced them to make explicit matters they usually accepted as known to others. Their exchanges with Hanssen were different from those they had with ordinary penpals, for her letters led them to attend directly to language and to receive her questions about their language as the starting point for subsequent letters. Their research made them take note of the rich patterns of language in what one student characterized as a 'little town school'. Knowing this little universe was a step toward preparing them to know the many uses of language which are 'out there' in the wide universe of mainstream institutions.

The tie-in nature of becoming literate

These students, through collaboration with researchers and teachers, are becoming literate; they are not simply acquiring literacy skills. Both groups of students, previously relegated to classrooms in which they were rarely regarded as experts over any kind of knowledge, have been allowed to assert themselves as authorities over the important domain of knowledge about language. They have had to accept themselves as experts who have information which others value and want but must receive in writing. Thus their oral discussions in class, as well as their prewriting and rewriting, have purposes; they are improving their chances of 'making sense' to a distant reader who will hold them accountable for their language skills as well as their knowledge about language.

Their research reports, as well as analysis of their writings, indicate that they recognized the tie-in nature of language – the similarities and differences of types of talk and kinds of writing. In their letters, they wrote in personal evaluative terms about their findings, process of research, and hope that they were pleasing the researcher. Yet in their reports, quantitative listings, categorizations, and interpretive essays, they wrote of this same material in different ways. Students seemed to accept the need to become competent in expressing themselves in various forms of communication, and they used their talk in class to prepare for their written arguments, descriptions, and personal letters.

The work of James Cummins, Lily Wong Fillmore, and Merrill Swain has, in recent years, alerted us to the various functions of language and the different kinds of cognitive demands which come with social interactional language and academic tasks. Learners must, before they can become successful in using language for many functions, pay attention to the forms and structures of types of discourse. The work of Heath and Branscombe, and Hanssen and Ash involved students in cognitive academic talk and writing around topics about which they could express social and interpersonal views, but about which they ultimately had to be accountable as academic experts. Their topics for initial, repetitive, redundant, and multiply reinforced practice were, however, topics they knew well. They were immersed in the context of this knowledge through the uses of language which surrounded them daily; they had to decontextualize that knowledge to allow the distant researchers to understand what they knew. Through a variety of types of writing – personal interactive, field notes, interpretive essays, and descriptions of speech and literacy events – students learned to see the relationships among the forms of different types of writing designed to carry different functions.

Furthermore, by achieving success in different types of writing focussed on information they knew well, they avoided the initial failures which had for many of them accompanied their experiences in English classes. Captivated by writing and talking about an academic topic – language – students willingly engaged in numerous types of writing and repeated returns to observing, reporting, and interpreting materials they collected. The additional practice and reinforcement, which came through researchers' questions about their work, allowed them to acquire in a relatively short period of time skills which they had not learned in previous years of formal instruction around decontextualized information over which they had no ownership. For most of the students, within the first five letter exchanges 80–85 per cent of their words were spelled correctly, and they had left behind many of their mechanical errors. Modeling their correspondents' writing, they intuitively picked up features such as proper use and punctuation of salutations, closings, etc., and they imitated the structures of the opening sentences of paragraphs, as well as ways of introducing topics in their letters.

Yet another linkage between the skills practiced in their collection of language data and the usual requirements of English classes was their improved ability to observe. Numerous assignments, especially in ESL/EFL classes, ask students to observe contrasts between their own habits and those occurring in their new environment. Yet the skills of observing, recording, and analyzing such contrasts have not been practised on familiar habits. These students became experts over familiar materials before they were asked to compare and contrast unfamiliar materials. Consequently, when asked to compare and contrast materials given in textbooks, literature, or films, they had a habituated set of procedures, writing genres, and analytic steps to follow. They were able to tie in knowledge about their own field work experiences to decontextualized foreign information or situations.

The tie-back nature of becoming literate

For those of us who have come from mainstream homes where we were oriented to composition-centered tasks and academic uses of language from our earliest communicative experiences, the implicit rules of academic language seem natural to us. However, we have learned these rules in a rich context of numerous supporting, reinforcing activities. For most of our students, however, we have to make explicit the academic habits of using oral and written language which the school requires, and we have to provide social interactive meaningful occasions for repeating these habits again and again. Since we cannot know the specific first language socialization of the Indo-Chinese, Middle Eastern, African, or Latin American students in our classes, we can solicit from them as much as possible about their first language socialization through asking them to recollect and collect as much as possible. However, this information will not be sufficient to guide decisions about particular uses of language with which they may be unfamiliar. Thus, ESL/EFL teachers must incorporate into the classroom a variety of types of writing and talking about writing; furthermore the content around which these occasions of talking and writing focus should ideally be familiar. To complicate learning a new language, by asking that new content be learned as well, is to make extraordinary cognitive demands on students. Thus, we begin with what they know – their own language socialization – and we help them make explicit in their second or foreign language what it is they do know about their oral and written uses of language (see Vann 1981).

Tying back classroom activities to first language socialization necessitates making explicit the nature of academic language socialization. Language becomes the object as well as the vehicle of study. Turning students to the active study of their own uses of language enables them to verbalize for teachers and for themselves comparisons and contrasts between first and second language uses, on the one hand, and between their oral and written language uses in either one or both languages, on the other hand. With the interpretations of language researchers to facilitate their thinking about the meanings of these differences for pedagogical practices, teachers and students have a context for considering not just what these differences say, but what they mean for classroom practice. The research of anthropologists and social historians who have examined literacy across cultures and time periods lends emphasis to the need to link reading and writing habits to speaking habits (see Davis 1975, Graff 1981 and Goody 1977). This historical and sociocultural work indicates that the adoption and retention of literate habits is highly interdependent with early language socialization. Maintenance and extension of types and functions of literacy depend upon participation in redundant, multiple, and reinforcing occasions for sharing orally the meaning of written texts. Olson (1984) has under-scored this point for individuals as well as for societies in his identification of distinctions between *say* and *mean*. Successful achievement in formal education depends on being able not only to say or report something but also to tell what it means. Such a task requires interpretation – reconciling what the data or text says with what the student knows. Students who come from homes in which their first language socialization includes daily such occasions for interpretation are usually able to take up school tasks much more readily than those students who have not experienced repeated occasions for having to articulate the meaning of words, events, and texts.

Briefly, the following early language socialization experiences seem to correlate positively with academic success and the retention of literate habits.

1. *Participation in talk delineating the sequence or the problem-and-solution aspects of ongoing actions.* From descriptions of the process of getting dressed which a mother might narrate while dressing a young child, to a football coach's explanation of plays, students may hear this type of language. The extent to which preschoolers are asked to produce such talk varies greatly across cultures, and yet the ability to sequence events, explain step-by-step procedures, and talk aloud about ways to solve problems is critical in academic tasks. Branscombe's students collected such data on the younger children in their families by simply recording all the types of questions adults asked preschoolers for several days at different points during their research. They were then able to compare the types of questions asked at home with those used most frequently in classrooms at school.

2. *Participation in situations in which adults expect children to compare one phenomenon (e.g. action, scene, character, object, occasion, or written text) with another.* Adults rarely ask young children directly to make comparisons, but they will model analogical or metaphorical reasoning through their own use of and commentary on proverbs, stories, or statements of comparison and contrast ('Look carefully. That boot isn't like your other one, is it?'). The subtle need to compare one situation with another and to carry the meaning of the first to the second is most often realized in storytelling. Adults

53

may tell tales about their own or others' misdeeds as children and leave a heavy moral point hanging with the story. For their own children, they may state only a brief portion of the story as a reminder that current behaviors are similar to those of the story or they could lead to similar consequences. Without formal explication of the similarities and differences, children learn to link one occasion with another and to draw the meaning of such comparisons for their own behavior. Students in the classrooms described here collected tales from their communities as well as proverbs or aphorisms used by adults to call up metaphorical linkages in their children. In mainstream literate homes and in classrooms, numerous occasions demand that we be able to compare one scene or situation with another without full explication of the similarities and differences.

3. *Participation in verbal explanation of cause and effects.* Students in Branscombe's and Ash's classrooms had to explain cases of miscommunication by identifying sources or causes of the failure of one speaker or writer to connect with listener or reader. They recounted cases in their daily lives when adults or peers asked them to explain causes and effects: 'What did you think would happen if you left your skates on the stairway?' 'What did you think the coach would do if you missed another practice?' In their classrooms, they began to identify their teachers' requests for explanations of causes and effects and to link these requests with certain types of discourse, such as argumentation, persuasion, generalization from specific facts, etc.

4. *Participation in verbatim or near-verbatim retellings.* Students in Branscombe's class read books to younger children in their families and asked the youngsters to retell the stories. They listened for occasions when adults at both home and school asked for retellings and asked questions which prompted students to tell about events in the order in which they occurred or in the same way they had been given in a printed source.

5. *Participation in storytelling.* Stories include an animate being who moves through a series of events with goal-directed behavior (N. Stein 1982), and familiarity with these in oral or written form enables students to participate with ease in several types of classroom activities. Textbooks across the curriculum contain stories placed within the expository text to increase students' interest and to provide variety in forms of genre. Students in the classrooms described here collected stories and analyzed the structures of those they judged as 'good'. They could then apply their standards to stories they found in textbooks or other classroom readings. Intuitively, they came to understand how the expected structure of stories helps listeners and readers anticipate what will come next in both oral and written stories.

These five situation types occur repeatedly in classrooms. Collection, identification, and analysis of language outside of the classroom or through recollected experiences of early childhood can help ESL/EFL students bring to consciousness the structures and implicit assumptions which surround these situations in academic performance. The more extensive and intensive a student's out-of-school experience has been with all of these types, the more likely the student will be able to meet academic performance requirements in school. We can begin to compensate for a lack of experience with these situation types by turning students' attention to their existence in their current environment beyond the classroom.

Conclusions

Being literate in today's formal education system means being able to talk and write about language as such, to explain and sequence implicit knowledge and rules of planning, and to speak and write for multiple functions in appropriate forms. Literate understanding requires far more than basic literacy skills, and the current emphasis on basic skills to eliminate the 'literacy crisis' will not give us literate students. The kinds of activities described here in the classrooms of Branscombe and Ash brought teacher, researcher, and students together in the study of language; through this collaboration, students improved their handling of basic mechanics and came to understand what it means to be literate speakers and writers. Improving their basic skills in English and their facility in spoken and written English came as part of the natural process of meaningful research on the types and functions of language in their daily lives.

Jerome Bruner reminds us that 'Learning is most often figuring out how to use what you already know in order to go beyond what you currently think' (1983a: 183). These students, teachers, and researchers working together played out Bruner's insight into learning. Language use in every moment is a reduction of uncertainty, but the uncertainty is never totally reduced. I have argued here that the attempt to reduce students' uncertainties about language should not come through teacher imposition of rules of grammar and occasions for practiced drills of decontextualized and depersonalized tasks. Instead, together, students, teacher, and researcher can focus on what students already know to accomplish a joint reduction of the uncertainties of language. With such collaborative work, we can all better appreciate that a single piece of evidence of language use touches a world of antecedents and assumptions; if we follow these beginnings, they will lead us to the centers of social and cognitive worlds about which we can best learn together.

3 Collaboration: constructing shared understandings in a second language classroom

Donald Freeman

The frame

I ran into Maggie at the harvest festival. She and I have known each other, through mutual friends, for years and always seem to meet up in similarly chaotic circumstances. Although it was early October, the weather had turned nasty; rain and sleet were driving most people indoors amid the din of food stalls, games, and crafts of various kinds. As we crowded through a doorway, we exchanged pleasantries and somewhat on the spur of the moment, I began to tell her about the research project I had in mind. Her response was open and interested: 'Sure you're welcome to sit in classes, but I don't know what you're going to see.' (Field notes: 6 October 1988.)

So the project was launched with the kind of felicitous informality which came to characterize our work together. This chapter describes collaboration on two levels: how the students in Maggie's classes worked together to create a shared understanding of French, and – as a backdrop – how, with Maggie's help, I came to understand that process.[1]

The major themes

> Classroom education, to a very large degree is talk: it is the social use of language to enact regular activity structures and to share systems of meaning among teachers and students. . . . The questions . . . concern the ways in which teachers and students make meanings together with language, what they . . . do to one another through language, and how language is integrated into the activity routines of the classroom.
>
> **J. Lemke 1985: 1–2**

56

Like many projects which examine how people use language in classrooms, this inquiry started out with one focus and ended up with another. I began with an interest in the nature of possibility in the classroom: how the teacher defines what can or cannot go on in a lesson and how these boundaries of acceptability are constructed or negotiated through the teacher's talk and activity (Fine 1987). This image of the possible, it seemed to me, creates a sort of mental map of the territory in which the teacher operates and within which the students encounter and ultimately learn the subject matter. I had these preliminary directions in mind when I arranged to work with Maggie Brown Cassidy,[2] a French teacher at the local high school.

I am not sure when the research focus shifted, but at some point the boundaries of classroom activity became less crucial than the territory itself; I began to realize that my question about the nature of possibility was premature. I saw that I could not examine these boundaries without first having some understanding of the classes themselves; I had to understand what the boundaries defined. This shift came about largely independently of Maggie. While she had been intrigued by the first formulations of the research focus, she seemed to know on a tacit level that we were examining the shadow of the phenomenon and not the phenomenon itself.

In retrospect, I think my interviews with the students were crucial in redirecting the study. I asked them about what constituted unacceptable behavior in Maggie's classroom: what would get you thrown out of class. Two students made points which were pivotal. They each talked about misunderstandings between teacher and student which led to being thrown out of other classes. For one girl, it was an incident in an art class:

> I got a detention in my art class my freshman year with Mr Lyons because he was describing this box and he said, 'OK, now this is a solid box.' And I said, 'No it's not, it's hollow.' And he gave me a detention for it; he was in a really bad mood . . . I couldn't believe he gave me a detention for that because I even said it to myself, I didn't say it out loud.

(Field notes: 18 November 1988)

For another student, the misunderstanding had to do with confusion over directions:

> The other day I was in my history class and a girl didn't understand and she asked a question and then she got it and she was telling . . . explaining it back to the teacher so she would make sure that she understood it and he just got really mad at her and [said], 'I am the teacher. I will tell you how it goes.' And she got kicked out . . . and the rest of the class was very tense.

(*ibid.*)

Initially these incidents struck me as misunderstandings which resulted in a heavy-handed exercise of the teacher's power over the student. There was certainly an air of injured rectitude in the way the students told me about the incidents. But I began to see more in their stories; in fact, the punch line – being thrown out of class – was not the key. In each case, there had been a breakdown in the perception shared by the teacher and the student. In the art class, there had been a breakdown in the shared perception of the content, the hollow box which the teacher wanted the students to accept as solid; in the history class, there had been a breakdown in common perception of the activity. To the art teacher, it became a challenge to his *authority*; to the history teacher, a challenge to his *control*.

Authority over content and control over activity became a central framework for understanding the teaching and learning in Maggie's classes. It generated many questions: is authority absolute or is it shared? Is control by fiat or by consensus? Imposed or negotiated? Clearly a forty-five-minute class period is riddled with opportunities for negotiation and for misunderstanding of these choices. How does a teacher build the shared understanding of authority and control in the class which is crucial to successful learning and teaching? Thus the focus of the study was shifted; it was now on the nature of Maggie's classroom: how authority and control were distributed, through pedagogy and interaction, to build a shared understanding of French.

Maggie has a fairly consistent, articulated view of teaching and learning; she talks about the subject matter, French, as both content and activity.[3] Our study honed that definition; it became clear that the subject matter is not the French language itself, but the interactions which generate it. Interaction produces talk which is channeled or transformed into content. Thus her pedagogy is primarily concerned with shaping interaction, through authority and control, to generate and perfect content.

The context: Brattleboro Union High School and Maggie's classes

> Gluing the [haves and have-nots] together, as always, is a majority of the middle class, which more than anything else has given Brattleboro its identity. It's a regular kind of people town.
>
> **From the detective novel *Open Season*, set in Brattleboro (Mayor 1988: 49)**

Constructing shared understandings in a second language classroom

The great majority of children in Brattleboro attend the public high school. With a student body of about 1,600, it is actually a 'union' school, serving the town of Brattleboro and six surrounding communities. Children from outlying towns go through sixth grade in their town schools and then come to Brattleboro. There are periodic discussions about the pros and cons of this arrangement, one which is common in many rural areas. Fiscally it seems the only way for small towns to finance secondary education, however it is not without an emotional price, a feeling of loss: of individuality, of immediate control over education, and of innocence. At Brattleboro Union High School – or BUHS – some argue, the 'rural' children will get 'swallowed up', they aren't known by name, and they are exposed to 'town influences'.

Maggie teaches in the newer wing of the high school. Her classroom is:

> . . . down the hall from the health office, across from the gym. The room itself is light and warm, with formica and metal desks and chairs in a loose semi-circle. At some point they may have been consciously laid out, but with successive classes the furniture arrangement has taken on a casual, slightly unkempt look. The room appears in the best sense lived in; it shows the signs of previous tenants – some paper on the floor, a forgotten coat, books and boxes stuffed on the shelves. It has the feel of a studio, perhaps because of the three easels leaning in one corner and the overstuffed armchair in one corner; people come to create something here. The room shows an emphasis of activity over place. Maggie remarks: 'I should get some more posters and stuff on the walls' (there are some here and there). Her voice trails off, then finishes strongly with a ring of recognition rather than defensiveness, 'but what's the point, I don't think that's what they're here for.'

> (Field notes: 13 October 1988)

This year Maggie is teaching all four sections of French II and one of French IV/V, an arrangement which allows her a fair degree of freedom in organizing the curriculum within the level. The French II classes are heterogeneous in terms of age and academic ability (see Appendix); although a foreign language is not required for graduation, there is a strong ethos of interest and support in the school and the town.

Maggie's teaching is like a Moebius strip; it has a fluidity in which process and subject matter meld into one, as in the following class quiz:

> Today, Maggie is giving a quiz in her French II classes. It covers basic vocabulary of quantities – 'a box of . . . ', 'a jar of . . . ' – which you would need to buy food. The students have generated the phrases in previous classes: brainstorming them in English, using them with vocabulary for food which they have already

studied, and practicing them in role plays. Now they are
responsible for them in written form. As they enter the class, there
is the usual pre-class patter with some reference to the quiz . . .
'Will *all* the stuff be on it?', 'How many are you going to ask us?',
'Did you study? I didn't . . . '.

As the quiz is given, it unfolds in an incredible elegance of
technique. The activity is built not on authority, but on a
symmetry of roles; a carefully crafted interplay and balance of
control and initiative (Stevick 1980). The kids dictate the items to
each other: one will say a phrase in English while the others write
it in French. They dictate as many as they can think of, about
twenty-five items in all, with occasional prompting from Maggie.
She then tells each person to choose their 'best twenty', the twenty
items which they are most sure of. As the students dictate these
items back to her in French, she writes them on the board. There
are comments, cries of glee, and exaggerated groans as the details
of written French emerge: 'Is it correct without the "s"?', 'Do we
have to have that thing [the circumflex accent] over the "i" in
"boîte"?' It is a constant give-and-take of detail, combined with
the friendly banter of a group engaged in a common task.

Maggie tells them to look hard as they mark their mistakes in a
different color pen. 'If you miss one, it's minus one [point]', she
says. Kids concentrate as they correct the quiz which they have just
given themselves. The roles are ever-shifting, yet they are also
clear. 'Moi, je vais calculer les points eh . . . Toi, tu soulignes les
erreurs.' [I'll add up the points, you just mark your own mistakes.]
The interaction among the kids and between them and Maggie is
constant; there is a sense of movement and play which keeps things
alert and always in flux. The activity is founded on the ongoing
exercise of choice within boundaries, with direct and immediate
knowledge of results.

(Field notes: 18 November 1988)

The delicate sharing of authority and control is evident here; authority
over language and control over activity shift back-and-forth from
teacher to students and back again. Which raises key questions: how do
the students understand the subject matter, French? How are activity
and talk interrelated in the construction of that understanding? How
does Maggie exercise her knowledge in the process of their learning?
These questions stand out against the fabric of teaching and learning in
Maggie's classes.

Teaching and learning

> Success [in language learning] depends
> . . . on what goes on inside and between
> people in the classroom.

> **E. Stevick (1980: 4)**

The students are brainstorming quantities of food items, while
Maggie records them on an overhead transparency. Terry, a tall,
open-faced, blond boy in a blue T-shirt and grey work pants, says:
'How about beer in a six-pack or by the case?'
Maggie: Some of us buy it by the container.
Terry: Well, *some* of us can't buy it anyway . . .
Maggie: (chuckling) Right.

About ten minutes later, the theme resurfaces as students are
practising the French language they have created:
Terry: Une litre de bière. [A litre of beer.]
Student: Don't we have beer on the brain.
Maggie: Don't knock it, at least it's in a bottle not a case.

There is laughter and Terry seizes the moment:
Terry: How come you're not marking down my checks?
(Maggie makes check marks in her grade book to record
participation.)
Maggie: I have two. Did you say more?
Terry: Naw, I guess that's right . . . I was just hoping.

(Field notes: Class 2, 10 November 1988)

Two elements, participation and humor, are fundamental to
Maggie's teaching and they are intimately related. Humor is a vehicle for
participation: by making jokes students participate and thus they
contribute. On a deeper level, both humor and participation share a
common root, which Maggie refers to as 'energy', central to her view of
teaching. 'Energy' runs through her talk about teaching on all levels. One
afternoon, she characterizes the last class of the day as being like 'a
bunch of spent [nuclear] fuel rods'. At another point, in talking to a boy
after class about his rowdiness and inability to concentrate, she asks:
'What class do you have before this?' Before he can respond, she answers
herself, 'That's right you have gym, well no wonder *your energy's all
over the place*' (my italics).

When asked to define this 'energy', Maggie simply calls it 'the willingness to speak'. Yet as I watch and think about her teaching, it seems
far more pervasive and powerful than that. Maggie is unable to pinpoint
what it is; like a fish, she doesn't see the water. In rereading my field
notes a key emerges:

> The class seems pretty chaotic in some ways. There is constant
> activity about and in spite of the task: kids talking about things
> outside of French at the same time as they do the pairwork. They
> seem able to carry on two conversations at once without losing
> track of either. It's almost like the one supports the other, because
> she lets them use their energy the way they want to, they are able
> to do the work.
>
> (Field notes: 11 November 1988)

Energy seems to be a raw social force which occurs naturally when
adolescents meet. It is created through interaction; the teacher's job is to
use it for learning. Limiting what goes on to acceptable, 'on-task' interactions would be akin to 'shutting down the reactor' which is the source
of this natural social force.

Energy is the matter out of which teaching and learning are fashioned.
Maggie states her view succinctly: 'It is often easier to take energy and
direct it than to create energy in a class.' The challenge becomes how to
manage this energy without curtailing it. Humor and rambunctiousness
take on a new dimension in the social interactions of the class; they are
the exercise of raw social energy which depends on risk, the risk of trans-
gressing the limits of acceptability in the class. In the risk, there is the
vulnerability of being caught and the adrenalin of success. Maggie recognizes this intimate connection of risk, success, and enjoyment in learning: 'I don't know how you can learn a language if you're not enjoying
it. It's so risky and it's so scary and it's hard work.' Maggie's pedagogy
lies in transforming the raw energy of social risk-taking in the class into
the risk-taking of speaking the second language. To that end, she encourages, cajoles, coaches, and directs students as they use their own energy
to learn.

The interaction which generates social energy requires a basic human
respect and the ability to learn self-control; it also requires an emphasis
on the collective. Interactions go on 'between and among people'
(Stevick 1980), so coherence in the group is crucial. Maggie says about
her teaching: 'In general [it] is moving much more in the direction of
working together, the whole class working together in order to learn in
every way.' The inherent problem has been how to recognize individual
contributions to the collective effort.

In Maggie's classes, students control their involvement in a given task
or activity. She consciously eschews the usual teacher role of calling on
students to participate, believing the student must be free to participate
voluntarily. With colleagues in the department, Maggie has fashioned a
simple system to record student participation. They receive participation
grades based on check marks earned on a daily basis throughout the
term; these in turn become part of their overall course grade. There is an

acknowledged sense of reasonableness in the system, as a student explains:

> You always get a check if you try, I mean she's not going to *not* give you a check for raising your hand and saying something and saying it wrong. You contributed something and you made a mistake that probably other people have made and you probably helped other people even more.

(Field notes: 18 November 1988)

The students seem to feel very much in control of the system. Far from being pressured or arbitrary, it seems to be open, accessible, and for the most part fair. Often in class, they remind Maggie to mark down checks, and she is quite detached about it. 'Tell me if you did your homework and I'll mark down a check,' she'll say, indicating again that the students have ultimate control over what goes in the book. But there is more to this system than simply a fair representation of the students' efforts. Check marks are the currency of formal interaction in the class, they identify the interactions which contribute to what is being learned, to the formation of a common understanding of the target language.

What is striking in our collaboration is that Maggie is largely unaware of the central role that the concept of energy plays in her teaching. As I identify it as a theme in the data, she responds immediately almost as if it were something she had known and yet forgotten. In an almost classic interplay of my view as an outsider and hers as an insider, we fashion a shared understanding of this central aspect of her teaching. In a sense, the understanding is as clear as it is unnecessary. Our collaboration only serves to articulate what is intuitive for Maggie; she can certainly operate without it. Yet if energy helps to explain the flux of control and interaction in classes, it leaves largely unanswered the question of how the students are developing their understanding of French.

Language and text

> All too often, teachers organize reality
> and turn over that organization, full-
> blown, to the students to remember until
> test time.
>
> **T. O'Brien (1989: 362)**

The textbook is the usual source of content in the great majority of foreign language classrooms. Both the target language itself, in the form of vocabulary and dialogues, and explanations about it are found in, and

63

often presented from, the text. The text is often also very instrumental in structuring the activity in the class. Students first encounter the language in prepackaged dialogues, they practice it through oral and written exercises from the text, and are tested on their grasp of the language as presented in the form and explanations of the text (Freeman 1991). Authority, and to some extent control, are fused in the text. The not-so-subtle message to students is that the content is outside of them and must be internalized, that the new knowledge is fixed in a pre-existing structure and must be accepted as presented. Thus it is not surprising that most students, particularly at the secondary level, find foreign language study inflexible, static, and unreal.

Maggie's approach contradicts these norms. She does not use a textbook, the content is not written down ahead of time. Rather it evolves through the students themselves. She works through a carefully developed procedure of brainstorming, transcription, and enactment by which the students in effect create the language which they then learn to use. She says, 'I've resisted having a textbook; it's much too easy for them to leave it [the language] within the covers of the book.' Students echo her view, as one observes: 'I think you should teach [French] from the teacher. . . . You can probably learn more from a teacher because they're a human being and they're there talking to you and the book is just laying there open.'

Participation in class activities with the language generates the written text for the students.

> As students are correcting the sentences they have written for
> homework by comparing them with what she has written on the
> overhead projector, Maggie remarks to them: 'What you have here
> is going to be . . . it's like a text you know. It's your reference. If
> it's not correct, you're going to be learning all the wrong stuff,
> because that's what you have to refer to; you don't have a text-
> book. So work with a partner, make sure that what you have, that
> both you and your partner are pretty sure that what you have is
> correct.
>
> (Field notes: Class 2, 2 December 1988)

Her statement holds the kernels of two central tenets of her approach to subject matter, as well as authority over and control of it. First, that language originates with the students and develops through their attention to it, and second that they are responsible for that evolution individually and collectively. Thus both authority and control are ultimately shared. She says:

> They [the students] somehow haven't succeeded [in learning
> French] until they can help the other person do it right. They can't
> just [say], 'Well thank God somebody around here can pronounce
> it right, now I can go on to the next thing.'

There are two types of learning going on in Maggie's classes: each individual student's evolving understanding and mastery of French and the students' collective development as a group which can work together for the effective learning of everyone. By way of these processes together, authority over the language shifts from Maggie to the class collectively and individually.

Students recognize this collective responsibility. They see the role of group work in French as different from what it is in other classes:

> There's also more working in groups [in French than in other classes]. In other classes you just sit there as an individual, but like in French you sit there together and try to figure it out together. If the person next to you doesn't understand, they like ask you and if you do that in any other class, you'd get your head taken off.

(Field notes: 18 November 1988)

Interaction creates and corroborates knowledge. French is constructed by the students in relation to each other, with the occasional necessary input and verification from the teacher. This seems to make intuitive sense to the students:

> [French]'s a speaking skill, you've got to learn to practice with other people. It's like almost a social skill.

(Field notes: 18 November 1988)

Since there is no textbook, there is no absolute source of reference, no canon of explanations. A shared understanding has to evolve through use and interaction in the class. The students become responsible not for something outside themselves, but for the growing understanding of French which they themselves create through interaction with the teacher and with each other.

Phases of learning: constructing a shared understanding

There are three principal phases in the learning process in Maggie's classes: creation of new material, investigation and negotiation of form and explanation, and ritual performance of shared understandings. These phases do not take place in a linear progression; they overlap, often occurring and reoccurring many times within one lesson as well as over the course of several weeks.

In the first phase, the students generate the language through brainstorming activities, with help from Maggie. In the second, they sort out the language, often over days. As they use it in practice, they create both an understanding of the French itself and their own common metalanguage in which to express that understanding. At this point, the flexibility and free flow of energetic activity is crucial; without it, the students would be unable to interact to create common explanations. In the third phase, they rehearse the common explanations by collectively performing them. This stage is highly impromptu, with Maggie triggering the performances. There is a fourth phase, which could be called mastery, which is invisible: as students use French appropriately, it blends into what is the ongoing activity of the class.

The key to these phases arose out of the different relations of talk and activity in the lesson. From Maggie's perspective, these relations were guided by her intention to orchestrate student energy within a basic progression of presenting and eliciting new material, practicing it in structured situations, and ultimately using it more freely in role plays. For me, the major question became how students were learning the material through this progression. As I isolated segments with similar patterns of talk and activity, I tried to articulate to Maggie how I saw them as similar. Often she would see the segments in terms of the point of the activity; comparability was not her concern. Like standing too close to a pointilliste painting, she saw the discrete dots, patterns of color, and how they were put together; I saw the image which they represented, yet was often unclear how or why she did what she did.

Phase 1: Creation of new material

The first phase in constructing a shared understanding of French comes when the students are brainstorming language, in a mixture of French and English, around a focus which Maggie sets. Maggie intercedes as necessary to help with content or to direct the activity. Overall, the control and authority are shared in this phase as students participate in developing the content.

> The students are brainstorming vocabulary for quantities of food items for a picnic. Maggie (MC) records the French on the overhead projector.
>
> S1: Pickles . . . 'cornichons'?
> MC: A big jar or a small one . . .
> S2: (tentatively) 'Une bouteille'?
> MC: No, that's a bottle. A big jar is 'un peau'; a little one is 'un bocal'. (she writes both) What comes in 'une bouteille'?
> SS: Wine? Coke? . . . How about milk?
> MC: No, that's 'un carton de lait'.
>
> (Field notes: Class 2, 4 November 1988)

Often at this stage Maggie will explicitly help students to link the new French vocabulary with English cognates. This is the only point in the learning process where she directs their attention to the relationship between the two languages.

'Courir': 'to run'[4]

Students are brainstorming verbs for what they might do that evening.

S: What's 'run'?

MC: 'To run' . . . You run at night?

S: Yeah. (MC writes 'courir' on the board.)

MC: The past is 'couru'. What English word is related to 'courir',

5   meaning 'to run'? What's running water?

SS: Flows?

MC: In a river . . .

S: Connecticut (referring to the Connecticut River which separates Vermont and New Hampshire).

10   SS: (laughter) No!

MC: The running water in the middle of the river which is dangerous.

        [

S: CURRENT.

MC: The current, right?

15   SS: Very good. How'd you get that?

MC: How about a guy – usually a guy, sometimes a woman – who is a messenger? What's the word for

                           [

SS: Court? Courier. COURIER.

MC: 'Courir' is 'to run' and 'couru' is the past.

(Field notes: Class 3, 1 December 1988)

This type of vocabulary work, which is brief and occurs only when new French words are being introduced, has a tight teacher focus. Maggie controls the activity to exercise her authority over the content. Questions or prompts, which require one-word responses from the students as a group, often generate guessing (see lines 6, 8, 13, 18). Through the exchange, a scaffold is built out of what the students know, to house the new material. The energy in such interactions is quite high; the whole group works together in a give-and-take with the teacher which is reminiscent of a tennis volley (see lines 4–6, 7–8, 11–13, 16–18). This varies the standard Inquiry–Response–Evaluation structure (Cazden 1988: 29) found in most classroom discourse, concentrating instead on the exchange of Inquiry and Response. The Evaluation is handled implicitly (lines 7 and 11) when Maggie continues the exchange with a question, thus indicating the response was what she had in mind. Only in line 14 does she explicitly confirm the response and finally, in line 19, summarizes the whole exchange to bring it to a close.

New language is then practiced through various situational and role-play activities. On the surface, it appears that students are practicing the structures and vocabulary – the form of the language – through these interactions. However there is more than just practice involved; these times also provide the forum for articulating a common set of explanations for how French works. While Maggie's control in the first phase is explicit and tight, it shifts dramatically in the second phase. Here the students assume the major role in developing their understanding of the language by rehearsing the explanations which Maggie has originally introduced, with her and with their peers, in reference to their own use of the language.

Phase 2: Investigation and negotiation of form and explanation

In this phase, the form of the language and explanations for it are investigated, negotiated, and ultimately agreed upon, in peer work and directly with the teacher. In both instances, the control over activity and the use of authority is loose and open-ended. In learning the form and explanations for it, the process is as important as the outcomes themselves because the former is collective while the latter are ultimately individual. The following excerpt shows the flow of control and authority in this phase:

'It's feminine' (1)

Students line up at the overhead projector, having volunteered to write up sentences from their homework. Those who remain seated are comparing and correcting their own versions of the sentences. Maggie is circulating, helping individuals. Mark and Tony are at the overhead projector; Mack has just gone back to his seat after writing up sentence 1.

M = Mark; T = Tony; R = Mack; S = other student

The sentences on the overhead projector are:
<1 J'ai parlé avec mon ami.>
<2 J'ai mangé du chocolat.>

	M:	I hate this . . . How do you say 'candy bar'? 'Un chocolat', is that good enough?
	MC:	(from across the room) Oui. 'J'ai mangé du chocolat.'
	T:	(mugging) The drug dealer's going down on it.
5	S:	(near the overhead projector) You're totally out of it . . .
	S:	Oh, Mark, doesn't . . . [incomprehensible]
	MC:	(to Mack who has returned to his seat, reading from the overhead projector) Mack, 'J'ai parlé . . . ' Regarde la question, eh.
10	R:	(calls from his seat) Avec.

> M: Want me to write that for you 'big Mack'?
> R: Yeah.
> M: (as he changes Mack's sentence on the overhead) Avec ma.

(Field notes: Class 2, 2 December 1988)

The collective aspect of learning in this phase is apparent. The sentence in French, which has been individually created by Mack, becomes the collective text when written on the overhead projector. When Maggie calls attention to an error in Mack's sentence (line 8), he corrects it verbally from his seat (line 10) and Mark offers to make the physical correction on the overhead (line 11). A similar exchange occurs at the end of the next excerpt (lines 33–4) when Doug corrects Mark and Tony's sentence.

In the process, Mark switches from off- to on-task behavior (lines 1–6 *v.* 11) without any direction from the teacher. The freedom which students have to manage themselves in this phase seems directly linked to their willingness to take risks with the language in front of their peers. Thus social risk-taking is integrated with linguistic risk-taking; risk with peers is allied with risk with content. This pattern is illustrated more clearly in subsequent excerpts.

Metalanguage was a crucial clue to identifying this second phase of learning. It provides students with a social means to talk about the content. In applying metalanguage to the French they produce, the students express, with varying degrees of accuracy, their understanding of how French works. As they reflect on, learn to express, and explain to each other the mechanics of French grammar, they build a shared view of the language. Peer interaction is critical at this phase because the understandings which they create are social, tested through interactions with other students and with the teacher.

In the following excerpt, which continues the one above, Mark and Tony explain to each other, erroneously, why the past participle, 'allé', in the sentence 'Elle est allée à sa chambre' has two 'e's.

'It's feminine' (2)

D = Doug; M = Mark; T = Tony

(a few seconds later)

Sentence on the overhead projector: <6 Elle est allée à sa chambre.>

> MC: (from another part of the room) Attends une seconde pour 6
15   parce que . . . [Wait a minute to do 6 because . . .]
> M: (at the overhead projector) Oh yes, that's what I want to know
>   . . . about the two 'e's on 'allée'?
> MC: Oui . . .
> S: That's for feminine.
20 (Other talk; Mark and Tony are at the overhead projector)

M: 'Chambre' is feminine, 'marché' is not, right?
<9 Je suis allé au marché.>
T: (writing on the overhead projector) Je . . . n'ai . . .
                                     [
M: ne . . . that's right
25   T: suis . . . pas . . . allé
                       [
M: ma chambre. If it's 'ma chambre' then it's
two 'e's. (Tony writes 'à marché')
M: Marché (under his breath) au marché.
T: (mugging as he finishes the sentence) Eh bravo.
30   M: Au marché . . . au marché, AU MARCHÉ.
(Tony has left the overhead projector)
S: (nearby) AU.
D: (the next person, already at the overhead projector) That's
what I just . . . 'au'?
35   M: 'Au', not 'à', 'au'. (Doug changes the sentence to read 'Je suis
allé au marché')[5]

(Field notes: Class 2, 2 December 1988)

This excerpt shows rather clearly the social dimension of shared understanding at work. It also reveals what some would call the perils, and others the strengths, of peer work (Cohen 1986). The grammatical explanation (line 19) is accurate, but its applications (lines 21 and 26–7) are mistaken (see endnote). Does peer work create the mistake or does it simply make the mistake public and thus audible? Were the teacher to maintain tighter control with less peer work, she might spot Mark's mistake and correct it. However it seems more likely that tighter teacher control would probably silence this type of peer cross-talk and thus drive such mistaken understandings underground. Because Mark and Tony are getting the right answer in this instance, she would have no access to their misunderstanding. However given the social nature of understanding in Maggie's classes, through repeated peer explanations it is more likely that Mark and Tony will realize their mistake, although it does not happen immediately in this instance (see Edwards and Mercer 1987 for other examples).

The excerpt also presents an interesting image of learning. The students' explanations for the French they are using result in student performance which is sometimes accurate and at other times erroneous. However even these matches between explanation and performance are not always clear; sometimes students do the right thing with the language for the wrong reasons, as Mark and Tony do in the excerpt. The students are involved in an ongoing process of sorting out what they understand and what they are confused about by comparing their understanding to the collective explanation, which is shaped, although not controlled, by the teacher. Maggie seems to recognize the situation by acknowledging through the structure of her teaching that common understandings take time to develop. While she might insist more closely on accurate form, it would not necessarily give rise to a clearer, more uniform understanding of the subject matter.

The following excerpt also illustrates the second phase of investigation and negotiation; it shows how one student's misunderstanding is addressed through interaction to create a shared explanation. The exchange here occurs over the phonological confusion between 'manger', as the infinitive 'to eat', and 'mangé', as the past participle, which are pronounced identically. In this instance, Maggie is more centrally involved, although the explanation and adjudication of the correct form are still left to the students.

The infinitive

J = Jack; K = Kris; T = Terry

MC: OK, *alors*, I want you to be correcting your own papers. And it's . . . you really need to focus here because . . . a lot of it sounds the same . . . 'travailler' with an 'er' sounds like 'travaillé' with an 'e' accent, but it makes *all* the difference
5   she emphasises 'all' with her voice). OK, une question . . . Terry raises his hand) Oui, Terry?

T: Est-ce que tu as mangé le dîner? (Did you eat dinner?)

MC: (transcribing on the overhead projector) <Est-ce/ que/ tu as mangé/ le dîner?>

               [

10 S: (under his breath) Oh my god.

             [

K: I thought it was an 'r'. (referring to the 'é' at the end of 'mangé' which is the past morpheme)

MC: You thought it was an 'r' . . . (addressing the class) Why? How did we put them up on the board? What did it mean
15   when you put them up like that?

                  [

J: that was the infinitive

                      [

MC: That's the infinitive which means what . . .

J: That's just the name of the verb.
20 MC: That's right, it means 'to eat'. (She points to 'mangé' on the overhead projector.) This is . . .

SS: . . . the past. (completing her sentence)

MC: . . . the past.

S: Wait a second.
25 K: I did it all wrong then.

MC: (to Kris, matter-of-factly) Well, fix 'em.

Donald Freeman

S: (from another part of the room, checking his paper) Perfect
       . . . alright.
(A couple of minutes later, Kris continues.)
30   K: I guess I don't know what 'infinitive' means.
       MC: (in a private voice, to Jack) Can you tell her what the
              infinitive means, she says she doesn't . . .
                                             [
       J: The infinitive? Well, it's just,
              (pauses) it's just the word, it's just the word itself.
35   S: (helping out) The name of the verb.
       J: Yeah it's the name.
       S: (somewhere) 'To eat.'
       MC: What . . . what . . . what verb means putting food in your
              mouth?
40   S: (somewhere) The verb 'to eat'.
       MC: Manger, 'er'.
       K: Oh, and this means past.
       MC: That's right. This means really . . . 'eaten'. 'I have eaten.'

(Field notes: Class 3, 2 December 1988)

Kris recognizes that she does not understand the past participle when she sees Maggie transcribe 'Est-ce que tu as mangé?'. Rather than ignoring the difference, or making covert corrections by copying the right version without understanding her mistake, she risks going public with her confusion. Her statement (line 11) echoed by Maggie, leads to two realizations: first that the form is wrong (line 25) and then that she doesn't understand why (line 30).

Kris's statement here (line 30) is a major social risk; it also precipitates social interaction in which the mistake is investigated and a shared explanation for it arrived at. This interaction requires a different kind of talk. Kris's admission creates a genuine need for metalanguage; it is impossible to explain her mistake without words for both the mistake and the explanation. To refer only to the French is to confine explanation to the level of form; metalanguage is the only way to combine form and explanation. Student control over metalanguage in this phase is a crucial mechanism in building their shared understanding of how the French language works and thus their common authority with it. It also indicates to the teacher the level of their understanding.

Maggie's role here is highly facilitative; she does not invoke her authority. When Kris realizes her mistake, Maggie tells her to fix it (line 26); when she realizes she does not understand, Maggie turns to Jack for an explanation. By doing so, she integrates authority for explanation with control over peer activity, giving the message that form is means to understanding, which is what is crucial. This response triggers Kris's second question about understanding which Maggie turns into an opportunity to construct a shared understanding of the problem. When I ask her, in another context, why she does not provide such an answer directly, Maggie replies: 'Oh, I could tell them, but they get sick of hearing me talk. Besides, I think it sticks better when it comes from them.'

In this process of sorting out the language, students interact constantly with each other; there is no external reference invoked. Occasionally they will refer to previous learning, as in the following excerpt.

> Maggie is transcribing homework sentences which students have written in the *passé composé* (past tense) onto the overhead projector.
>
> M = Mike; B = Bob
>
> M: Uh . . . faire du ski? [To go skiing.] Est-ce que tu as *faire du ski? [Did you go skiing?] No?
>
> MC: C'est différent, la forme est différente. [It's different; the form is different.]
>
> 5   B: (faintly) Fait.
>
> M: . . . fait . . . du ski. Oh. Mrs Wallace (French I teacher) kept telling us it was 'faire'. Whenever I wrote it she'd mark it correct.
>
> S: Not the past . . .
>
> 10   B: That's future!
>
> M: (feigning contrition) Oh, oh, excuse me.
>
> (Field notes: Class 2, 2 December 1988)

While Mike playfully evokes a past explanation (lines 6–8), perhaps hoping to create a conflict in authority between his present and former teachers – Maggie and Mrs Wallace, the shared understanding in the class outweighs his version (lines 9–10). Thus Maggie avoids the role of arbiter of the language, turning it over to fellow students as she does in *The infinitive* (lines 33–4). In instances where the students' collective understanding is inadequate, primarily when an explanation is first introduced, she does step in. After that time however, she leaves the students to negotiate and thus build up their understanding. She does participate in their discussions, as in *The infinitive* (lines 41ff.), but she does not insist on her authority. In this way, Maggie creates a scaffold through her initial explanations and introduction of necessary metalanguage, through triggering their application, and through her participation in students' investigations and negotiations of form.

An important counterbalance to this attention to form is the ongoing emphasis on meaning. It is crucial that the language be anchored in the student's reality, to sustain interest and more importantly to decipher its accuracy. Accurate language, in Maggie's view, is not simply formally correct; it must also be true of or for the speaker. At one point, she admonishes the class:

> Go through the questions a couple of times until you're pretty comfortable with them. And answer them truthfully. Don't just answer 'yes' because that's easier. If you did the thing, then say you did; if you didn't, say you didn't. And if you can't figure out how to put it in the negative, just ask.

(Field notes: 5 December 1988)

Here form is clearly cast as subsidiary to meaning.

The following excerpt illustrates this interaction of form and accurate meaning. The students are asking and answering questions about what they did the previous night. One student, Michael, claims to have been skiing, which is unlikely because there has been little snow. The formal issue at play is the shift of the preposition 'du' to 'de' in the negative.

Skiing

MA = Michael

S: Est-ce que tu as fait du ski? [Did you go skiing?] (laughter)
MA: Oui, j'ai fait du ski. [Yes, I went skiing.]
MC: Oui, il a fait du ski. (Skeptically) Hier soir tu as fait du ski, Michael? [He went skiing. Last night you went skiing, Michael?]
S: Last night you did?
5   MC: OK, ça va, eh. Est-ce que Michael a fait du ski? [That's OK, did Michael go skiing?]
SS: (somewhat confused) Non? Oui.
MC: Oui ou non, Michael? [Yes or no, Michael?]
MA: Non.
10   MC: Je dis ça parce que c'est important pour le négatif, eh. Alors, est-ce que Michael a fait du ski? Non, . . . [I'm asking because it's important for the negative . . . So did Michael go skiing?]
SS: (various versions of the negative) Il n'a pas fait de ski/ *Il n'a fait du ski pas.
15   MC: Attention eh . . .
SS: (in increasing agreement and unison) Il n'a pas fait DE ski.
MC: Il n'a pas fait *de* ski. Alors Michael, est-ce que tu as fait *du* ski?
MA: Oui j'ai fait du ski. (Class erupts in laughter.)
20   S: Oliver North!
MC: C'est bien. David, est-ce que tu as fait du ski?
D: (hesitantly) Non, ah, je n'ai pas . . .
                                   [
SS: fait de ski.
SS: De ski/ négatif.

(Field notes: Class 2, 2 December 1988)

Michael prevails in his statement (line 19), to the evident skepticism of his peers (line 20). Rather than sacrificing her commitment to his right to say what he chooses, Maggie moves to David (line 21) to clarify the grammatical issue (line 24). By granting students control over their meanings in the target language, Maggie shares an important aspect of her authority. The students are granted the capacity to know what they mean, even if they don't know how to say it. This creates an important counterpoint within the class since it encourages risk-taking with the language and limits what can be corrected by others to what they know to be untrue.

Phase 3: Ritual performance of shared understandings

During the third phase of learning, the French which has been sorted out can become a ritual performance, bringing form, meaning and explanation, through metalanguage, together. When the students encounter the French through use, they rehearse their shared explanation using their metalanguage. They thus share authority for the explanation and control the giving of it. The following excerpt illustrates this process with the use of 'de' in the negative, where 'des' had been used in the question.

'It's negative'

I = Issac; B = Bob (his partner)

(Issac raises his hand, indicating that he wants to take part.)
MC: Issac?
I: Est-ce que tu as fait des devoirs? [Did you do your homework?]
B: Non, je n'ai pas fait de devoirs . . . [No, I didn't . . .]
5   MC: Oh là là là là bravo! (falling intonation)
S: Très, très bien.
MC: Très bien . . . why was that so 'très bien'? What was special about that?
S: It was polite.
10 S: He said it right.
(Laughter/talking: MC starts to say 'Why' . . .)
MC: Let's have an instant replay there. This was music to my ears. Once more please.
S: Now they won't be able to say it
                                    [
15 I: Est-ce que tu as fait des devoirs?
B: Non, je n'ai pas fait de devoirs.
S: 'cause he didn't do his homework.
S: He said 'des'.
        [
S: DE (loudly).

20   MC: The 'de' . . . why did he say 'de'? The question was in . . .
            (drowned out)
      SS: (in chorus) Because it's NEGATIVE!
      SS: (various people saying) Oh . . . bravo . . . très, très bien . . .

(Field notes: Class 3, 2 December 1988)

The shared understandings which have been evolved are now part of a common lore. This phase represents the ordering of an understanding which all, or at least most, students can see and voice. An individual student's contribution (line 4), precipitates some group entertainment (lines 5–6). Picking up on the students' reactions, Maggie formalizes the performance (lines 12–13) for which students offer their explanations. At first these are intuitive (line 10: 'He said it right'), in anticipation of the next phase of mastery when such use of the language will no longer be remarked on. Then on analysis (lines 17–19), students offer two explanations; one based on meaning (line 17: ''cause he didn't do his homework') and the other based on form (lines 18–19: 'He said 'des/ DE'). The formal explanation prevails (line 22) because it is shared, while the meaning is by definition individual, and the performance is complete.

The creation of a shared understanding

The process of evolving shared understandings of what to learn and how to learn it is at the heart of what makes Maggie's classes work. It takes place against the backdrop of constant social interaction, or 'energy', and is intimately tied to sharing authority and control. Table 1 summarizes the interrelation of four major themes in Maggie's classroom: interaction and social energy, risk-taking, authority over content, and control over activity.

There is an intriguing symmetry in the overall shape of the learning process. While the first and third phases tend to be more tightly focussed and controlled, the second is more open-ended and individualized. The focus of the first phase grows out of Maggie's unique position as the knower of the content; she has the authority over the content and the control over the activity. Students take over that control, practicing the content and evolving understanding of it, first individually and then in progressively more collective ways. Through practice, they gain the authority which comes from understanding the content. The mark of having achieved a collective or shared understanding comes when they can perform it, as they do in the third phase. Here authority and control are integrated in a ritual.

This symmetry involves differing types of interaction and uses of social energy. In the first and third phases, the interaction is primarily teacher–

TABLE 1. SUMMARY OF THE THEMES OF AUTHORITY AND CONTROL

Excerpt	Phase	Interaction and social energy	Risk-taking	Authority over content	Control over activity
'Courir'	1	High; tightly focussed	Minimal	With teacher	With teacher
It's feminine		Diffused among peers	Social (with peers)	Distributed among students and teacher	Turned over to students
The infinitive	2	Diffused among peers	Social and linguistic	Delegated to students by teacher	Shared between students and teacher
Skiing		Mid-level; created by tension between form and meaning	Social and linguistic	Split: student controls meaning, teacher form	Shared; student: meaning, teacher: activity, students: form
It's negative	3	High; group effort	Minimal; exercise of known language	With students	Teacher orchestrated

student, with Maggie providing a structure of questions and prompts to which students respond. In the second phase, which makes up most of their classtime, students are involved primarily in peer interaction which gives more or less free, or at least open-ended, run to their energy. Thus they mix talk in French with talk about it, and talk about it with talk about other topics. In a very real sense, this process which can appear chaotic and unstructured is when understanding emerges. Students are free to risk, and therefore they tend to show their imperfect grasp of the content. If, as in many other foreign language classes, they were confined to accurately reproducing linguistic form, neither they nor the teacher would have any sense of whether the understandings which underpinned that formal production were appropriate or not.

Thus Maggie has been able to make public the process of creating and internalizing the language precisely because she allows the talk and activity in her class to be largely self-regulated. Students come to control themselves in their interactions; that control goes hand-in-hand with authority over the language. Both involve the responsibility to an inner sense of rightness: for appropriate behavior and for accurate language use. This responsibility is individual and collective. Maggie is a resource for the language and a source for criteria and explanations of correctness. Likewise she is the source of activity in the classroom and a resource for successful accomplishment of that activity.

Collaboration: some closing thoughts

> A way of seeing is always a way of not seeing.
>
> **K. Burke (1935: 70)**

My last set of field notes for the project reads as follows:

> I met with Maggie this afternoon to go over the transcripts and get her reactions to my analysis of them. We sat in the kitchen, drinking tea and talking as her younger daughter, Susanna, alternately amused herself and tried to get involved. I'm not sure what I expected – or wanted – from the meeting, perhaps her definitive statement that I was right or wrong in my approach and analysis. Our conversation was very comfortable, although somewhat disjointed as it always is with little kids around, but most of all profoundly in the present. I realized from it that this is first and foremost her teaching I am writing about, not some abstraction.
>
> (Field notes: 5 January 1989)

As we reviewed this analysis together, Maggie found most of it apt and true. She commented that it gave her a sense of coherence that she did not always feel in the midst of things, and that this sense was affecting her ongoing teaching in positive ways. In thinking it over, I realized that was in fact what our collaboration had borne: a shared understanding of her pedagogy.

Teaching is a phenomenon she lived and I described; she did it and I tried to find words for what I saw and heard. The relationship worked in large measure because it was founded on the 'believing game' (Elbow 1973). I believed there was meaning and logic in her practice to be uncovered and Maggie believed, from our initial meeting at the harvest festival, that I would be looking in that way. Within this framework, the interplay of our points of view helped to move something which was private, intuitive, and unreflected into the public forum of writing and talking, the construction of our shared understanding expressing what she had done and I had found in her classroom.

Appendix

TABLE 2. MAKE-UP OF FRENCH II CLASSES (FALL 1988)

	Class 1	*Class 2*	*Class 3*
Total number of students	14	16	25
Number of students by grade	1: 12th 2: 10th 11: 9th	1: 12th 12: 10th 1: 9th 2: 8th	5: 11th 6: 10th 14: 9th
Gender:			
Girls	8	8	17
Boys	6	8	8

Characteristics of the three classes in the study

Each of the French II classes in the study varies in size and age grouping. Class 1 is relatively quiet, perhaps because it is small and primarily ninth graders, most of whom did not know each other previously.

Class 2, in contrast, is rambunctious and energetic. Most of the students know one another from French I. In addition, there are two rather outspoken eighth graders, one who speaks French at home in his Franco-American extended family and the other who has spent time in France.

Class 3 is Maggie's largest, with 25 students, the majority of whom are ninth graders. The class does not know each other very well and seems to be dominated by two immature ninth-grade boys.

Endnotes

My grateful thanks to Maggie Brown Cassidy for the collaboration which made this work possible, and to Courtney Cazden for her comments on an earlier version of this paper.

[1] Although the researcher and the context are continually present in any study, that fact can be obscured when research is reported in a third-person, abstracted voice. However, collaboration between researcher and subject is neither impersonal nor acontextual; I think it is important to make that fact visible to the reader. Therefore, throughout this paper I have decided to maintain, and make evident, my first-person voice as writer-researcher and to emphasize the setting and context of our collaborative work.

[2] With the exception of Maggie Brown Cassidy, all the other names in this account have been changed.

[3] Research into teachers' ways of thinking about their practice indicates that although they often talk of them as separate elements, teachers actually think about activity and content, both in planning and retrospective analyses of lessons, as integrated wholes. See Carter and Doyle 1987; also Freeman 1990a.

Donald Freeman

⁴ *Key to transcription symbols:*
  S refers to a single student speaking.
  SS refers to more than one student speaking at the same time.
  MC refers to Maggie throughout; fictitious versions of other students' names (with their gender maintained) are included only when they are referred to in the body of the conversation.
  [= overlapping speech.
  Capital letters indicate words which are said more loudly than the surrounding speech.
  < > = what has been written on the overhead projector.
  * denotes an utterance which is grammatically incorrect; I have used it only where information about correctness is critical to understanding the interaction. I have marked the date and class in which the data were collected at the end of each transcript; for further information on composition of the classes, see Appendix. I have also indicated any speech transcribed from field notes, without aid of tape recorder.
⁵ Mark realizes that he doesn't understand why there are two 'e's on 'allée' (lines 16–17). The explanation which a student (line 19) offers is correct – 'That's for feminine' – however Mark misapplies it (line 21) to sentence 6, <Elle est allée à sa chambre>. So he derives the correct form of the past participle for the wrong reasons. Although the noun 'chambre', is feminine, it is the pronoun 'elle', and not the predicate object, 'chambre', which controls the addition of the extra 'e'. When they write up their sentence, Mark applies the same logic (lines 26–7), only to have Tony change the predicate object to 'marché' which is masculine. Their sentence, <Je suis allée à ma chambre>, would have been wrong – Mark/Tony as its authors are male thus 'allé' would not need the extra 'e' – but when Tony changes the predicate to 'marché', they again make it correct for the wrong reasons.

4 Context and cooperation in academic tasks

Bernard Mohan and Sondra Marshall Smith

This chapter will investigate how a group of Chinese students participated and succeeded in a graduate adult education course, despite the fact that they had scored below the required level on a language proficiency test (TOEFL). Rather than taking a view of language learning conceived in abstraction from sociocultural proficiency and content learning, this study will use the theoretical perspective of 'language socialisation', which views language learning and cultural learning as interrelated, and which seeks to understand the role of language in the process of forming social practices. Consequently, language socialisation will be contrasted with language acquisition. Central to the study is the notion of academic tasks as sub-tasks of a larger cultural activity, learned cooperatively.

Background

The eight subjects in this study are 'student-trainees' sponsored by the Canadian International Development Agency (CIDA) to study in Canada for one year. They are part of a large bilateral program negotiated by the Canadian and Chinese governments to expand China's resource pool in the areas of agriculture, forestry, communications, transportation, and human and social development. The common prerequisite for training in all fields is an adequate knowledge of French or English and their respective cultures.

The students in this investigation were able to accomplish the academic requirements in a graduate course despite their lack of background in the field and their limited proficiency in English. The study seeks to understand how and why they succeeded. By examining the entire cycle of the course and the surrounding environment, the study takes a broad view, considering, for example, the background of the students, their preparation for the course, their cooperation with the professor and other students, the nature of their tasks, and other factors. However, it is not our intention to identify what cultural learning occurred and had been learned, but rather to examine how these students integrated the content matter, cultural learning and language that they were exposed to in an actual course. Further, it is not our purpose to note specific language learning or linguistic aspects. Instead, the study views the course more broadly as a language socialisation process.

Task as focus

'Task' was chosen as a focus for this study because there is evidence that task is a unit of analysis common to both language teaching and learning, and content teaching and learning. Without a common unit of analysis it would be difficult to see the relation between the Chinese student as a second language learner and the Chinese student as a learner of subject matter. With a common unit of analysis it is possible to make some assessment of proposals for relating the language syllabus to the content syllabus and of the research issues that lie behind these proposals.

In a detailed, constructive and critical review of the literature, Crookes has marshalled evidence 'of the potential strength and utility of "task" as a major unit of analysis throughout all educational research and design' (Crookes 1986: 6). Communicative tasks appear in *Communicative Language Teaching* (Littlewood 1981) and similar tasks have been found useful in experimental research in second language acquisition (SLA) (e.g. Long and Porter 1985). Moving from the language classroom specifically to classrooms generally, Doyle (1983) draws on an extensive literature review to present a view of the school curriculum from the perspective of the student as a collection of academic tasks. In addition, beyond education, Crookes indicates that task is an important unit of analysis in the world of work; he cites research such as Peterson and Bownas (1982) who review job-related task classification, covering both jobs as a whole and task structures within jobs. More recent developments add to this evidence: in second language teaching e.g. Nunan (1989a), second language acquisition e.g. Long (1989), and education in general e.g. Marx and Walsh (1988).

Important educational design implications follow from the position that task is a common unit of analysis for language learning, education and work. Long and Crookes argue that task provides for an 'integrated, internally coherent approach to all six phases of program design and one which is compatible with current SLA theory' (Long and Crookes unpublished: 46). In their conception, a task-based syllabus will be based on a needs assessment of the target tasks of content classrooms or the world of work, and will derive pedagogic tasks from such target task types. In other words, the tasks of the language syllabus will relate developmentally to the tasks of the content classroom or work world, and the research basis for this relation will be, firstly, SLA research on tasks and secondly, research on content classroom and workplace tasks.

But there is a problem. For this program of educational research and design it is not sufficient that task be a common unit of analysis. A common unit does not guarantee that different research approaches cannot begin from the same unit and produce results which are irrelevant or even contradictory to each other. There are at least two research approaches to task and language: the input and interaction approach in second language acquisition, and the language socialisation approach. We will argue that they differ in their assumptions about task, in the scope of phenomena they consider, in the methods they use, and in the results they produce. This raises the question of whether these approaches are contradictory or complementary, and whether this program of educational research and design is feasible.

We will first consider the assumptions about task in the second language acquisition (SLA) input and interaction approach and then we will consider the assumptions about task in the language socialisation approach. We will consider assumptions about 'context' also, since that is another central concept on which they differ.

SLA input and interaction approach

SLA research tasks are given below. They are fairly typical of the literature on input and interaction (Young 1988), and also of the literature on second language communication processes (DeKeyser 1988):

1. Picture description task, e.g. a learner of English is given a coloured photograph of a familiar object and asked to describe it in English so as to identify it clearly for an English-speaking hearer.
2. A twenty-minute interview with a native speaker of English, during which discussions ensued on everyday topics such as school, holidays, cooking and sports.

SLA researchers interested in input and interaction have examined similar tasks seeking those types that favour language acquisition: Pica and Doughty (1985, 1986); Long and Porter (1985); Gass and Varonis (1985); Long (1989). These studies look at various aspects of interactions: one-way tasks, two-way tasks, teacher-to-student and student-to-student, the object being to determine what task types and what group membership facilitate discourse features of modified interaction. As Young (1988: 122) explains: 'the term "interaction" has been used in the literature in a narrow sense to mean oral exchanges in the target language between a learner and one or more interlocutors who are focused on some kind of activity in which the meaning of unclear words or structures is clarified.' Categories listed by Long (1989) which have been frequently counted in studies to measure interactional modification include confirmation checks, comprehension checks, and clarification requests. Pica and Doughty give the basic rationale for such studies: 'In keeping with second language acquisition theory, such modified interaction is claimed to make input comprehensible to learners and to lead ultimately to successful classroom second language acquisition' (Pica and Doughty 1986: 322).

It is important to note that 'task' is here seen in the tradition of psychological experiments: the participants in the task are 'subjects', engaged in an experimental task; task characteristics are seen as independent variables; and characteristics of task discourse are considered to be dependent variables. In order to relate task characteristics to discourse features, and aggregate across individuals, it is standardly assumed (see Todd 1981: 220) that: (1) all subjects share the same 'definition of the task'; and (2) the 'definition of the task' is constant for the duration of the experiment. As we will discuss later in this paper, task is viewed very differently in the anthropological tradition where one participant learns about the task from another during the course of the study.

The theoretical basis for the above studies is ultimately related to Krashen's input hypothesis which is centred on a single claim: 'comprehensible input is the true and only causative variable in second language acquisition' (Krashen 1987: 40). More explicitly, for the learner to develop in language competence by acquiring a new grammatical structure, the learner must understand input which 'contains' the new structure. Krashen claims that the learner does this by relying on 'context': the new structure is comprehended by relying on contextual and extralinguistic clues. In one of the very few studies which takes account of this, Wesche and Ready (1985) studied the speech adjustments made by two psychology professors in their lectures to first language (L1) and second language (L2) students. The authors point to several contextual and extralinguistic differences between the L1 and L2 lectures: more frequent use of gestures with the L2 students, more time spent at the blackboard and greater schematic and representational information written on the board. In other words the professors supplied more contextual support for the L2 students.

Thus the input hypothesis depends on what should be called the context hypothesis. But how exactly the context hypothesis works is left unclear, despite its major importance. Its apparent assumptions are: (1) that contextual information is 'given', known information (2) which operates on the sentence. We are not led to examine issues of great concern in the anthropological tradition: (1) how contextual information becomes known, and is socially constructed; and (2) how it operates on units larger than the sentence, such as the task. This is not the place to examine in detail the conceptual and empirical weaknesses of the context hypothesis (see Mohan and Helmer 1988) but it is notable how this approach based on comprehension has little connection with comprehension research on formal and content schemata which are of central importance in reading and subject matter (see Carrell 1988). Largely ignored has been a major category of contextual information: 'the background knowledge (particularly sociocultural knowledge) which the learner brings to the interpretation of discourse' (G. Brown 1989: 98).

Language socialisation

An example of a task from the present study, a course assignment from a content classroom, is given below:

> Course assignment #1: Provide a comprehensive [written] description of the organisational context and client system [for the adult education program you have chosen to describe] and explain how these characteristics may influence later steps in the planning effort . . .

This task was initially very difficult for the Chinese students. We were interested in how the instructor arranged the course interaction so that this task (and the other course assignments) apparently became understandable and 'do-able' for the Chinese students.

This task is simultaneously a language task of writing and a content task. It raises questions both of language learning and of content learning (which can be seen as a sub-part of cultural learning). Both of these aspects are taken account of in the language socialisation approach which treats the learning of language and the learning of culture as integrated processes. The young child learning language is simultaneously learning about the world. Language socialisation means both socialisation to use language and socialisation through language. To language learning is added a theory of learning as a linguistic process (Halliday and Hasan 1985: 49). Language socialisation considers both the development of language and the development of knowledge (which can then play the role of contextual information in the interpretation of discourse).

A useful distinction between language acquisition and language socialisation has been provided by Schieffelin and Ochs: 'the study of language acquisition has as its ultimate goal an understanding of what constitutes linguistic competence at different developmental points. Whereas, language socialization has as its goal the understanding of how persons become competent members of social groups and the role of language in the process '(Schieffelin and Ochs 1986: 167). Thus while many L1 and L2 researchers of language acquisition consider the

85

sentence or the utterance exchange as the natural frame for linguistic inquiry, language socialisation researchers consider how vocal and verbal activities are socially organised and embedded in cultural systems of meaning and interaction, and thus often take as their unit much longer stretches of interaction (Heath 1983; Ochs 1988).

The language acquisition / language socialisation contrast can be clearly seen in the work of one L1 researcher. During the 1970s first language acquisition researchers such as Snow (Snow and Ferguson 1977) sought to understand the nature and importance of an adult's linguistic input to a young child while his or her language skills were developing. The special language that occurs between caregivers and young children became known to some as 'motherese'. (Krashen's views owe an obvious debt to this work, via the concept of 'foreigner talk'.) In this approach, language acquisition was treated as a separate topic from learning culture and social context (Snow and Goldfield 1983: 552). In later papers (Snow and Ninio 1986) Snow took the view that the processes which make language acquisition possible required investigations of the social context as well. In her example of the task or situation of recurrent picture-book reading sessions by a mother and child, the child not only participates increasingly in the discourse interaction as the sessions continue but also begins to acquire the 'contracts of literacy' (books are to be looked at, read, and discussed, not eaten, ripped or thrown). Participation in the picture-book reading task, knowing what to say when, calls for both language and cultural development.

Bruner (1983b) provides a further example of language socialisation, giving significant attention to task (also called 'activity') and context, with parallels to the earlier work of Halliday (1975). Following an emerging trend 'to look increasingly at the contexts that enable human beings to act as they do'(Bruner 1983b: 124), Bruner describes in detail the actions, sequences and roles played by two caregivers and their young children, in their second year of age, during games such as peek-a-boo. In the beginning of the study the mothers initiated the games, played both roles, and maintained all the routines. Quickly the children began to respond orally; then they participated actively. In doing so, they mastered the language, transactional routines and concepts which could be applied elsewhere, such as mastering fundamentals of linguistic reference. Bruner observed that '[these] lessons are obviously as much cultural as they are linguistic. Language acquisition seems to be a by-product of cultural transmission. The engine that drives the enterprise is not language acquisition *per se*, but the need to get on with the demands of the culture'(1983b: 103).

At the core of Bruner's thesis are two primary concepts: first, human action is systematic and ordered, and much of our cognitive processing appears to operate in support of goal-directed activity; and second, human cultural activity is extraordinarily social and communicative (1983b: 25). In Bruner's data, the game is the unit of cultural activity. According to him 'each of the games played by children and their parents is a self-contained "form of life". The games are, in a word, an idealized and closely circumscribed format. They have "deep structure" and a set of realization rules by which the surface of the game is managed' (1983b: 46). The game provides a structured 'format', a patterned situation of moves, that enables the adult and child to cooperate in passing on the language and culture. As the child becomes familiar with the moves of the game he or she takes the initiative and learns to execute the role of the agent as the mother hands over control. Thus the child's learning is dependent on rich routines which can be diversified, to allow for the increasing initiative and competence of the learner as he or she executes the moves.

What relevance could peek-a-boo have to the study of second language learners in a graduate course? To see the general features of Bruner's approach, it is helpful to view it through the Vygotskian concept of the learner's 'zone of proximal development' (Cole 1985: 155) (see page 91) and to identify the following as research issues: the processes by which novices come to adopt the role of experts in culturally organized activities; the interactional nature of their progress, which can often be described as an increase in control or responsibility; and the ways experts structure interactions so that novices can participate in activities that they are not otherwise capable of. Cole gives further examples of how cultural activities are learned: Lave's (1978) study of tailoring practice in shops in Liberia showing that direct instruction was less important than how apprentices were engaged in productive work through which they became familiar with later steps in the tailoring process; and Childs and Greenfield's (1982) description of learning to weave among Zinacantecan weavers, noting the role of prior observation and graduated social guidance by adults and showing how adult task-based talk varied with the specific weaving task and the child's level of skill.

In the Vygotskian framework, as we can see from the above examples, task (as 'activity') has a central place, but it is task as a cultural, social activity, and not merely as an experimental task, which may be uninterpretable outside of its original culture (Cole 1985: 150). Furthermore, we can distinguish the adult or *expert's task* (the full process of book-reading, peek-a-boo, tailoring, or weaving, for example) and the *novice's task* (initial participation within the context of the full activity) which is progressively expanded into the expert's task.

The learner's understanding of the *context* or environment of his or her actions (e.g. what you need to know to do tailoring or weaving) is expanded as the learner's task expands, the context is socially constructed by the *cooperative* work of expert and novice, and the context both illuminates and is illuminated by communication within the task. Understanding of the context is not initially a given. And there is a range of communicative ways of learning: while the learner's participation in the cultural activity is a central means of socialisation, it is not the only means; observation may be important, as may comment, discussion and explanation. Vygotsky saw the task as both a unit of cognitive organisation within the individual and as a unit of social organisation within the culture. Moving beyond the more obvious implications of this, we can ask how far the correspondence holds between psychological and social aspects of the task.

The input/interaction view of SLA focusses on the negotiation of language input within a task; this perspective of language socialisation focusses on the negotiation of a task so that a learner can participate in a cultural activity. In the input/interaction view, task and context are assumed to be givens; in the language socialisation view, task and context are under development. Both approaches deal with task and context, but deal with them in very different ways. One takes a psychological view of language, the other a social view. Are these two approaches to task contradictory or complementary?

Cole (1985: 158) suggests that task or 'activity' can be a link between psychology and anthropology. Seen in Vygotskian terms as both a unit of cognitive organisation within the individual and a unit of social organisation within the culture, the task allows a complementary division of labour: psychologists can study the cognitive aspects of the task by controlled laboratory-based analysis of individual human subjects; anthropologists can look at the task as part of a social organisation created within the reciprocal cultural action of the human community, and will study this holistically by observation in the field. Can any similar division of labour be made for the two approaches to task under discussion? It may be that a division of labour can be made between the experimental study of microprocesses of discourse below the level of task and the naturalistic study of macroprocesses surrounding the task. If so, this study will provide an example of the latter.

In the investigation at hand, we have chosen to use a case study approach to explore how the group of eight Chinese graduate students fulfilled the academic requirements for their course of study. The theoretical framework outlined above necessitates that the entire cycle of the course be scrutinised in order to understand how tasks were completed. Where Bruner used the game and moves in the game as the contextual units, this study will use the course, and the tasks of assignments within the course as contextual units.

Data have been gathered from a variety of sources: extensive field notes gathered from participant observation, interviews with each of the students and the professor, all of the students' assignments, materials distributed from the course, and a field diary. In addition, there was ample opportunity to meet and discuss issues informally with the students over a five-month period. This provided an abundance of data from which to draw.

Case study

A group of Chinese students were participating in a graduate adult education course (ADED XXX) at the Western University. Two distinct student groups composed the class. There were eight Chinese students and six other graduate students, who were native speakers of English (NS). The NS were graduate students in the adult education department and had taken several courses in this field. They were all older than the Chinese students and had several years of professional experience in related fields.

The Chinese students were attending the course in order to gain an understanding of the field of adult education, but they were not registered for credit. Their objective was to become knowledgeable about the field of adult education in order to establish an adult education institute in their city in China. Their motivation to succeed was high. All were young, bright, with reasonable levels of English (they would score approximately 500–550 on TOEFL). Their undergraduate studies included: physics, marine engineering, pharmacology, chemistry and English literature. None of them had any background in either program planning or adult education. They were unfamiliar with the routines and expectations of graduate-level work in a Western university. Prior to and at the beginning of the course, they expressed apprehension about whether they could fulfil the requirements.

ADED XXX – Adult Education Program Planning Practice – is a regular departmental offering which examines the application of planning and evaluation principles in specific adult education settings and explores the practical utility of various approaches to planning and evaluation. The prerequisite for ADED XXX is a companion course which provides theoretical and conceptual perspectives in adult education. The Chinese students had not taken the prerequisite.

In the next sections we will discuss the course plan, the course process, and the assignments. The case will be viewed as an example of learning a cultural activity, through the language socialisation perspective. This enables us to see how a number of familiar and 'taken-for-granted' details of university graduate courses can fit into a larger pattern.

89

Course plan

The instructor introduced the students to the course in a standard but effective way. He had prepared a detailed package of course materials which included the course schedule, the assignments, the required readings, and a list of expected outcomes. The following topics were covered in the course:

1. planning as an anticipatory decision-making process
2. analysing the planning context and client system
3. identification of educational needs
4. developing educational objectives
5. formulating an instructional plan and an administrative plan
6. developing an evaluation plan.

Required readings and lectures were keyed to these topics and there were five assignments which matched topics 2–6 exactly.

On the first day of the class he distributed and discussed the materials. Students were introduced to the overall philosophy and conceptual basis of the course, the professor's background, desired outcomes from the course, and students' responsibilities. There was a discussion about the marking scheme for the assignments and the scope expected.

Simple as this was, the Chinese students took great comfort from it. They said that it gave them a clear view of exactly how the course would be structured and what they must do, for they could refer to the outline and see how various sections related to one another. In particular, they could link lecture material and readings to the assignments. They cited their awareness of the total organisation of the course as a significant contribution to their success.

A special aspect of the course organisation deserves comment. The instructor had designed the course to be task-based, and it was centrally organised around student assignments which were integral to the course. As a course in 'Adult Education Program Planning Practice', a central aid of the course was to 'study the process [of program planning] and practise making the kinds of decision which must be made'. Accordingly, the major piece of student work in the course was to plan an educational program for an actual case or for a hypothetical case (which was provided). This large task was broken down into five steps which were the basis for the five assignments of the course which guided the student through this task and which were the main basis for evaluation. As noted above, the assignments matched the course topics and the required readings. Moreover the instructor clearly signalled a strategy of using the assignments as the focal element in the course, drawing together knowledge gained from sources in the course and elsewhere. The course outline stated:

> the objective of these written assignments is to provide an opportunity for you to apply, in a systematic way, the knowledge and insight you have attained through reading, discussion, and experience. Critique from class participants and feedback from the instructor are intended to facilitate your increased understanding about the process of planning educational programs.

The professor reiterated this point during the first lecture.

This aspect of the course has many of the features of learning a cultural activity described in the discussion of language socialisation above. Program planning is a culturally acknowledged activity existing in the community. The instructor plans that students will learn by participating in this activity, if only by simulating it. The instructor as expert enables the novice to participate by breaking down the activity into sub-tasks. These sub-tasks are designed to be within the capacity of the novice when guided by the expert (within the 'zone of proximal development'). The result is that these assignments are not unconnected cognitive exercises; they fit together as guided participation in a larger activity and are intended to develop understanding of the larger activity.

Course process

The instructor guided the day-to-day process of the course so that its various parts could create a context of information and interactive support for the course assignments. These parts, homework and classwork, were already coordinated through the course outline, which was followed closely. Homework consisted of course readings which matched the assignments. Classwork consisted of lectures, small-group discussions, and, for the Chinese students, morning group tutorials.

The lectures set up the knowledge needed for the assignments. The small-group work offered an opportunity to apply the lecture information to a new situation or to examine an aspect of it in greater detail. This meant that the Chinese students had another chance to hear (and comprehend) the information again. The morning group tutorials gave the Chinese students 'sheltered' situations in which to ask for assistance or clarification. The Chinese students reported that this coordination enabled them to maintain a sense of coherence throughout the course. In the words of subject 7: 'All topics are related, following step by step, specific and logical from beginning to end.' We will discuss lectures, group discussions and tutorials in turn.

LECTURES

The structure of the lectures was predictable since they followed the course outline. Topics of the assignments were the focus of the lecture preceding the due date, so that each lecture presented the content and the methodology needed for the subsequent assignment. The professor highlighted this point during the first class. In other words, it was a deliberate strategy to tailor the lectures to the content of the assignments. For instance, during one evening the professor reviewed on the black-board a sample budget which could be applied to a continuing education program. The next assignment, due the following week, included a section in which the students were to propose a budget for their hypo-thetical program.

He often referred to the course readings during his lectures and occasionally asked students to examine some aspect in detail or used passages on an overhead projector. During the first lecture, he offered hints on how to use the print material in relation to the assignments and how to work efficiently: 'Keep a list of the assignments in front of you when you are doing your reading. Make a notation if it relates directly'; 'Refer to your notes when doing assignments'; 'Don't reread the articles six times.' Even with this guidance the Chinese students sometimes found it difficult to access ideas in the reading material: ' . . . the content and the lecture were very related to one another. But sometimes the content wasn't so easy to find, for example in the evaluation section' (subject 6).

The professor's instructional style was also clear. Each section of the lecture was summarised, and he often previewed a topic and then reviewed it as a conclusion. Frequently, important concepts or vocabulary were 'revisited'; for example, the notion of planning as an 'anticipatory decision-making process' was mentioned in lecture 1 and again in lecture 6. He constantly rephrased ideas, repeated new words; clarified concepts; and defined words or terms that might be unknown to the students. His speaking style was slow, calm and direct during ordinary conversation and in class. He was conscious that half the students were non-native speakers and thus he avoided jargon, slang or idiomatic references. In addition, the professor illustrated his remarks with frequent concrete examples. In short, his lectures were very repetitive, giving the Chinese students ample opportunity to hear the important point and relate it to an example. Every student interviewed commented that the lectures were understandable and well organised.

Although the professor presented the lectures at the front of the room and directed most of the interaction, he made it clear that the class was an open forum for student participation and invited student comment. In fact, it was only the more outgoing students (subjects 5, 6, 7, 8) who ventured to speak publicly in front of the whole group. These four subjects were all males. Only on two occasions did two female students ask a question while class was in progress. 'I was reluctant to speak in front of the whole class' (subject 3).

DISCUSSION GROUPS

Discussion groups took place around tables and the seating arrangement (roughly two native speakers, two Chinese per table) was deliberately staged to foster interaction among the students. Discussion topics were based on the course reading and were assigned by the professor to the whole group. But the Chinese were not equal partners in the discussion. When the Chinese students were asked whether being involved in the discussions facilitated their understanding, all eight said that they found it useful to hear the ideas of the other students. When asked how they felt about participating, two of the eight said they felt nervous; three commented that they didn't always understand the task and for that reason didn't participate. 'I felt afraid to participate [in small-group discussion] because I wasn't sure if my understanding was correct' (subject 2). Also, they sometimes did not understand the comments of the other students. In some instances they were reluctant to break into the conversation. On the whole the Chinese students were much less vocal than the native speakers. It seemed that the Chinese students participated in the discussion when they were able to be prepared rather than spontaneous: 'I didn't participate as freely as I do in my native language. You have to organise and that means slowly, not quickly, before you can express your own ideas' (subject 6). From field observation it was noted that the Canadian students rarely asked the Chinese students for their opinions or directly included them in the conversations. Nor was there much informal interaction and spontaneous mixing. Sometimes the Canadian students engaged one or two Chinese in conversation during the coffee breaks, but the conversation was exploratory, with the Canadian asking questions about the Chinese situation, rather than a mutual exchange. The Chinese students rarely initiated conversation with the others and did not engage in small-talk patterns that are normally associated with casual conversation.

GROUP TUTORIALS

The Chinese students used their morning tutorials with the professor to ask questions about the previous class, the reading material or the assignments, rather than raising those concerns in front of the group. 'We always asked questions in the morning [group tutorials]. I think we felt we had better control and we were not worried about wasting other students' time' (subject 7).

An additional factor was the way in which the instructor made himself open and accessible to the students: 'He made ESL students comfortable. He talk to them and give them opportunity to talk' (subject 5). Student participation was highest in the tutorials but was not limited to them. As the course evolved their confidence and knowledge increased, and they began to speak more frequently during the group discussions and the lectures.

Assignments

The professor's policy on assignments and evaluation treated the course assignments as steps in a developmental learning process, with inter-active, formative guidance from the instructor. He did not see the assignments as a series of final, summative assessments. He expressed the view that a teacher's first responsibility was to provide every support to the students in order to help them learn. He reiterated this point during the course section on evaluation when he remarked that evaluative procedures should help students to demonstrate what they know rather than penalise them for what they do not know.

The professor had designed the assignments in a way which could assist the learning process. As mentioned earlier, the assignments simu-lated the process of program planning, starting with 'Analysing the planning context' and ending with 'Formulating a summative evaluation plan', so they made possible a cumulative learning effect, rather than being random and isolated tasks. Moreover, all five assignments had the same pattern: each had a central focus, such as assessing needs, design-ing an instructional plan, and so on, followed by a series of questions which led students through the complete assignment. In some cases there were helpful, explicit rules stated for completing questions, for example, 'use proper form and avoid fussiness', 'if you plan to use a questionnaire then attach it'.

The professor encouraged students to approach the assignments developmentally during the first session of class, when he offered some guidelines to everybody about the quality expected on assignment papers. He advised students not to be 'too concerned about the first assignment, just do it. They'll get better and better with each one'. Concerning the assignment papers of the Chinese students, he stated that he did not expect graduate-level writing from them. As Bazerman (1980: 658) suggests, the professor wanted them first to become familiar with the 'conversations of the discipline'.

How did the professor mark the assignments? An examination of the marked assignments showed that, in general, surface-level errors were largely ignored, but misconceptions regarding the specific topic of the assignment were not. Students were not penalised for incorrect spelling, faulty grammar or stylistic weaknesses. In the area of content, the professor seemed to give the students ample praise for their efforts. Correct responses were reinforced with a check mark for every correct point. If the student expressed a point particularly clearly, or offered a new idea or a creative solution, such as, 'use sentence completion to obtain needs assessment from prospective candidates', the professor would write a positive comment beside it.

The assignments were marked in such a way that the professor tried to guide incomplete or inaccurate answers by posing a question, for example, ' . . . it is necessary to ask client representatives. How will you do that?' (assignment 1, subject 8). 'What authority does the program planner have?' (assignment 1, subject 2). Those that were blatantly incorrect were treated with an emphatic 'No', plus a question or two to direct the student to rethink his or her reply. For example, ' . . . your questionnaire is very obtrusive. Why not . . . '. With answers that were not well formulated, or those that were mildly off the mark, the professor would pose questions to help the student clarify the answer, for instance, 'What are the prerequisites?'

The professor's approach can be summarised as this: pay great attention to content and structure feedback so that the student can achieve the desired outcome. Pay little attention to form and rhetoric if they do not interfere with meaning. Structure the tasks and the desired outcomes so that they are within the grasp of the learners, and provide detailed guidance for development along the way.

Despite the support given in the initial phase of the course, all of the Chinese students stated that they felt considerable anxiety about how to begin assignment 1. 'For the first unit, we had lots of questions. We don't know what he means and what he wants us to do' (subject 1).

There were, in fact, a variety of difficulties that the students faced in working through the assignments. As might be expected, students encountered language comprehension problems, but these were compounded by a number of other factors. Several students (subjects 1, 2, 4, 7) acknowledged that even if the course had been given in China using a Chinese context, they still might have encountered difficulties because in their own work history they had no experience with program planning, administration, evaluation, budgeting. More generally, the students had only vague notions about adult or community education endeavours, and knew little about Canadian society. 'It is very confused for me. If it was Chinese society we could explain but in Canada I'm not sure' (subject 7). Additionally, students had to proceed in ways that were very different from their previous academic experience:

> We didn't find what sentence gives a very clear answer to the
> question, so you have to answer yourself. You have to reorganise
> and do your own concept. In Chinese text you'd never find this.
> There would be definite answers or definitions . . . Another
> problem is to organise. I'm not familiar with how to organise. I'm
> familiar with logical and mathematical [material] but not this
> form. Also to think about it is different than to write about it.

(Subject 8)

Interaction with other students and the professor was helpful with these difficulties:

> The first time I don't even understand what the assignment said. So I asked my colleagues to clarify some problems for me . . . Then I ask the professor to give me more explanation, so I understand.
>
> (Subject 7)
>
> Every time before he wanted us to do an assignment he always explained what he wanted, a little bit for us. I'd write it down, then I'd go back and do the assignment. I referred to the readings and my notes and his explanations.
>
> (Subject 1)

To determine how far the assignments had accomplished the required tasks, the papers were coded according to the percentage grade, the rank accorded by the professor, and other comments and remarks written on the completed assignments. As a cross-reference to the professor's grading system, the assignments were reclassified according to three basic categories (Incomplete, Complete, Extended) as developed by Schmidt (1981). The assignments were ultimately successful.

Student performance fluctuated in the first three assignments, but all students were able to complete the final two assignments well. Although five students accomplished the first assignment in a basic manner, three did not, and in two cases, two questions were not attempted. Six students held their own in the second assignment, but two produced barely satisfactory papers. In assignment 3, all but one student slipped to a lower score. Comments from the students indicated that they had trouble with certain concepts in their assignment. By assignment 4, all students comprehended the nature of the task and completed it in an extended manner. This pattern was maintained in assignment 5.

Although the students found themselves muddled and stretched intellectually, they appreciated the struggle to complete their tasks. When questioned about their feelings regarding their work, some comments were: 'Even though I know my assignments weren't good, I spent lots of time at it' (subject 6). 'It's very important for us to get some outcome [output]. It's a pressure for you to do the things [but] producing something is good for us' (subject 4). 'I think I have a good basic grasp of the material now' (subject 2). 'Just after finishing this class, I am excited and want to step right into adult education' (subject 6).

Conclusion

This study has attempted to discover how and why a group of Chinese students was able to succeed in a graduate-level course, despite the obvious deficiencies of inadequate background knowledge about adult education and limited language skills. It became clear, too, that there were difficulties other than language that these students faced: course content assumed knowledge of Canadian society; and course process differed from the 'culture of the classroom' in China.

The students' achievements have been examined from the perspective of language socialisation which places much greater emphasis than second language acquisition research does on the role that sociocultural context plays as an environment for communication. Thus we have examined the whole course, the relationships between course processes and course assignments, and the assignments themselves as examples of student tasks. This study shows how these course elements worked in concert in an actual situation. A number of the features we have noted are familiar and rather expected characteristics of competently taught graduate courses. They are 'taken-for-granted' features which need to be looked at systematically for their communicative importance. The main focus of this study is the way the plan and the conduct of the course enabled students to complete their assignments successfully. Specifically this process operated at the level of the organisation of the whole course, the organisation of the course process to support the course assignments, and the organisation of course assignments. The study indicates that the organisation of the course was particularly cohesive and was clearly communicated to the students at the beginning of the course. Course processes provided background knowledge and feedback that enabled students to participate successfully in the assignment work. The assignments were integral to the course and were coherent with each other, and there was a clear format to each assignment. The assignments were not isolated exercises but engaged the students in the work of the course as a whole.

In other words, the main focus of this study was the way the course enabled a student to develop the background knowledge and access the guidance needed to support work on the assignments; that is, the way the course supplied and developed the *context* for the learner's tasks, a context that was constructed by the *cooperative* interaction of the instructor and the students.

This focus contrasts in several ways with work on tasks within a SLA input/interaction framework. The input/interaction approach looks at interaction within a task. The task, as an experimental task, is assumed to be consistently and constantly understood by the subjects. Context, as in contextual and extralinguistic cues, is taken as given. In this study, context was regarded as being under development: the course was intended to develop the contextual knowledge and skill required in educational program planning; in this it was doing what any subject matter course aims to do – develop subject matter understanding. In this study, the tasks were content course assignments rather than experimental tasks for second language research. The students had little understanding of them initially, but improved considerably as the course progressed. Their understanding developed; it was not constant and consistent. In this study, we looked at how the interaction surrounding (not just within) a task developed the learner's contextual understanding of the task. To draw these contrasts with work on tasks in the input/interaction framework is by no means to say that such work is misconceived and inadequate; it is to say that there are very different approaches to the study of language and task. It is also to say that there are possibilities for complementary relationships between the two approaches: the input/interaction approach looks at communication processes within the task; this study has looked at communication processes around the task.

The approach taken in this study was a language socialisation perspective, where language and cultural knowledge were viewed as being learned together, as parts of the learning of a cultural activity. Learning in this graduate course showed a number of similarities to other cultural studies of learning. Participation in the cultural activity of program planning was a central thread. (Contrast this with those input studies where the emphasis lies in listening to lectures.) During the course, these students, or novices, became more expert in the culturally organised and recognised activity of program planning. Their progress was reflected in an increase in control of the activity, as they performed their assignments more confidently and successfully, and as they completed the parts of a whole program plan. There was considerable evidence that the instructor, as expert, had structured the course interaction and the series of assignments so that the novices could participate in the activity and undertake tasks that were beyond their unaided capabilities, but within their 'zone of proximal development'. It also seemed clear that the students saw their assignments not as isolated exercises, but as sub-tasks within the larger activity of planning, and that their understanding of educational planning expanded as they worked through these sub-tasks and as they related background knowledge and theoretical material from the lectures and readings to their assignment work. That is to say, their contextual understanding of the activity developed. These features, of course, are familiar features of university courses and of language socialisation studies. But these features form a coherent pattern when the course is viewed as an example of guided participation in a cultural activity.

Learning from this graduate course also showed a number of differences from cultural studies of learning where the novices were young children or the activity was, like weaving or tailoring, more physical than symbolic. As a communicative means of learning, participation in the activity was a common feature, as was commentary on a learner's performance. However, repeated engagement in routine practices was not a feature of this graduate course. Instead there was much greater reliance on discussion and explanation of the activity. Future work within the language socialisation perspective could well examine the more complex issues of analysis that arise here. What are the relationships between cultural activity and discourse connected with the activity as they are revealed in the process of cultural learning? Are there exact parallels between the cognitive structure of the activity and the social processes that enable its learning, as Vygotsky suggested? How do the communicative processes of learning a cultural activity differ between first and second language learners? Answers to these questions will add a new dimension to our understanding of the relation between task and language.

5 Collaborative writing as a literacy event: implications for ESL instruction

Denise E. Murray

Introduction

In 'real-world' contexts, writing is not a solitary enterprise; it is a social act. In communities, members talk about their letters and notes, asking for advice on their writing (e.g. Heath 1983); in the workplace, managers and others discuss their memos and reports, comment on, add to, and change each other's texts (e.g. Doheny-Farina 1986; Halpern 1985; Harwood 1982; Murray in preparation; Paradis, Dobrin and Miller 1985; Selzer 1983; Spretnak 1982) or delegate their writing to another (Flatley 1982). These researchers demonstrate how writers in the real world collaborate, and how their text is formed by the context while at the same time creating the context. The studies cited report that such collaborative writing is a common occurrence in the community or workplace. Parallel to this research on real-world writing is the pedagogical focus on cooperative learning (e.g. Kagan 1986) or collaborative learning (e.g. Bruffee 1984). In response to this growing body of research and pedagogical theory, writing theorists are calling for collaborative tasks in the teaching of writing (e.g. Doheny-Farina 1986 and Odell 1985) driven by a socially-constructed theory of writing (e.g. Cooper 1986). Such theorists and practitioners have begun to realize that while the cognitive approach (e.g. Flower and Hayes 1981) has shown us important insights into some aspects of the writing process, it has ignored the way in which context and writing interact. These writers all make the same claim: writing is not a solitary act (as claimed by Ong 1982 and Olson 1981); rather, it is the result of the interaction among people, contexts and texts. In other words, writing occurs in a community (Nystrand 1982), for a community.

If we want to ensure that our ESL writing classes prepare students for their life outside the classroom, we must give them opportunities to experience collaborative writing. However, of the little research conducted on collaborative-type writing, only Heath's account of community literacy and Doheny-Farina's account of writing in an emerging organization detail *how* members collaborate to produce a written text. If we are to incorporate collaborative strategies in the ESL writing classroom, we need to have greater specification of exactly how native speaker participants collaborate. We can then determine effec-

100

tive ways of using collaborative writing in the ESL classroom. In this chapter, I report on research that shows how members of a group collaborate to produce written text in a specific setting, one in which ESL professionals produce texts about their professional work. I then discuss collaborative classroom writing tasks, based on the research findings.

Types of collaborative writing

Interaction on paper

From examining collaborative writing in a number of settings, I have identified several key characteristics concerning the ways in which people collaborate. Collaborative writing can be divided roughly into two types: those in which the majority of the interaction occurs on paper and those in which the text is constructed through oral discussion. The former is especially the case in the review of books or articles for publication, where the reviewers and editor make notes on the writer's draft and also write additional comments. The literature on workplace writing has mainly focussed on such critiquing of drafts of reports and memos. The notes and comments usually take two forms: surface editing for spelling, infelicities of grammar, etc. and global comments on content. The former address the actual writing, but the latter do not. This seems to be the model that most of us use when responding to student papers, as discussed by Zamel (1985), a model that has been shown to be inappropriate for both native speaker and non-native speaker student writing. In the workplace, too, such responses can create conflict. Paradis, Dobrin and Miller (1985) found that the process of close editing, while vital to the production of documents at EXXON ITD, was a major source of conflict. Staff took criticism hard, believing supervisors were controlling them through their written product. Novice employees included information such as the process of solving the problem that managers were not interested in hearing. Both problems stem from a failure to clarify organization, audience and purpose before documents are written. That paper collaboration works reasonably well for book and article reviews may be the result of those writers being more conscious of audience and purpose than students or workers. However, as co-editor of *The CATESOL Journal*, I have found that conflicts do arise. One contributor testily wrote: ' . . . enclosed is the *third* draft of my paper. I hope this meets with approval.'

Collaborative writing as a literacy event

The second type of collaborative writing, I would claim, is what Heath calls a 'literacy event', and is the one I will discuss and then use as a model for classroom writing. I focus on this type because it is the least studied, but is very common in workplace settings (see, for example, Faigley 1985). Heath points out that many of the texts read and written in communities are part of a literacy event, i.e. an event that '[has] social interactional rules which regulate the type and amount of talk about what is written, and define ways in which oral language reinforces, denies, extends, or sets aside the written material' (Heath 1983: 386). In participating in and examining several collaborative writing literacy events, I identified a number of distinctive features (what Heath would call 'social and interactional rules') for those events that participants considered successful and that resulted in a satisfactory written product.

Source and nature of the data

I am and have been involved in a number of collaborative writing efforts, several as a board member of CATESOL (the Californian affiliate of TESOL). I am chair of a CATESOL committee on teacher education, and the California State Government and Department of Education have recently made several moves affecting ESL teachers. As a professional organization, we wanted to respond with position statements and testimony at public hearings. Consequently, we have recently developed a language policy, competencies for ESL teachers and two responses to changes to current and proposed teacher certification of ESL teachers. These pieces of writing have been produced over one- and two-day meetings, sometimes in people's homes, sometimes in hotel conference rooms. The cast of characters has changed for each document. The social and interactional rules of collaborative writing that I will identify below are common to all the collaborative writing sessions I have analyzed. To illustrate these social and interactional rules, however, I will use only data from one of these collaborative writing events and use mostly examples from the same segment of the discourse. This will make the chapter more coherent because I will not have to keep explaining new data and their context.

The illustrative writing event used here covers an evening session in a hotel meeting room and an all-day session in one member's home in February 1988. The task before the group was to develop competencies for ESL teachers teaching elementary and high school students. We brought a number of documents to the meeting, including: (1) 'Suggested courses for a "model" Certificate Program', an earlier 1981 CATESOL document; (2) 'Suggested competencies for teachers: English language development instruction', a document originally developed by CATESOL and changed by the state; and (3) 'Subject matter assessment of prospective English teachers', a document developed by the

California State University to provide guidelines to teacher education programs concerning the competencies required of teachers of English in California's high schools. The group consisted of six members (pseudonyms are used): Dawn and Lynn were both high school ESL teachers, Sam, Tina and Elizabeth taught in ESL teacher education programs in three different universities, and Paul was an ESL/Bilingual Administrator in a school district with students from kindergarten up to high school (K–12). This entire session (and several other collaborative writing events) was tape-recorded and analyzed to determine the social and interactional rules that produced successful collaborative writing.

The group had met for a full day two months previously and had written a first draft that provided a general conceptual outline and brain-stormed competencies within four major categories: language, language acquisition, teaching ESL and culture.

During the session referred to here, participants negotiated meaning, objectives and text as they developed a three-page draft of 'Competencies for teaching English as a Second Language (ESL) in grades K–12'. In later drafts, as a result of input from non-group members, such as the Board of Directors, formatting changed and some language was edited. However, the text negotiated over the day and a half contained the content and organization of the final product. How did this group move from brainstormed lists to a coherent, professional document? Although I participated in this literacy event, I will use 'they' rather than 'we' throughout the description and analysis of the data to maintain anonymity for all participants.

Social and interactional rules in collaborative writing

The data used here to illustrate the social and interactional rules of collaborative writing are from only one meeting. However, the characteristics themselves were identified through the analysis of several other successful collaborative writing enterprises. Collaborative writing was essentially a social process through which writers looked for areas of shared understanding. To reach such an understanding, participants functioned according to several social and interactional rules: they set a common goal; they had differential knowledge; they interacted as a group; and they distanced themselves from the text. Each of these strategies is described in detail below.

A common goal

Group members shared a higher order goal. While specification of the goal was sometimes negotiated during the process, without a shared overall goal, the enterprise would have become a discussion, not collaborative writing. In the particular session focussed on here, all members wanted to produce a written document giving the qualifications necessary for a teacher of ESL in grades K–12. How such a goal was realized, of course, depended on the information brought by group members and how they jointly negotiated. This realization will be described below. In addition to a broad common goal, writers all agreed that, although organization and style were important, the focal concern was content. Members agreed that they had some (as yet not clearly defined) content to make available in written form.

Information gap

For tasks to be truly communicative, Morrow (1981) claimed that participants must have different knowledge, that there must be a gap in information between the participants. Interestingly, Morrow's requirement of an information gap for communicative tasks in the ESL classroom was an important principle in the collaborative writing project described here. Because of this information gap, group members had to negotiate content, style, and even the goals of the writing. Although they were embarked on a common task, the collaboration was not pre-scripted. Doheny-Farina (1986: 180) also found that 'a successful organization fosters collaboration among individuals who represent different constituencies who have different interpretations of the organizational context'. In her work on community literacy (1983), Heath also showed how literacy events involved speech community members with varying levels of understanding of the text and its context. In my data, the information gap took two distinct forms: the gap between the intended audience and the writers; and the gap among the collaborative writers themselves (of both content and style).

GOALS AND AUDIENCES

For collaborative writing, as for any oral or written text, there must be a communicative goal or purpose. The broad goal of this group was to produce a document detailing the competencies required for ESL teachers of grades K–12. Although, on the surface, this goal appeared straightforward, it was not. Not all members held the same view of what 'competencies' meant. Although all participants had worked on competency lists for ESL content, they were less sure of what a competency for a teacher might entail. In a discussion of the competency related to sociocultural factors in language acquisition, Elizabeth read from an outside document: 'knowledge of how sociocultural and economic environments influence language acquisition.' When Dawn asked her to repeat this (since only Elizabeth could see this document), Elizabeth began: 'knowledge of . . . except I don't want knowledge or understanding.' She rejected the terms 'knowledge' and 'understanding' because she did not view them as demonstrable competencies. However, while the entire group rejected 'knowledge', even though it appeared in two of the official documents from which the group was working, it accepted 'understanding' on the basis that this required action of some sort on the part of the learner/teacher.

The audience for the text was less clear, resulting in some early confusion and disagreements. The teachers in the group rejected the use of jargon (technical terms such as 'code-switching') on the grounds that it would 'frighten teachers', that they might know the concept, but not necessarily its technical name. Once this objection was raised, the group discussed audience, deciding that there were two audiences: (1) teachers, and (2) teacher education institutes and government bodies. For the former, they did not want to use jargon. For the latter, they believed it was essential to identify topics clearly so that teacher preparation programs did indeed cover the areas of knowledge they believed to be essential for an ESL teacher. The group therefore decided to produce two documents, one for each audience. Further, they agreed to have a longer, more detailed document for the teacher education institutes and government organizations. For the teachers, they agreed to use only major headings and sub-headings so that the specification of particular areas such as diglossia would not appear in that document.

In addition to defining the audience for the text, the group established that a gap of knowledge existed between the group and the audience. Thus, in discussing the competency referring to sociocultural factors in language acquisition, Sam raised the question of how the audience might interpret the heading in the document they were working from, the original CATESOL document, 'Suggested courses for a "model" Certificate Program', which states:

Sociocultural factors in language acquisition

This course may include such issues as the following: language in contact; social roles and language use; codes and code-switching; diglossia and ethnic language variation; societal bilingualism; pidgins and creoles; societal attitudes toward language use; language planning; language shift and maintenance; sensitivity to cultural differences; men's and women's language; speech acts; discourse/conversational analysis; language repertoires.

Sam began this segment by stating that: 'I have a little bit of a problem with this whole third paragraph and that is that all these issues or at least many of these issues can be looked at without the question of being factors in language acquisition. And I think we need to reword it slightly at the beginning so that [the] context is more clearly spelled out.' He knew his audience of teacher educators and worried that they would attempt to use a general course in sociolinguistics to meet this competency, thus not addressing the issue of second language acquisition at all. This gap in knowledge between audience and writers was reduced by the writers changing the heading to 'Understanding how social, cultural, and economic factors affect first and second language acquisition'.

DIFFERENTIAL KNOWLEDGE AMONG PARTICIPANTS

The six participants in this writing event brought different knowledge and different perceptions to the writing process. Three participants were practicing ESL teachers to whom the competencies would apply, while the remaining three were teacher educators who would have to fit the competencies into their particular training programs. Within each subgroup, members had differing knowledge bases. Sam, Tina, and Elizabeth brought the perspective of teacher education programs from three very different institutions. Lynn, Dawn, and Paul brought the perspective and knowledge of teachers in the classroom, again in three very different settings and with three very different experiences of teacher education. In addition, Lynn and Elizabeth brought knowledge about how the credentialling system works in California, both having worked closely with the state departments that have responsibility for teacher standards. In addition to their differences in knowledge of content and audience, the group brought different knowledge of writing style to the task.

As a result of these differences in background knowledge, in one negotiation concerning how to identify competencies that relate to social factors in language acquisition, the three teacher educators took the information lead, providing arguments why certain terms and organization were ambiguous, while relying on the three teachers to be the audience to be convinced by their arguments. In the negotiation that followed Sam's concern about the heading for the competency on sociocultural factors (discussed earlier), primarily Sam, Elizabeth, and Tina held the floor. In this case, they had the knowledge of how teacher education institutions might interpret such a competency, that is, institutions might use a general course in sociolinguistics to meet this competency without addressing the issue of language acquisition. They were therefore more concerned about the way this competency got written than were the three teachers, who were more concerned about the jargon used in the list (as discussed earlier). While it took almost fifteen minutes to resolve the heading for this competency, all agreed on the list very quickly, deleting some of the items from the original document since they did not fit this category (see discussion and transcript below). This transcript also demonstrates how style as well as content was negotiated. To do this successfully, members needed a metalanguage. Elizabeth, for example, talked about the 'title' and the 'colon', the latter being vital to her argument. She tried to speak the written text she had in mind so that other group members would 'see' the written text.

DOCUMENTS TO WORK FROM AND TEXT OWNERSHIP

Another aspect of information gap that was pivotal in collaborative writing was the use of outside documents as an aid in invention. In the first CATESOL collaborative writing project in which I was involved, the group had no external documents to work from and, after the first brainstorming meeting, one participant wrote a first draft. In subsequent meetings, this participant found it difficult to surrender ownership of her text. Any negotiations for change were interpreted as attacks on her draft. Her ability to take this stance was enhanced by her relative prestige among the group. Having learned from this experience, in the next collaborative effort in which a group developed a language policy, I brought along a number of *outside* documents, including Australia's Language Policy. This latter document, which no participant 'owned', became the focus of attention, the source of new information and new language.

In the collaborative writing session used here, the group also began with a number of outside documents. Two of the participants (Sam and Tina), however, had worked on one of these documents. However, that was seven years previously and the current task had a different focus. Thus, neither Sam nor Tina took the stance of owning this text; rather, it became an impersonal resource.

The outside documents provided a useful starting point for getting started, but they were also useful during the whole writing process, providing a reference point that could also be a point of departure. In the discussion over how to describe sociocultural factors in language acquisition, the three members actively participating in this discussion came to a standstill in their discussion. Every suggestion was rejected and Sam kept returning to his original concern that programs would use general courses in sociolinguistics to meet the competency, courses that did not have a second language acquisition focus. The impasse was broken by reference to the outside document, 'Subject matter assessment of prospective English teachers'. The following excerpt from the transcript demonstrates how this reference freed participants from their own stance and perspective.

Transcript 1[1]

Sam: I don't see any way personally now maybe you can show me and I would be tickled to death . but anyway to recast the things are listed here so that they each one become that . . .

(Silence)

5 Elizabeth: What . . . they've got under the language competencies
     in the CSU thing is knowledge of how sociocultural and
     economic environment influences lang language
     acquisition and use that might must make a better title
     than sociocultural factors in language acquisition.
                 ⌐
10 Dawn: Read it
     again.
  E: Knowledge . . .
  S: OK.
  E: of how except
       [
  Tina: Uh uh.
15 E: I don't want knowle knowledge or understanding
              [
  D: No.
  E: of how sociol cultural and economic environments
     influence language acquisition and use
                [
  T: Uh uh.
20 E: and then colon with these
             ⌐
  D: understanding.
              [
  E: you can
              [
  T: That's right.
  E: and then you've got the word 'affect' already in that title
25   they've got influence
       [
  D: Uh uh.
  E: and you're just listing the social, cultural and economic
     environments in fact.
             ⌐
  S: Do we have any . . . socioeconomic
30   things listed here?
  E: Well . . . uhm . . . th some of them are
              [
  P: soc societal attitudes
  E: societal attitudes.
  D: Uh uh.
35 T: Language planning.
       [
  E: Language planning they're economic
                ⌐
  S: So long as
     we're going to have it part of the general statement we
     need to have some sort of specificity on it.

40	E:	I agree . . . but I'd like to leave out speech acts and discourse and conversation analysis . . . I don't think they fit in that set of categories.
	P:	I'm having a small problem with the title now that we've got uhm you know the one that you just said
		[
45	D:	Uh uh.
	P:	[unclear] because I think that's Sam's position doe does not necessarily apply to second language acquisition unless unless it's stated the statement as read from here applies to native speakers.
50	D:	Uh uh.
		[
	P:	We need to
		⌋
	T:	Well then should we expand it to say again specifically to influence first and second language acquisition and use?

Once Elizabeth read from the document (lines 6–8), all members of the group participated in what Tannen (1984) has called a shotgun style. The preceding discourse had been marked by long silences, hesitations, and dialogic talk between Sam and one group member at a time. This later segment was marked by increased pace, constructive overlap, and participation by all members. In this enthusiastic rush, Dawn supplied the word 'understanding' (line 21) to replace 'knowledge' that Elizabeth had rejected; Elizabeth suggested substituting 'affect' (line 24), which had been previously discussed, for 'influence'; Sam asked whether they wanted to include economic factors (lines 29–30); Elizabeth abandoned speech acts, discourse/conversational analysis (lines 40–2); and Paul asked whether the statement applied to *second* language acquisition (lines 46–9). Within two minutes, the group has decided on the draft version of this competency as follows:

> Understanding how social, cultural and economic factors affect first and second language acquisition: societal attitudes toward language use; social roles and language use; languages in contact; codes and code-switching; diglossia and ethnic language variation; multilingualism; pidgins and creoles; language shift and maintenance; language and gender; language repertoires; and registers.

At later meetings, the heading was altered slightly to ' . . . language acquisition and use' and the list was collapsed into three main categories. However, the stance and content agreed upon at the February meeting remained; Sam's basic concern was resolved, largely due to reference to another document.

Denise E. Murray

Group interaction

For participants to write collaboratively, they also used interpersonal communication strategies and skills, including those of choice and feedback that Morrow identified. Several interaction strategies were vital to the outcome of the collaborative writing.

SMALL NUMBER OF PARTICIPANTS

As in any group work, collaboration is not possible with large numbers of participants. The group size for the project reported here was six. Research on group work (Shaw 1986) has shown that five is a maximum size for problem solving, ten for discussion and fifteen for reaching a decision. Further, this research shows that odd-numbered groups work more efficiently than even-numbered groups since the group does not collapse into dyads. This group of six worked well, but at any one time only three or four participants were active, depending on the topic and the knowledge each participant had of that topic, as seen in the excerpt below from the discussion on sociocultural factors in language acquisition.

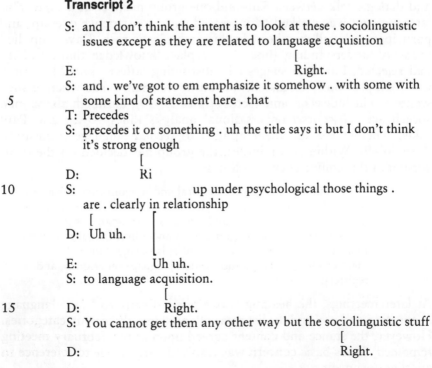

Transcript 2

```
        S:  and I don't think the intent is to look at these . sociolinguistic
            issues except as they are related to language acquisition
                                                    [
        E:                                             Right.
        S:  and . we've got to em emphasize it somehow . with some with
  5         some kind of statement here . that
        T:  Precedes
        S:  precedes it or something . uh the title says it but I don't think
            it's strong enough
                        [
        D:              Ri
  10    S:                          up under psychological those things .
            are . clearly in relationship
                    [        [
        D:  Uh uh.

        E:              Uh uh.
        S:  to language acquisition.
                        [
  15    D:              Right.
        S:  You cannot get them any other way but the sociolinguistic stuff
                                                                [
        D:                                                         Right.
```

110

S: doesn't have to be seen in the language acquisition con context.

L: Right.

20 D: Well then we need to uh

T: keep repeating it in each of the
specificities.

D: Yes . . . their cultural backgrounds . . . as related to language in
contact or something.

    [[

25 S: Well I   I I think rather than repeating it all down
the line

D: Yes.

T: Cultural factors.

    [[

S: It's   it's in this first phrase the course may include
30 such issues as uh . . . we're not talking about courses at this
point in time.

D: No we're
talking about , uh, just the definition of what we mean
by sociological factors in language acquisition.

    [[

S: But I I think   I think that . that phrase we again
35 need to repeat uh that we're

    [

D: Yeah.

S: only referring to this in relationship to language acquisition.

(Silence)

D: Well it needs to be inherent to these . things we list.

40 (Silence)

LEADERSHIP

The collaborative events I have examined all have a designated leader
or chairperson, but the groups met informally, as groups, not chaired
meetings. In the example problem discussed above, Elizabeth, the chair
of the committee, did not take a turn until ten minutes into the
discussion. She allowed Sam to hold the floor (see Transcript 2) and
discuss his problem and the other participants to suggest several
solutions. She intervened after four suggestions had been rejected in
order to clarify a point that Sam was misunderstanding. She then took
this opportunity to make her own suggestion and engaged in a dialogue
with Sam, with only the occasional backchannel or 'Right' from other
participants. To the group, she was clearly the leader. However, she did
not take the floor until everyone had had ample opportunity to participate or unless one person was holding the floor to the exclusion of all
others.

Denise E. Murray

OTHER PARTICIPANTS

In the writing session I have been using here, all participants felt free to contribute at any time, but also gave the floor to one person for longer than in casual conversation. In the discussion in Transcript 2, the group saw clearly that Sam had a problem that was very important to him. At first, the other participants were not clear that this was a vital issue. However, they allowed Sam the floor. Moreover, two participants used constant backchannel to let Sam know he had the floor and that they were attentive to his concern. Then, as the three teacher educators discussed the problems that might ensue if the heading was not precise enough, the others began to offer their own suggestions. But even these suggestions were directed more at Sam than the group. He was allowed to interrupt (e.g. lines 25, 34), participants helped him find words (e.g. line 6), and generally supported his dominance of the conversation. Sam controlled the discussion until Elizabeth intervened as leader. However, even this intervention did not clear the floor for much participation by others. It was not until her suggestion of the language from the subject matter document that the group began working together to produce the written text. This did not mean that the group had not been working together before. Members were agreeing to allow Sam the time to elaborate his concern.

In the collaborations I have studied, silence was not awkward, as in face-to-face casual conversation. Group members saw silence as thinking time (as in lines 38 and 40 above). No one rushed to fill the silence. Further, the time for the entire task was open-ended; members felt they could take the time to discuss issues thoroughly. It seems that collaborative writing could not be achieved under a pressure of time. Indeed, no group members ever tried to rush closure to the project, preferring to meet again rather than produce a document they were not all confident in.

In all the collaborative writing sessions I studied, one member appointed him or herself as scribe. Sometimes, the role of scribe changed at various stages of the production. In each case, the person who became the scribe did so because he or she had less to contribute to the discussion at that particular point. In Transcripts 1 and 2, Dawn was the self-selected scribe at this stage of the session. Her contributions to the discussion were largely conversational, not content. She agreed, backchanneled, and echoed other speakers, showing that she was a participant; but she did not make any major contributions of new information in these segments.

In no case was the scribe the actual chair of the committee. Since both chair and scribe can appear to have a large degree of control over the final decisions and therefore the final document, these roles were filled by different people. In addition, the role of scribe changed so that another member could assume this measure of control. While all members took notes and made changes to their own documents, only the scribe was responsible for accurately capturing the language agreed on by the group. In addition, the scribe was responsible for typing up the draft on a computer during the session, as discussed below.

Distance from the text

To see their collaborative text as an audience might, these collaborators used two strategies: they produced many written drafts during one session, and they moved away from the text in time and space.

WRITTEN DRAFTS

Although much of the collaborative writing session was a literacy event with discussion and talk around the topic, in each case group members felt the need to produce written text quite early in the process. By preference, the groups met in people's homes so that they would have access to a personal computer. When they had to meet in hotel rooms, they used butcher paper and white boards to write their brainstormed ideas and drafts. In the more successful sessions, the scribe went to the computer once the group had reached consensus on one issue. In the session already discussed, the scribe did not produce a computer print-out until the group had agreed on both the psychological factors and the sociocultural factors that affect first and second language acquisition. Then, the scribe, with one other person to help, went into the computer room and typed in the latest draft. The remainder of the group had coffee and chatted about other matters. No substantive work on the document was done while the scribe and others were absent. Once the scribe had produced a rough draft, she made copies for all members who then began further refinements and revisions. Since these participants are from a highly literate culture, and the final product of their collaboration was to be a written text, they found they needed a written version to refer to. Once they had made so many changes on the current draft that it was almost illegible, they wanted a clean copy. In this way, they did not overburden their long-term memories. At the same time, they did not compose at the computer since they did not want to be constrained by the text until they had reached some consensus.

NEED TO GET AWAY FROM TEXT AND RECONSIDER

Each document took more than one session to write. At the end of a session, group members would take away the latest draft or the chair would type it up and mail it immediately to the group members, who would then reconsider it over several weeks or sometimes even months.

By constantly coming back to the text as a new reader, the participants were able to identify language or content that needed changing.

Theoretical implications

As yet, we have no theory of collaborative writing. We do have a cognitive theory of the writing process (e.g. Flower and Hayes 1981) and we do have a theory of literacy events as a type of speech event (Heath 1983). The research reported here, as well as that of Doheny-Farina are first steps towards situating the writing process within a literacy event. Doheny-Farina does not make this connection with Heath's 'literacy event', but I believe it provides an important theoretical perspective on the enterprise of collaborative writing. The research reported here indicates that collaborative writers use a number of social and interactional rules: agreeing on a common goal; contributing differential knowledge; determining the knowledge of the audience; interacting as a group; and distancing themselves from the text.

Although the cognitive model includes the 'task environment' as part of the context for writing, it does not specify just how this task environment operates. The research reported here suggests a number of aspects of the context of writing that should be accounted for in any theory of the writing process: the ways in which social interaction is *part* of the process; the effect of intertextuality (other texts) on the invention process; the negotiation of different points of view; the relationship between talk and text.

Pedagogical implications

Some scholars are questioning the isolated view of invention and arrangement that often prevails even in classes subscribing to the view of writing as a process (e.g. Cooper and Holzman 1989). While peer responses are encouraged, often they take place in limited ways; ultimately, the single writer is responsible for his or her final text. While teachers engage in conferences with students, these conferences are non-directive; the student is responsible for both content and language. This approach is based on the Platonic view that truth is discovered through an internal apprehension, a private vision. Although the pedagogy attendant on this view encourages the writer to interact in dialogue with members of the class and/or the teacher, it is only with the goal of finding what is authentic in the writer, not of jointly discovering meaning. This monologic view of writing is counter to what actually takes place in real-world contexts. Thus, if our writing programs are to help our students in their lives outside the ESL classroom, we need to develop teaching strategies that will provide opportunities for collaborative writing. But these opportunities need to be based on what actually happens as native speakers collaborate in literacy events.

How can we develop classroom practices that encourage collaboration? Based on the social and interactional rules of successful real-world collaborative writing strategies, I have worked on and used several writing assignments that require collaboration for their completion. In each case, group members have differential knowledge.

> Each collaborator should then try to discover the point of view of the other writer(s), state that point of view, and recognize how and in what cases that point of view is valid. Most important, the collaborators should be prepared to alter their own views as they strive to understand those of their fellow collaborators.

(Doheny-Farina 1986: 181)

But, for these activities to be successful collaborative enterprises, the teacher also needs to guide students to select leaders and scribes, discuss group interaction techniques, provide sufficient time over an extended period, and have students produce written drafts throughout the process.

GROUP PAPERS/REPORTS

For each of these tasks, the group must have a leader and a scribe, usually determined by the group. I usually choose groups of five students with different points of view on the task at hand. I also have students discuss and then define their audience in writing. They must include in their definition what the audience already knows about the topic. I discuss with them what I have discovered about successful collaborative writing and encourage them to use the rules and strategies used by native speakers. Most importantly, I provide ample time for groups to circulate back to their texts as many times as they feel necessary.

'Jigsaw' (Kagan 1986) is one of the most successful models for creating a setting for collaborative writing. It refers to any activity where each member of the group has part of the information and the group has to create the whole jointly from their separate parts. For writing, such an activity might be breaking a paragraph into its separate sentences, assigning one sentence to each member of the group, and then having the group reconstruct the whole paragraph. From the sentence level, activities can move to the paragraph level and so on. This activity, requiring no invention on the part of students, allows them to focus on collaboration, on listening to each other's point of view, and on reviewing the text in writing.

I also model collaborative writing by constructing a whole text on the blackboard jointly with the class. The ideas for the text sometimes come from a picture composition or from a topic the class has discussed. Here, I again focus on collaboration, on listening to each other's point of view, and on reviewing the text in progress. Sometimes I act as both leader and scribe; sometimes I have a student take one role while I take the other; other times I have two students take these roles.

A more sophisticated activity for more advanced ESL students which I have found successful is where each group member makes notes on some experience or knowledge not known to the other members of the group and the group then uses the information from all group members to construct a text. A theme I have found successful is the experience of culture shock as an immigrant. The group collaboratively prepares a text that can be submitted to a class, school or local newspaper. Or, so that students feel less ownership of the information and are thus more willing to negotiate the text, I have them interview members from their speech community on a particular theme. Successful themes have included culture shock, cultural values, legends and tales from their culture, and life stories of respected older members of their community. Each member of the group then translates and transcribes the interview. The group then collaboratively constructs a text on that theme. As they negotiate the text, they have to decide what information is the same, what is different and what themes run through their interviews. They then have to develop a coherent text that uses the information appropriately for their particular audience. Sometimes this audience is members of their own community, such as young children. These texts can be used as cultural resources in their own school settings or in others.

Similarly, groups can write a narrative jointly. I give each student a character sketch and the group has to construct the story using the characters of each member of the group. For research papers, each student can collect different information from library sources. On a project on a famous person born in the same decade as they were and how that decade affected the person, one student collected biographical information of the famous person, one collected political information of the decade, another collected social information, while another collected information on the social environment of the particular person. Although each topic formed a separate section of the final report, all topics had to be integrated to develop the overall thesis.

WRITING CONFERENCES

I mentioned earlier that teachers often respond in conferences as if writing were monologic. If writing outside the classroom is collaborative, then our conferences should better approximate collaborative writing. For fear that we appropriate our students' writing, we often go to the other extreme and give them little or no guidance at all. I can remember so many times saying to a student who could not find the words or had no ideas, 'Well, what do *you* think about X?', constantly placing the responsibility for the writing on students who were novice writers, who had not become members of the 'literacy club' as Frank Smith called it. We as their teachers must help initiate them into the rites of this club. How can they become members without knowing the rules? Without knowing what is acceptable behavior and what unacceptable? How can they become members without a mentor, their teacher, who is there to guide? I am not calling for teacher appropriation of student writing. Nor am I calling for autocratic control. However, I do feel we need to be more directive and show our knowledge and reactions to their writings in our conferences. We have an information gap situation – we know the conventions of writing that they may not yet fully comprehend. Therefore, we need to establish some ground rules, tell them when their writing does not meet the acceptable rules of the club, and when it does. We are not being honest if we appear to claim that 'anything is all right as long as it's how you feel'. When they get into the outside work world, they will soon find that everything is not all right. Different groups have different conventions and each set has to be learned. I learned one set for writing this article, but the conventions are different if I give it as a presentation at a conference or publish it in a journal for non-teachers. We can help our students more by directing our writing conference questions so that we model and teach as well as draw out.

Applebee and Langer (1983) suggest that teachers need to scaffold for the learner. In writing conferences, we can provide the learner with a scaffold for their writing, to work collaboratively with them through more informative questions such as the following:

1. Leading questions, e.g. 'Have you thought about . . . ?' 'What would happen if . . . ?'
2. Confirmation checks, e.g. 'Do you mean . . . ?' rather than clarification checks, e.g. 'Can you tell me more about that?'
3. Advice, e.g. 'You could . . . ', 'Why don't you try . . . ?'

If we apply some of the principles of successful collaborative writing in our classrooms, we will help our students write for the real-world contexts in which they must write. While we still do not have sufficient data on how people write collaboratively, the research reported here and the suggestions for classroom activities are a first step in that direction and a step towards developing a theory of the composing process that is based on what collaborative writers actually do.

Endnotes

[1] [= overlap

  ⌊ = latching

Part II   Focus on teaching

In this section, some of the themes and issues which emerged in the preceding section are taken up and elaborated upon in the context of collaborative teaching and research. The chapters provide the basis for a reconceptualisation of team teaching and collaborative research, and each is based on original data.

The study reported by Shannon and Meath-Lang is a thematic investigation of critical factors in successful team teaching relationships. By 'team teaching' the authors here mean ongoing, consistently present classroom collaboration as opposed to a shared assignment or alternate-days approaches. There is a paucity of literature on such professional relationships. There are, however, numerous anecdotal observations of effective team teaching – often accompanied by expressions of disbelief at the particular pairings. This study attempts to collect information more systematically. The authors interviewed and observed 25 language teachers at the National Technical Institute for the Deaf in the USA. All of the teachers interviewed had experienced two or more successful team teaching relationships and were known, through courses, presentations and affiliations, for cooperative work. The data from the study were analysed for emerging themes. The authors were particularly interested in the nature of the dialogue between collaborating teachers.

In Japan, the use of native speakers in English language classrooms to improve listening and speaking and to promote the concept of internationalism is becoming more and more widespread. However, when it comes to operating in the classroom, no one is quite sure how best to do this, and although broad guidelines exist, most Japanese and native speaker teachers are still confused about how best to work together. The chapter by Sturman reports on a project which involves the use of native speaker teachers in English language classrooms in lower secondary schools in Tokyo which was aimed at developing an effective model of team teaching within the Japanese context.

The study by Bailey, Dale and Squire is based on a collaborative teaching experience in an advanced oral communication course. They outline four general organisational patterns found in team teaching before describing the procedures followed in their particular course. In the body of the chapter, they highlight the advantages of collaborative teaching at each stage in the process. Like a number of other contributions to the collection, this study illustrates the different perspectives on the reality of the classroom which emerge when more than one interpretive account is provided of a particular classroom event.

Gebhard and Ueda-Motonaga question the usual approach to teacher supervision in which the supervisor observes, evaluates, and directs the teacher's teaching, arguing that this approach does not afford teachers opportunities to learn how to make their own teaching decisions. They offer an alternative approach to teacher supervision in which the supervisor directs the teacher through a process of exploration, rather than through the provision of prescription on how to teach. They suggest that it is through this process that teachers can learn how to make informed decisions about what to do in their classrooms. The authors illustrate the collaborative efforts of a supervisor and teacher of Japanese to explore teaching, beginning with a description of the teaching setting, followed by discussion on how the teacher and supervisor approached the exploration of teaching in this setting. They then present some of the exploration the Japanese teacher did, and finally present, in the teacher's own words, what she learned from the experience.

Schecter and Ramirez present a case study of a teacher research group in action. Action-based teacher research, i.e. research carried out by teachers in their own classrooms to solve particular problems, is becoming increasingly significant, both as a professional development tool and a source of data on language learning and teaching. In their study, the authors focus in particular on the kinds of support which teachers need if they are to conduct classroom research, the effects of becoming a researcher on teachers' views of classroom practice and themselves as practitioners, and the kinds of knowledge which teacher research can provide.

Budd and Wright describe a term-long experiment with a multi-national group of young adult EFL learners, to put into practice the ideas for a process-based, negotiated syllabus. It attempts to chronicle and analyse the experiment from the viewpoints of both learner and teacher, and relate observations made to the conceptual framework that provided the point of departure for the study. Data for the study come from journals kept by teachers and learners.

In the final chapter, Nunan presents a rationale for the development of a collaborative approach to language curriculum design between teachers and curriculum specialists. The adoption of such an approach within the Australian Adult Migrant Education Program (AMEP) is described, as is a national curriculum project, set up within the AMEP to realise the ideals of a collaborative approach to curriculum development. The author concludes that the quality of relationships and the sharing of responsibility are crucial to the success of curriculum development carried out on a collaborative basis.

6 Collaborative language teaching: a co-investigation

Nora B. Shannon and Bonnie Meath-Lang

Primo Levi, in the foreword of his last book of essays, *Other People's Trades*, says:

> Sometimes I am asked with curiosity, or even arrogance, why I write though I am a chemist. I hope that [my] essays, with their modest limits of commitment and scope, will make it clear that between 'the two cultures' there is no incompatibility; on the contrary, there is, at times, when there is good will, mutual attraction.
>
> (1989: 10)

In the final essay in the collection, 'To a Young Reader', Levi talks to someone who wants to tell stories. His advice includes holding onto your day job, giving writing a rest period, and having others read drafts. But his last line speaks to those of us motivated to collaborate: 'Oh, I forgot to tell you that, in order to write, one must have something to write' (p. 222).

This 'having something to say' is a reason why many language instructors choose collaboration with teachers of other disciplines. They see the need to have students' language grow and expand in the context of a technical area of another discipline. Other language teachers have the need, as Levi pinpoints, for someone to 'read' and respond to the texts of their classroom discourse. These teachers work with colleagues from both their own and other fields to create multiple perspectives and to broaden interaction, as well as to elicit feedback.

Descriptions of team teaching

An abundance of articles in various teaching journals in the late fifties and early sixties described teams in general and what they did. In the mid-1960s, with the move toward more open classrooms and school-within-a-school concepts, team teaching emerged as an innovative way to develop various staff utilization techniques (Singer in Beggs 1964). The Beggs volume in particular emphasized the importance of administrative support, and listed 41 school districts throughout the United States that were successfully using team teaching at the time. By and large, these articles were enthusiastic endorsements of team teaching, seeing it as an impetus for change in the role of the teacher.

A few years later, Hanslovsky, Mayer and Wagner (1969) explained and outlined a process for setting up a team situation from the viewpoint of three experienced instructors. They saw team teachers as separate from 'traditional' teachers. They emphasized throughout the book how threatening the teams could be to traditional teachers, parents and administrators, who have come to expect a single classroom authority and separate academic departments. On balance, however, these authors say that the opportunities for integration and real-life application of interdisciplinary knowledge outweigh the discomforts.

We have come a long way from the time that team teaching was considered radical, but there still remains a lack of literature on team teaching with second language learners in general, and deaf language learners in particular. We would point out here that deaf students share some issues with second language learners. As Swisher (1989: 240) notes, while deaf students' language learning histories may vary from those of ESL students, many have competence in a signed first language (Newport 1988), benefit from ESL teaching techniques (Goldberg and Bordman 1974), and demonstrate similar proficiency in written production (Langston and Maxwell 1988). There are also specific features of Deaf culture, in the presence of a visual language and its requirements (S. Rutherford 1988; Padden and Humphries 1988).

The points that are made related to team teaching and the education of deaf students emphasize a multidisciplinary and/or multi-modal approach. The centrality of language learning in deaf students' lives is the primary catalyst for the interactions described. Forman and Spector (1980), for example, prescribe a rationale for having an audiologist, a speech pathologist, and an English instructor work together to enhance students' productive and receptive communication skills. Stewart and Hollifield (1988) describe a bilingual curriculum requiring a team teaching approach, in which a deaf teacher uses American Sign Language (ASL) to teach Social Studies, and a hearing teacher uses Signed English and speech to teach language with connected materials. Additionally, there are reports of content-based language learning models followed by team teachers in particular courses (P. Brown and Slutzky 1986) and in secondary programs serving deaf students (Maxwell 1979).

All of these articles emphasize the desirability of the English language instructor working with a co-teacher in order to enhance the deaf student's Sign, speech or technical skills. We were interested, however, in examining the texts of team teaching relationships to analyze the attitudes and components necessary for positive team teaching experiences. We were unable to find this in-depth analysis in our review of general, second language, and deafness-related team teaching literature.

121

E

Methodology

The authors interviewed 25 teachers at the National Technical Institute for the Deaf (NTID) in the USA. These teachers work with deaf language learners at the post-secondary level, in a college offering a variety of technical programs, ranging from basic vocational skills to baccalaureate and masters' degree options. The admissions requirement to this federally-sponsored institution is an overall eighth-grade achievement level (age 12–13 years equivalent); 95 per cent of the students are born deaf or deafened shortly after birth, 30 per cent are bilingual in Sign Language. Therefore, NTID has established a comprehensive developmental/remedial language and communication program, staffed by English teachers, audiologists, speech/language pathologists, and Sign language instructors. This program offers courses to students, and provides professional development experiences in language to teachers in other disciplines. Many of the teaching methods employed are rooted in second language teaching.

The participants in the study

There were 25 teachers interviewed, thirteen female and twelve male. All of the teachers had experienced two or more successful team teaching relationships, and were known, through course listings, presentations, and professional affiliations, for cooperative work. There were fourteen teachers for whom language teaching and administration were primary professional assignments, eight specialists in the areas of speech and hearing, and four teachers from technical areas with a history of concern for content-based language learning. One English language teacher also holds certification in speech/language pathology and has functioned as a speech therapist as well as an English instructor at NTID. Five of the teachers interviewed have had training and experience teaching English as a Second Language to non-native speakers in the Peace Corps, at language institutes, and on church or humanitarian missions. Nine participants had previous experience in elementary and secondary schools for deaf students.

The mean number of years' teaching experience for the participants at the time of the interviews was 15.9. No one interviewed had fewer than seven years in the classroom. Additionally, 21 teachers were hearing and four were deaf.

We recognize that our effort to elicit the voices of teachers for whom collaboration has been a powerful and positive experience could have led to a rather homogeneous sample. Our interest in the factors that characterize successful team teaching, however, was the overriding principle in using a qualitative procedure which allowed us to focus on the text of these teachers' narrated experiences. Indeed, one of the participants in the study, while reflecting on whether or not shared philosophy is a necessary condition for team teaching, stated the methodological concern nicely:

> I have never really worked with someone with a different philosophy . . . but I think one could learn from co-teaching with someone having a differing philosophy – it could be an eye-opener. On the other hand, maybe we self-select – I keep finding myself with co-teachers the same age as I, Irish Catholic, and married with kids!

The various disciplines that are brought to bear on work with young adult, deaf language learners assured a diversity that was expressed in the interviews. While certain themes did emerge, the texts of each individual's experience documented a breadth and variety of perspectives on collaborative work.

Procedure

Qualitative research methods (Bogdan and Biklen 1982; Pinar 1975) were used to collect and analyze data. An in-depth, open-ended interview was conducted with each of the 25 participants lasting from one to two hours. The participants received, in advance of the interview, nine questions which they were asked to think about prior to the meeting with the interviewer. During the interview, they were free to follow the questions or add to them. The questions included requests to explain why certain partners had been chosen, ideas on conflict resolution, exploration of the dialogue between the teachers, and characteristic behaviors and concerns. The participants were encouraged to provide detailed experiences.

Interviews were transcribed verbatim, coded, and sorted independently into descriptive categories. These categories were analyzed for recurring patterns and themes.

We, the writers, were also participant-observers. Prior to the other interviews, we interviewed one another. We chose this involvement for two reasons. First, interviewing one another allowed us to pilot the questions and techniques that we would use in the subsequent interviews. Secondly, participant-observation in investigating collaboration afforded us a phenomenological perspective to bring to the interview texts. As the anthropologist Mary Catherine Bateson points out:

> The resonances between the personal and the professional are the source of both insight and error. You avoid mistakes and

> distortions not so much by trying to build a wall between the
> observer and the observed as by observing the observer – observing
> yourself – as well, and bringing the personal issues into
> consciousness.
>
> (1984: 161)

Additionally, we wanted to extend this opportunity for reflection as a participant-observer to our colleagues. After all the interviews were finished, we held a meeting with the teachers and asked them to explore team teaching metaphorically and/or visually, following the encoding-decoding approach of Freire (1970). The images and metaphors that the group discussed are reported below.

Interdisciplinary demands of the curriculum

As previous research confirms, courses that are cross-disciplinary, bimodal, or bilingual lend themselves to team teaching. Twenty-two of the respondents reported working across disciplines, four participated in bimodal courses and four taught bilingual courses. In specific instances, it appears that it is the content of the course or topic of the research that determines the collaboration.

> Yes, S. initiated the request with me because of my background in
> history, political science and social studies . . . we got the course
> up and running . . . After a while, we learned to float back and
> forth and rely on the content to help us do that . . . I'd talk about
> culture and political content, she would teach vocabulary, and
> language structures that were frequently occurring in the news.

> I became interested in Technical Report Writing specifically
> because I read a lot and was always interested in reading and
> writing and I wanted to get students interested in that part of their
> education. So I volunteered for the Tech Writing course because I
> was not confident to offer the course myself because I didn't have
> the background. I needed someone with an English background.
> By working with someone, I could use someone else's knowledge
> and see how they would approach that type of situation.

> There is no choice but to collaborate because of the kind of work I
> do. There are so many different disciplines: linguistics, psycho-
> linguistics, writing, pedagogy, psychology. But that's not surprising
> when you are dealing with teaching.

Seven of the respondents were involved across the disciplines of English/Communication and a technical field. Of those seven, four reported that in those situations, generally the technical faculty member took the initiative. In the studies cited above, this supports Maxwell's contention that the language targeted was determined by the content, and P. Brown and Slutzky's stated need to integrate communication skill development into the technical curricula.

Whether the course is cross-disciplinary, bimodal, bilingual, or intra-disciplinary, one of the reported advantages of having two professionals in the class was the diversity of point of view. Respondents reported that often in class the teachers or presenters would have different points of view, and that such disagreement could help students see that: (1) one teacher is not always right; (2) there are various perspectives on issues and within fields of study:

> When presenting, I don't think I do anything differently because of the other person, except if there is a question from the audience that the other person has more knowledge about, I let him answer it. Or if a question is controversial, both of us will answer so that the audience will see both perspectives.

> I'd have to be dead to say that working with others hadn't changed the way I look at things. Others' perspectives have to influence me. They have different experiences and a different knowledge base and so broaden my perspective. Once in a while, I've even changed my position because of others.

> The reaction of students was generally positive. Students did go through a period when they had difficulty accepting the differing styles of the team. These styles may not seem significant to the professionals, but they are to students. They had to resolve ways of talking and preparing for different teachers . . . but we did have a baseline communication established. I think this is good in communication courses because students were being sensitized to dealing with different audiences.

Fourteen respondents felt that having students see this diversity promoted dialogue and invited student participation. Some mentioned specifically conversation and expressive skill-oriented courses as being amenable to team teaching. Further, team teaching provided students with a visible connection across disciplines:

> There was certainly not a negative reaction. Actually, team teaching helped us come together as a group, pushing us away from the authoritarian model and our acting as group facilitators, v. lecturers – thus, we were able to elicit more from the students expressively, because they were not focussed on a central figure. I think students participated in classroom conversation more readily . . . They could see the relationship between different aspects of communication in the way L. and I related to each other.

While respondents agreed that some courses are better if they are team taught, five cautioned that there are some courses that should not be team taught:

> I think team teaching lends itself to group work, participation-oriented classes, interpretive information – not to individual-focus courses. In speech/audiology/language, for example, speechreading and language thinking skills emphases would be good for team teaching, not analytic, individual clinical material like auditory training courses.

Another reason may be because it is useful for teachers to maintain their autonomy. As one participant frankly stated: 'I think we all need to have our single-person classes too, for balance. I need my autonomy sometimes. It's nice to have the final say!'

These understandings of appropriate content certainly reflect previous literature on collaboration, but we found additional themes that underscore the complexity of thoughtful team teaching. A successful team teaching experience would appear to require factors beyond interest in the other teacher's area of expertise. We categorized these emerging themes as *the need for shared philosophy, the opportunity for reflection, ego strength*, and *metaphoric views of collaborative relationships*.

Shared philosophy and values

Every person interviewed expressed the need for collaborators to share a sense of common purpose. Sixteen of the respondents went beyond this mutual agreement upon goals, however, to state that compatibility in basic values and philosophy was necessary to a productive partnership.

> It is very important that team members agree on basic values. (They may disagree on how to act on those values.) For example: Do you accept that deaf people are equal to hearing people? Yes or no? This is one issue that we would have to agree on before we could begin. After those basic values are agreed upon, the team members may disagree about specific issues or ways to act on their beliefs, but the disagreement takes place within a professional framework . . . It is not a personal attack. If it occurs that you find no agreement on basic issues, then you have to stop working together. You can't sign your name to something you disagree with . . .

> P. and I had a common interest in curricular revision and in teaching advanced students with a more global approach. With L. it was different. He was assigned to work with an audiologist; I volunteered to work with him, because I think that inter-disciplinary combinations in teaching and curriculum are

interesting. Though our course was very different than originally conceived, that didn't bother me – you have to be flexible in these situations. P. and I shared certain beliefs about audition and language teaching having to be merged at the adult level. L. and I came to find out we had similar values about student performance, and our expectations of students . . .

I'm trying to remember how I first got involved; I'm not sure . . . I think I had heard about N.'s and C.'s use of reader-response theory in developing the seminar . . . I liked that theoretical model and I wanted an opportunity to apply it to teaching reading. N.'s talk about it convinced me that she and I had similar beliefs – the underlying rationale drew me to N. – I felt she and I were on a similar wavelength and we could communicate.

Interestingly, twelve of the sixteen persons who targeted shared philosophy as a necessary condition told us that similarity in *style* was less important, or wholly unimportant, as did four other respondents. In fact, stylistic difference was seen as an asset to one's own learning about teaching, and was cited as a potential pedagogical tool:

We very obviously have major differences in style, but not really in philosophy. I resolved the differences internally, because I felt they were mainly me . . . my caution, etc. I don't think she changed that much. I think I presented a lot on layout, process and structure of texts; all the imaginative came out of her, in part, because she is good at that; I'm more confident in the other . . .

Successful team teaching puts [differences] in perspective because your beliefs are basically in synch. I can say to J., 'Gee, isn't that kind of unstructured?' – and it's no problem. We have very different styles, but common concerns, and it's never in the way . . . I love to watch her teach.

Differences in style often centered on the issue of 'organization' – the collaborator was described as more or less organized – and these differences were generally viewed with good humor. Organized teaching partners were seen as desirable, but 'disorganized' ones were not that much trouble; the pairs accommodated this difference easily. At the other end of the continuum, more rigid, perfectionistic teachers were described as gradually relaxing in the collaborative process. The truly critical factors were values and theoretical bases.

The nature of the shared philosophies tended to center on beliefs about the learner and on deeply-held pedagogical principles. The first person quoted in this section, for example, had seen so much prejudice against deaf colleagues in his previous work experience, that he told us he needed to know the attitude of a collaborator on that point before any work would be possible (this person is one of the hearing participants).

Another respondent reflected on the fact that while she and her partner were committed to a particular mode of teaching, the reality of their situation was, in itself, informative:

> C. did change my classroom behavior. She made me relax more. Part of that may have been our difference in age as well as style. But seeing her in the classroom also made me more objective about her. She talked a lot about dialogical, liberatory education, but the reality of her teaching – and probably for all of us – is somewhat different. She actually dominates in her teaching more than she thinks. M. made me more realistic. The control issue was a recurring problem, and I think that's because in these situations, someone has to be the leader. But we learned to resolve that and relax with it. We found a quotation, 'If you and your partner always agree, one of you is unnecessary'. We kept saying that to each other!

Content-based philosophies were an important impetus to collaborative work as well. Those mentioned specifically in the interviews were needs-based approaches (Munby 1978; Meath-Lang and Albertini 1983), reader-response theory (Rosenblatt 1976; Shannon and McMahon 1989) collaborative language learning (Freire 1970), communication strategies and functions (Erber 1988), bilingual/bicultural education, and use of problem-solving strategies. We suspect that these approaches generally demand a significant level of classroom interaction to be successful, and thus may be particularly served by the mutuality and dialogue between team teachers and their students.

Team teaching as a reflective act

Philosophical stances and values orientation demand reflection. Participation in the interview itself provided collaborators with an opportunity to reflect on the teaching process in general and team teaching in particular. We were told this by all of the participants at least once. Additionally, nineteen people commented on reflection itself, and on how collaboration generates thoughtful, critical pedagogy:

> By recording autobiographically and dialoguing from that text, we can see how my teaching story differs from your teaching story. Team teaching enhances your self-respect, and also acknowledges that you're limited and need others' input, cruel as that is . . . Take advantage, I'd recommend, of the stimulation that team teaching offers. Students benefit from more than one perspective. Having another person look at the way you reflect on and write up a class validates, and helps you develop other ways of reflecting on what teaching means . . .

> We both had a similar tutorial function . . . at the time, she was
> new and I didn't know her well. But we quickly came to realize
> how well we complement each other – even to filing: I'm a lumper;
> she's a splitter! On the other hand, we both seemed to speak of
> similar philosophies; we are both upfront; we are both action-
> oriented. She *is* reflective and brings out my thoughts on all sorts
> of things; I can't speak for her, but maybe I do the same for her.
> . . . The push from our Chair was good; maybe we were both
> lacking in confidence. I'm not sure I would have gotten that
> committed without that push. She likes to meet every week and
> organize material; she's quite a 'bookkeeper' – I'm more realistic,
> but that's fine!

> Expectations . . . well, as I had hoped, it was very positive, and we
> plan to continue teaching together. And as I said, we had not
> talked about pedagogical philosophy before we taught together,
> but a funny thing happened in the planning meetings with other
> teachers of the same course. We found ourselves in constant
> agreement in disagreeing with other teachers! Especially in their
> assertions that students could not do the amount and type of work
> we were proposing. We both disagreed and stuck to our ideas
> together. I was also surprised by J. I had always thought of him as
> a 'touchy-feely' type – but he's tough with students, has very high
> standards and holds students to them. I had thought of myself that
> way, but he was *strict*.

In a somewhat rueful vein, twelve teachers told us that a measure of
self-consciousness engendered reflection. The self-consciousness tended
to disappear after a few sessions with the other teacher, however; the
unease was viewed as characteristic of the early developments in a
significant relationship:

> I was very conscious of both my team teacher and our student
> assistant at all times. They *did* influence my behavior; I was
> startled at how much I was teaching to the teacher as well as to the
> students' needs. There was trepidation . . . I felt constantly
> evaluated. It occurred to me, thinking about this interview, that
> at times, what was a supportive safety net was also a modest
> burden . . .

> I certainly felt more accountable with another teacher there. I felt it
> was important to try to be more creative, imaginative, and
> innovative with a colleague like that in the room!

For the most part, the self-awareness that comes with articulating one's
plans, ideas, and hopes to another professional was termed a sort of
growth as well as an opportunity to look at one's own teaching through
a new lens. The insights that accompanied collaborative work were
perceived as particular to the team experience and as a positive, ongoing
evaluation.

Bettering one's ability to talk about one's work was not the only benefit of reflective collaboration. Team teaching was also mentioned as producing more active, thoughtful listening. Students watch the teachers in dialogue with one another. Teachers observe interactions between students and the other teacher. This triangulated listening translates into immediate feedback.

> Sometimes I saw the team teaching as a skill test of how well I could appeal to people, how I could possibly teach teachers. Also – you know, especially teaching in Sign Language, I find that I need to dig deep for appropriate metaphors, analogies, and examples. And sometimes the students will 'fake it', and politely respond . . . so I find that I can read a fellow teacher's face better to see if my explanation is reasonable. I miss that when I'm teaching alone.

Over half the teachers in the study said that a necessary condition for richer reflection and dialogue was equivalent experience. The same level of maturity and expertise was seen as fostering reciprocity and professional development. During the interviews, the participants themselves disqualified supervisory teaching as team teaching. One person said, 'Call it mentorship or internship; it's not team teaching.' Other comments included these:

> I also think that teaching experience should be the same, or equivalent in number of years, etc. Because if one person is a 'mentor' or overbearing in what is not clearly a supervising relationship – like student teaching – I can't see team teaching working well at all. Authority should be totally equal . . . at least in situations involving teachers in the same discipline. Distribution of authority should be agreed on in advance, too.

> The only difference I really notice is that I don't talk as much – which is nice, not having to say it all. A difference I really like is that I strongly believe in teaching from personal stories. And if I don't have a story of my own, or one of my former students', there's another person in the room with a wealth of stories, especially if the person is an experienced teacher.

The insistence on an equivalent *amount* of experience, although not on similar experience, relates directly to the next category. Choosing to collaborate with a seasoned equal not only enhances the opportunity for reflection on one's teaching, but also begins to characterize the participants in this study themselves.

Ego strength

While some people admitted that becoming involved in team teaching is a respite from taking full responsibility for a class, there generally was an attitude among respondents that collective insight and collaborative wisdom yield better learning and classroom interaction. Often the initial motivation for teaching in a team was the admiration and respect that one person had for the other. Colleagues were described as 'respected tremendously' and, 'superbly skilled'. Twenty-two respondents said they felt that the other person knew more in complementary areas than they did.

> C.'s background in literature was very helpful. I organized the language of the course by genre, and C. had taught genres of literature to high school students. Since our students were first and second year college/vocational students, there was a nice continuity and contrast to observe from. C. was observant and a good chronicler, helpful, in curricular development and revision. She's willing to reflect on her teaching too – which some people won't do – and I need dialogue in teaching.

> I think Communication, English and technical teachers must co-teach in our enterprise . . . there is no way that I can know current thinking on language growth and that language teachers can keep up with the almost daily change in the technical field . . . All my co-teaching with language teachers has been positive. Maybe you have a greater tolerance for differences with people outside your own field – you give them the benefit of the doubt. It's more complex with 'your own kind'! I found the Communication people very professional, very intellectual in comparison with people from the technical school. That was stimulating. Plus I learned a lot from them about students' language processing, and how to express myself in relation to first and second language learning issues. In my own field, I had two team teachers I really learned from – one was a Deaf teacher. He and I could really help each other cross-culturally, plus he's a nice person. And, of course, J., who's a master in his field.

The respondents demonstrated that respect for the competencies of the other person did not in any way dilute their own sense of competence. We observed that the successful team members recognized the gifts, skills and expertise of the partner without feeling denigrated, or in any way less skillful. In fact, five respondents directly identified ego strength as a quality necessary for team teaching:

> You have to have enough ego strength to say what you think, be willing to state what you feel, discuss it and not just give in right away. You have to be willing to compromise, try something new and see how it works.

> I chose B. and J. because I respected them tremendously as
> professionals. In fact, it always worked when I made the choice –
> which I would do after a lot of thought and experience with the
> other person. I've had team teaching fail – with someone
> competent but not confident or convinced of her own competence.
> It seemed I threatened that person.

The respondents all observed something that the other person brought
not only to the team, but to the partner:

> A team does make a difference to the audiences for the [Sign
> Language assessment] presentations. People can see there are
> things that F. does well. It's true in the reverse. F. couldn't do it
> alone. He needs me there to carry out the lecturing. But, because of
> the nature of that project, there is a lot of concern for detail, data
> collecting and policies with schools. That's where he really shines.
> The project really is too much for one person to do. And each of us
> can do our own part better than the other.

> Over the years, most of my collaborations have been with speech
> therapists. I simply don't feel as qualified to give the kind of
> feedback that students need with regard to their speech processes.
> I know there is an attitude with some people in my field that if
> you're 'top-of-the-line' you should be able to focus on both
> productive and receptive elements in a basic language curriculum,
> but keeping up with one's own field is challenging enough. So I try
> to hook up with highly qualified people in other disciplines. I have
> my own expertise, and that experience tells me that I shouldn't be
> going it alone.

> I found myself impressed by J.'s approach to the class, even though
> I wouldn't have done things the same way . . . I get a high from
> thinking in a team. As a single teacher, I feel lockstep. I'm very
> rigid teaching alone. The selection of content and my approach in
> team teaching was more flexible and very different.

Consistently, participants reported a balance between the need for
having confidence in oneself and recognizing the gifts the other member
brings to the team. Additionally, respondents were reluctant to collaborate with a controlling person. As one participant said: 'Do not work
with a prima donna; I've seen people do that; some can't share the
spotlight, or the power.' Other respondents echoed these sentiments,
substituting terms like 'domineering' and 'know-it-all' for 'prima
donna'.

The need for a defined leader seemed to be more important when a
written document was the desired end result. In research and curriculum
development collaboration, the leader or first author was defined as the
person who wrote the first draft or had the original idea, no matter how
much responding the partner had done. In a classroom, however,

equality was the ideal, although it is difficult to achieve. Respondents reported times when the paper-shuffling member of the team was viewed as the leader by students and by herself. But this leadership role was not as effective as when each member had equal status in students' eyes as well as in the eyes of the team. One manifestation of this equality (in the classroom) is the presence of both team members in class:

> I think both professionals should be in the classroom at the same time – this isn't turn teaching. I think that's important because when something comes up in class that she knows more about, I can say to L.: 'You're the expert, jump in when your area comes up.'

We were told that flexibility is critical to maintaining strength in collaboration. In class, this flexibility was described as 'a song and dance' and 'developing a sense of timing that was tricky at first'. Respondents also saw the need to change the way they behaved during the collaboration:

> I had to be less aggressive and controlling in the team situation. L. would not break in on what I was saying on her own. I needed to give her an opportunity to say what she wanted. We decided that we needed to have one leader per class. If L. was the leader, I tried to remember not to break in but wait for an invitation.

> Working with B. on presentation changed the way I do things. The whole idea of including personal reflection in your own voice was different from anything I'd done. When I started writing with her, there was the demand that I do reflection on my own teaching and beliefs. That was very different for me. It was especially brought out when we asked D. to work with us . . . he was very uncomfortable about putting personal reflections in his own voice. I think it is an interesting development in language teaching and research with student-centered teaching in writing that is coming, and the teacher will have to share his own voice . . . I think that represents the different points of view on approaching writing.

Occasionally, issues would arise that the team would have to confront. Respondents disagreed on whether controversy should be faced in front of the students. Ten stated that controversy should be dealt with 'after class' and that one should never confront the problem in front of the students. Six others thought that pointing out differences in philosophy or approach could be helpful to the students. One participant said:

> One of the benefits to an audience of having a team is to demonstrate that the audience will need to be active in dealing with the information that is being shared . . . that the presenters are still actively considering the issues. But the collaborators are collaborators and not debaters. If they disagree too often during a presentation the audience will be forced to choose between them.

Relational metaphors

A striking feature of the interviews, which could not have been predicted by the initial questions, was the fact that every respondent resorted to describing team teaching in terms of other relationships. Nine persons interviewed stated that team teaching becomes 'more than just another professional relationship'. Six respondents characterized team teaching as an act of friendship metaphorically, and six others stated that collaboration had led to or deepened a friendship. One teacher said, 'I can't imagine team teaching with somebody I couldn't be friends with . . . ' Other participants supported this perspective, five actually using the term 'chemistry' to describe what happens in a positive collaboration:

> With that particular colleague, prior to the team teaching experience, we really had never discussed and had no idea of one another's pedagogical approach or teaching philosophy. But I admired my colleague's style and personality in other situations. I liked how he approached language, problem solving, and parenting (which we had discussed in depth on several occasions) . . .

> We didn't have a lot of expectations. I wasn't disappointed. I couldn't have worked with a better person. We became friends and went on to collaborate on papers. She took a 'leadership' role very quickly – generated ideas and she kept us on track. I learned a lot from her. It was a bit more work than I thought it would be, chatting about how it went, how it would go next year; finding time to be together and keeping it.

Two collaborators used a marriage metaphor to describe the kind of sustained understanding that team members need to develop.

> A good team is like a strong marriage. It's funny . . . when I had a difference with a team teacher in style and philosophy, my tendency was to withdraw, to run away. The person went to the Chair to complain. The Chair identified the problem as a philosophical difference, but even a helpful third party couldn't resolve it. We finally talked, and I was willing to work it out; but the other person said she couldn't cope. The result was turn-teaching, we taught alone on alternate days. That felt like a divorce to me . . .

> J. and I were in labs together five to seven hours a day for six years. We often remarked that we were together more often than most married people – and we began to act the part, which was scary! I remember when we went to a conference – our field is male dominated, so people always assumed I was J.'s wife. But we realized we were reinforcing that idea by the familiarity we had with each other. One night, at dinner, he took two desserts and I

started to lecture him: 'Now you *know* you can't eat that or you'll never sleep tonight and be awful for your presentation tomorrow!' It was just like my mother and father. He fired back, 'Can't I enjoy myself on a trip???' And we both immediately, intuitively saw what was happening and laughed. Most of the time that was an asset in the classroom or in a presentation, because we knew exactly what the other person would do in different student situations or in reaction to different problems.

Seven participants used parenting as a metaphor – with all the possibilities of being manipulated in the ways that parents are:

> Our philosophy was dead-on. If you don't have that, the students can play on [inconsistencies]. Like parents, you have to be careful of that in team teaching. I'd throw those issues right back on students. D. and I did divide up. She prefers to lecture; I prefer activities. She's not comfortable with unexpected answers. I love them.

> I would say [student reaction] was a mixed reaction – maybe the parenting model is appropriate, because two or three students under a lot of academic and social pressure would regularly try to manipulate us – ask an opinion of one and use it against the other. etc. Most were flexible and got used to it.

The parent and marriage metaphors were not gender-specified. Same-sex teaching pairs used these as frequently as male–female collaborators. The strength of the collaborative bond, in fact, blurred such distinctions for participants, even as they told us about them:

> One interesting feature of C.'s and my dialogue – which was constant – was the gender-indexing. For a course with film and interpretive reading, the female interpretation was critical – having a woman's views on how women are seen as central characters across time was important for both male and female students. And I think cross-sex dialogue more productive in team teaching situations. Maybe men and women are more willing to give one another feedback. I just didn't find that in male–male teaching pairs. Maybe we think really talking to one another is 'bad'. In team teaching with other men, I found it interesting how careful they were with me, how they didn't take risks. It often felt very controlled.

> E. and I had a teaching relationship that was kind of gender/parental with each of us taking a traditional role . . . E. the authority and me the nurturer. There was one exception. One time there were some students who were trying to say: 'I'm deaf and I can't write.' E. intuitively stepped back and let me handle it. It could be because I'm married to a deaf man and I don't take that excuse . . . Funny enough, with F. and J. our roles were against gender type: I was the authoritarian and they were the nurturers.

Trust and 'intimacy' – specifically mentioned – were recurring needs voiced by team teachers and collaborators intent on developing their relationships. A discourse that spilled into the personal and political, as well as pedagogical, was described:

> Teachers need to have a common theory but also something more to bind them . . . a chemistry of some kind. I think N. and I had that. There was no 'mentor' feeling or subservient feeling; we were true equals. That allows for disagreements to be resolved, even if they are very painful – it did for us. God, I remember her getting red in the face and how my gut felt when we had a major disagreement. But because we had a *relationship* – I mean, a real, significant relationship that was developing as we taught together – we accepted that those feelings were necessary to a developing, important relationship. Something happens in a real team; the potential for growth makes resolving differences a priority . . . Something has to connect between the people involved. I wanted to say 'respect' at first; but I honestly think you have to *like* the person you're with day in and day out (you can respect a person you dislike).

> The gender aspect is funny . . . I didn't expect this, but I seem to be more comfortable team teaching with a teacher of the opposite sex. I am hard-pressed to say why. I guess there's some intimacy in a team teaching context, and it seems natural and helpful to work with men. I've heard men say that of women team teachers as well.

> Agree to talk with each other about basic disagreements and not with a third person. The team has to develop trust. It's OK to talk with a third person but both members of the team need to know a third person is involved.

> You need to be able to talk about your teaching as an issue. Keep it self-aware, reflective of what is happening. Let the collaboration be an object of discussion. If that happens, you will be more likely to focus on students because everything will be out in the open. Recognize that it is more than just a professional relationship. There needs to be some kind of intimacy that develops. By intimacy, I mean talking face-to-face about the teaching relationship.

The need for trust is fundamental to important relationships. This was stressed by ten respondents, as well as the mutual respect mentioned by 22 participants. That insistence on mutual trust is consistent with the next theme; for the relationships cultivated by collaborators appear, to us, to have as one goal rigorous self-examination. The team relationship – significantly enough, for teachers of language – puts a real demand on the participants to find a language with which to identify the collaboration and sustain its dialogue.

Metaphors: the decoding exercise

After all of the interviews had been completed, twenty of the participants joined us for the encoding-decoding exercise. Freire (1970) proposes this technique as a way to approach an issue or problem differently, and thus objectify and 're-present' the theme being explored. Freire's context, of course, is that of dialogical education with students. In this participant-observer study, we had become students of our own situations in the interviews. Thus, engaging in a decoding exercise as a group, after conversing on some general themes and descriptions, seemed an appropriate method for deepening our understanding of the statements on team teaching that had been collected.

In our initial analysis, we observed the spontaneous use of metaphors, generally limited to other human relationships, sports (the application of the word 'team'), and the allusion to 'chemistry' between people. Freire's decoding refers to putting the issue or theme in another form: theater, music, dance, or figurative language are often mentioned as possibilities. Given the group's touching on metaphor in the interviews, one decoding exercise we posed involved finding four *conscious* metaphors for team teaching. The alternative exercise we gave asked the group to draw a picture of team teaching. The participants met in small groups of three or four people, and convened to report their metaphors and drawings to the larger group after half an hour.

Both the metaphors and the drawings revealed a complexity of attitude not immediately apparent in the interview texts. While the interviews focussed, for the most part, on successful team experiences, certain difficulties were reported as a matter of course. The greater part of the conversation for every participant, however, was positive and supportive of collaboration. The metaphors and drawings showed a darker side of the experience of collaboration, often lightened by humor, but somewhat more ambiguous than the general statements of support we had seen. Where the greater part of the texts had been positive, most of the metaphors and drawings portrayed some struggle.

Two drawings were produced. One portrayed two halves of a completed jigsaw puzzle, slightly out of line, but moving toward interlocking. The other drawing showed a classroom with two tiny teachers and several very large students. In the full groups, the participants interpreted these, with the consent of their originators, to mean: (1) the steady progress that must be made to 'blend the voices' of collaborators (in the case of the puzzle); and (2) the result of team teaching frequently being a de-centering of teacher authority and concomitant growth in the students (in the classroom drawing). Interestingly, these drawings validated comments in the texts; but were produced by sub-groups whose members did not include those who had made such statements.

The metaphor exercise was more productive, from the standpoint of quantity of responses. There were twenty metaphors generated in the meeting. Some were specific to team members themselves. For example, the metaphor 'Team teaching is a walk in the woods with Ebenezer Scrooge and Peter Pan' referred to one of the teams we interviewed, a quiet, scholarly researcher who often portrays himself as a curmudgeon, and his dramatic, extroverted young teaching partner in a creative writing course. Others were elaborate and somewhat situation-specific. Six metaphors were transparent and repeated across more than one group with slight variations, however:

1. Team teaching is like watching a film with your eyes closed.
2. Team teaching is two sides of a coin – without both, it has no value.
3. Team teaching is like trying on someone else's clothes, trying to make them fit and still look like yourself.
4. Team teaching is split-brain soup!
5. Team teaching is traveling without a map.
6. Team teaching is a piece of fruitcake . . . it has lots of ingredients, and takes time to mature. People love it or hate it; some tolerate it when it's in season.

As in the interview texts, more sports and relational metaphors were created or repeated. 'Dating' was added to the list of relationships that team teaching and collaboration resemble: 'Like dating, team teaching is finding a common language, trying to impress another, and feeling sensitive to scrutiny!'

In the discussion that followed the sharing of the drawings and metaphors, most participants noted the seemingly more ambivalent stance of the 'decoded' representations of team teaching. We pointed out, though, that these ambiguities were at least touched upon in the majority of interviews, and were consistent with the complexities of language, timing, and relationships most respondents had mentioned. Indeed, the decoding exercise validated a number of points already raised, particularly with regard to ego strength and necessary types of support. Because our object was to elicit characteristics of *successful* experiences, the interviews followed that direction. The decoding exercise served a valuable purpose in reaffirming the complexity and difficulty of collaboration, even for those who have experienced powerful team relationships, and who share common convictions about language teaching. As one participant wryly commented in the course of the discussion: 'Team teaching is not for sissies.'

Conclusions and recommendations

There are some reasonable conclusions we can reach regarding the elements of successful team teaching. First, team teaching situations require compatible philosophy and appropriate content. Participants generally felt that while shared values were important to success, that was not the only criterion. The amount of experience and the personality of the teacher, as well as his or her value system, are all important when determining the make-up of a team. Regarding content, interactive group courses that demand dialogue and sharing of perspectives appear more conducive to team approaches than courses that are receptive, discrete skill-based, or information transmitting. At the same time, while the content of the course is important, it will not carry a team teaching experience to a productive conclusion. Not every experienced professional can or wants to teach in a team. The interaction of both the teachers and the content demands thoughtful planning and consideration.

Administrative understanding is crucial to successful team teaching. As Hanslovsky, Mayer and Wagner said in 1969, administrators need to be convinced of the worth of team teaching to the students' education. This is true today. But there are two administrative *caveats*. First, team teaching should not be viewed as a solution to time constraints or to staff efficiency issues. All of our respondents indicated a strong need for *more* time to negotiate and dialogue. Ten people specifically said that there was a need for structured, planned time together, many emphasizing the need for a debriefing that would enable the team to see what worked, what didn't work, and where they were going next. The second issue is related to how members of a team are chosen. Eight respondents reported that they were assigned a partner. Sometimes, these pairings were successful, but 100 per cent of the incidental reports of unsuccessful teams in the interviews were teams that were assigned by administrators, not selected or recruited by a team member. This would indicate to us that administrators should have a hands-off policy where possible in the assignment process and allow collaborators to self-select.

At the present time, there is an increased emphasis on collaborative writing and collaboration between students and teachers in the classroom. Our recommendations for further study are mindful of this pattern. It would be helpful, as some of our respondents noted, to gather information regarding *students'* perceptions and attitudes toward collaboration in order to identify and assess the issues that arise. Methods of evaluation used by collaborative teachers and the grading of collaborative classroom projects should be examined in this context. The purposes of both teacher and student collaboration would benefit from a comprehensive overview, and would also inform the evaluation of these experiences. Finally, another area of study should be an examination of the discourse of team teaching situations. In characterizing the kinds of dialogues that successful teams have, between themselves and with their students, we may be able to document a truly inter-subjective language learning experience. And that was the single shared goal of every teacher in this study.

Endnotes

The authors would like to thank the participants in the study: John Albertini, Gerry Bateman, Donna Burfield, Frank Caccamise, Carol Cuneo, Larry Hunt, Jacky Kelly, Ron Kelly, Anne Kingston, Harry Lang, Gene Lylak, Ed McGee, Michael McMahon, Elaine Milton, William Newell, Linda Palmer, Pamela Rohland, Larry Scott, Glenda Senior, Brenda Whitehead, Robert Whitehead, Dorothy Wilkins, and Paula Wollenhaupt.

This research report was produced at the National Technical Institute for the Deaf, USA, through an agreement between Rochester Institute of Technology and the US Department of Education.

7 Team teaching: a case study from Japan

Peter Sturman

Introduction

The Koto-ku project is a cooperative venture between the British Council Cambridge English School (CES) and the Board of Education in Koto ward in southeast Tokyo. The project began in the light of changes in English language teaching in Japan as the need to communicate in English became more apparent throughout Japanese society. A second factor that has influenced the development of similar cooperative ventures throughout Japan has been the internal and external pressure on Japan to 'internationalise', i.e. to become more integrated into the international community. Team teaching has developed as one attempt to satisfy these two needs. In the Koto-ku project, qualified and experienced ESOL teachers from the Cambridge English School, British Council, Tokyo work alongside their Japanese counterparts to team teach English to first-year lower secondary school students. The two groups of teachers have different pedagogic principles and different ideas about what constitutes good teaching material, a good lesson and a good teacher. Consequently there has had to be a considerable amount of compromise from both sides to produce an appropriate methodology and effective materials for the team teaching.

The project is now in its fifth year and is considered to be a qualified success in terms of its teaching aims and a great success in terms of international and personal cooperation. This has not always been the case, however. This article will outline the background and organisation of the project before looking at the preparation necessary for team teaching to be successful and the problems that can limit success. A final evaluation of the project from the perspectives of the students and the teachers, both Japanese and from CES, will argue that despite all the potential and actual problems faced by individual teachers, the students enjoy this kind of teaching and the majority of the teachers respect and support the project.

Background to the project

There is a long tradition of using foreign teachers in Japanese schools, but there was also, by 1985, a growing awareness that the teaching of

English throughout the Japanese education system was going to have to change drastically. Even after a combined total of six years of lower and upper secondary school English and a possible further four years at university, the end product was a person who knew a great deal about the grammatical rules of the language and had an impressive range of vocabulary, but could not apply that knowledge either to understand or produce written texts (without a great deal of painstaking effort) or to hold even the most basic of conversations. It is interesting to note that even with, or perhaps despite, this 'failure' of the formal education system, English is popular throughout Japanese society. There has been a spectacular growth in the number of private *ei-kaiwa* ('English conversation') schools – to the extent that there as many advertisements for English schools on the Tokyo subway as there are for package weddings.

The Ministry of Education (*Mombusho*) has been widely criticised for the apparent failure of the system. This is not entirely fair, as Mombusho's stated objectives for the teaching of English are not, as many people believe, simply in terms of the acquisition of vocabulary or grammatical rules. For example, one of the three objectives for first-year students in lower secondary school is: 'to enable students to hear [*sic*] and speak on simple matters using primary English' and, by the end of the first year, the student should be able:

> a. To grasp the main points in topics and to understand the necessary contents.
> b. To speak without missing important things, by arranging what one intends to express.
> c. To reply accurately after catching the intention of the speaker.

> (*Course of Study for Lower Secondary Schools in Japan*, Ministry of Education in Japan, Science and Culture, 1983: Section 9)

In 1985 the Education Board of Koto ward approached the British Council for advice about introducing native speaker teachers into their schools with the broad aim of improving the students' English. A pilot project was outlined in a series of design documents produced between March and September 1985 and this was approved by an advisory committee. The aims at the beginning of the project were:

1. to improve the students' speaking and listening skills;
2. to increase the students' motivation to study English;
3. to influence teaching methodology by example and cooperation.

A schedule was eventually agreed for a pilot project in nine schools and from October 1985 to March 1986 48 first-year classes received a total of fifteen 'team-taught' lessons per class. The British Council undertook to supply trained teachers and to provide professional support and services to the project. The project was extended to all 23 schools in the ward in April 1986, which coincided with the formal opening of the British Council Cambridge English School in Tokyo. The CES eventually took over the responsibility for the project although the CES management's priority had to be the establishment of the new school.

Project organisation

Of the 23 lower secondary schools in Koto-ku, some are large, with six first-year classes and some are small, with one or two first-year classes. Generally, one Japanese teacher will be responsible for all the first-year classes but in larger schools there may be two, or even three teachers sharing the classes. In any one year of the project, there may be 30 or more teachers involved. These teachers have no choice about whether or not to team teach with the CES teachers, and although some actively look forward to team teaching, some feel extremely nervous about it and some even feel hostile towards it. The project is not popular among the CES teachers and although nearly all the CES teachers who have worked in Koto-ku said they found it both interesting and rewarding, most felt that one six-month session there was quite enough.

The Japanese school year begins in April but the team teaching does not begin until September in the second term. The students have therefore had one term of English – usually three, 50-minute lessons a week in coeducational classes of about 40 students. They are supposed to have learned the alphabet – both capital and lower-case letters – in primary school, but in many lower secondary schools much of the first term is taken up with revision of this. In nearly all cases September is the first time for the students to meet a 'foreigner', and if the Japanese teacher has prepared the students well for the team teaching, they are usually in a state of high excitement, eager and willing to try something new.

Preparation for team teaching

Team teaching preparation begins in April with the organisation of the timetable. The schools are divided into two groups; the first group receives a CES teacher over a ten-week period from September to mid-November and the second group from mid-November to mid-December and then again from mid-January to late February. Of the three English classes per week, two are team-taught and one remains for the Japanese teachers alone. Each class receives a total of fifteen team-taught lessons over the ten-week period. CES teachers work in two lower secondary schools at the same time, usually alternating between them, but sometimes having to teach in both on the same day. A one-hour liaison period is arranged every week for the two teachers to meet to discuss the content and method of teaching the lessons. If a CES teacher is working with more than one Japanese English teacher in the same school, they may have to arrange several different liaison periods.

Ten professional-support workshops are held during the course of the team teaching period. These workshops last for two hours and are all held at the Education Centre in Koto-ku, except for the first one in late April which is held at the CES. These workshops have played an essential part in the project although the content has varied over the years. The Japanese teachers are always asked what they would like to see as the content. This has ranged from explanations of the underlying principles of communicative teaching to practical language development sessions on, for example, how to explain changes in the teaching schedule over the telephone, discussions on the differences between approaches to education in the UK and Japan, and language games and quizzes. The central theme has always been that the workshops are a forum for the discussion of the project – the principles, the materials and the method – and to get to know each other more informally. The end of the workshops coincides with the Japanese equivalent of pub-opening time and this may also have played a part in developing an awareness of each other's perspectives.

The CES teachers meet as a group once every two weeks to discuss the material and any problems that have come up. If everything is going smoothly, these meetings become unnecessary but they are valuable in maintaining a sense of team spirit. This team spirit can be very import-ant as it is quite easy to feel isolated when working on one's own in a Japanese lower secondary school. The Japanese teachers also meet as a group but usually only once at the end of the project in order to evaluate it. Their comments and criticisms are then passed on to the CES coordinator.

The first workshop of the team teaching year usually takes place in late April and all but a few of the Japanese teachers attend. By the fourth year of the project only about 40 per cent of the Japanese teachers were completely new to team teaching so there were fewer fears and anxieties to calm and there was more support from experienced colleagues. How-ever, many of the teachers who have already taught on the project, did so in the first two years when the materials, methodology and whole approach were in their infancy. Many of these teachers did not enjoy their first experience of team teaching and are anxious to see if there have been any improvements.

The main part of the first workshop is taken up with watching a video of a team-taught lesson. The video shows a full lesson in which the two teachers are obviously comfortable working together and the students respond extremely well. They should do, as this lesson was rehearsed the day before and the only things that were new to the students were the video camera and about 30 observers. The two teachers in the video had worked together for three consecutive years so the lesson can hardly be said to be representative of team teaching, but it was never meant to be. The video demonstrates some of the approaches that can be taken to team teaching and shows that the material can, and in fact should, be adapted to the particular class to be taught. It also shows that the students will respond to English *in English* without being intimidated by a big, frightening foreigner and that both the Japanese teacher and the CES teacher can make mistakes without looking stupid to the students or to each other. In particular it shows what I believe to be the essential components of successful team teaching: mutual personal and professional respect, adaptability and good humour. The problem with this type of video is that many teachers consider it to be prescriptive rather than descriptive and feel that team teaching must be done this way. As a result, much of the rest of the workshop is taken up with discussion about how exactly to adapt the material to students of different ability, and how to alter the approach for teachers with different personalities who would not feel comfortable taking a similar approach to the one on the video. The Japanese teachers are encouraged to take an *active* rather than passive role in the team teaching and to argue back strongly if they do not agree with something, and not to think of the CES teachers as 'foreign experts' to be deferred to.

Some details about the project are sent out to the CES teachers before they come to Japan, but when they arrive one full, four-hour session is set aside to discuss the project, look through the materials, isolate possible problems and generally make sure that they go into the schools with the best possible approach and attitude to the teaching. The main focus of the session is to try to explain the principle of 'flexible equality' that has come to be seen as the best way to deal with the problem of teacher initiative, roles, and responsibility in the classroom. This is of particular concern to the Japanese teachers and has been one of the two consistent problems mentioned by the Japanese teachers in their end-of-term analysis of the project (the other being the teaching material). It is essential that the CES teacher is always conscious of the fact that the class 'belongs' to the Japanese teacher, and is always sensitive to the relationship between the Japanese teacher and the students. Team teaching means working together – not independently – in the same classroom, understanding each other's pedagogic principles, even when it may be difficult to agree with them, and being sensitive to each other's professional position in the classroom. The CES teachers also have to be willing to listen to the Japanese teachers' views and opinions, try to understand what is really being said when the language of communication breaks down and realise that the Japanese teachers know more about the students than they do. The CES teachers must remember that they have been invited into the schools to help, to encourage and to motivate both the Japanese teachers and students and not to discourage or dominate either. Obviously it is essential that the two teachers share the teaching aims for the lesson and that they both accept the lesson plan and material. The three underlying principles of 'flexible equality' are:

1. to work with the Japanese teachers to teach the students, using material and methods that are acceptable and appropriate to both teachers in a way that is sensitive to the Japanese teachers' relationship with the students;
2. to discuss in the liaison periods before teaching commences, the exact roles of the two teachers for each stage of the lesson and to make sure that the Japanese teacher does actually agree with the final decision rather than simply appearing to agree with it;
3. to be prepared to adapt the materials and methodology according to the Japanese teachers' ideas, and to be particularly sensitive when trying to persuade the Japanese teachers to accept something that they are apprehensive about.

In the week immediately preceding the start of team teaching, the CES teachers visit the Japanese schools to meet the Japanese teachers for the first time, to be introduced to the principal, vice-principal, headteacher, office staff, kitchen personnel and other English teachers. This is also the opportunity to discuss the very first lesson and how to teach it. A special 'initial' lesson has been prepared which is supposed to introduce team teaching to the students and teachers. It involves simple task-based listening exercises, pair and open-class speaking exercises, task-based reading and writing exercises. All of these involve manipulating language the students *should* already know, in ways that may be new to them. The students will be under stress because of the new activity style but not, theoretically, because of the language content. The lesson is accompanied by very clear 'stage-directions' for the two teachers and it is supposed to be an enjoyable, interesting and valuable introduction to the team teaching session.

Team teaching problems

In an ideal situation, there are no problems. Both members of the team immediately find that they like each other as people and respect each other as teachers. They both consider the project to be valuable for themselves and the students and, although they may have reservations about several activities or whole lessons, they feel confident enough to discuss their feelings honestly and openly and to change the materials or methodology as appropriate. They are prepared to spend extra time on making good picture cards and on improving the prepared materials and enjoy the process of teaching together, even when things do not go as well as expected. They are prepared to accept the responsibility for things going wrong, and to shrug off any such setbacks as simply part of the learning process. In reality, things are very different, and in this section, I shall outline a number of problem areas.

Personality

When you have to work closely with someone over a period of ten weeks, it is obviously easier if you like each other. Unfortunately no one can guarantee that this will be the case and the least that either teacher can hope for is that they will not actively dislike the other. Some people are more difficult for one person to get on with than others. I found it impossible to get on well with one particular Japanese teacher, and she with me; yet the following year a different CES teacher worked with the same person and they got along wonderfully.

Respect

Professional respect does not develop automatically and it can only develop over a reasonable period of time as the two teachers begin to appreciate each other's qualities when working together. The Japanese teachers have consistently requested that the CES supply teachers for a two-year commitment to teaching in Koto-ku so that the Japanese teachers know whom they are going to be working with; unfortunately the CES has been unable to do so. Respect for each other can develop for a number of reasons: commitment to teaching, classroom personality, willingness to spend extra time on the teaching, attitude to the students and to classroom discipline, originality of ideas, underlying pedagogical principles or even simply the ability to cope with a difficult situation. Respect can also develop for less obvious reasons on a teacher-by-teacher basis. I found myself respecting one teacher for the way she was genuinely delighted when the students responded well and another teacher for the way he caught an escaped snake, the pride of the Natural Science class. There may be universal qualities to a 'good' teacher, but teachers working in different institutions, with different types of students and different pedagogical assumptions may find that the definition of a 'good' teacher varies with the institution's philosophy and aims. This will influence the respect accorded one teacher by another from a different institution.

The CES teachers and the Japanese teachers often have different definitions of what constitutes a 'good' teacher. If the CES teachers sometimes complain that the Japanese teachers spend too much time lecturing the students on 'behaviour', the Japanese teachers complain that the CES teachers do not spend enough time on grammatical rules and explanations. Or, if the Japanese teachers complain that the CES teachers ignore the importance of the examinations, the CES teachers complain that the Japanese teachers do not know enough about communicative teaching, and so on. Under such conditions, it becomes more and more difficult to respect your partners until you understand the different situations they work in and the pressures they work under. A complication for CES teachers is the fact that lower secondary schools and private language schools have very different expectations, as can be seen from Table 1 on pages 149–50.

Attitude to team teaching

Team teaching receives a great deal of media attention in Japan and there are books, articles and letters to newspapers and magazines describing the best and the worst examples. Team teaching can significantly help to change the nature of English language teaching, but this is not its sole objective in Japan. It is also hoped that team teaching will encourage the development of a more 'international' perspective in Japan. As a result, there are three different perceptions of the role of the foreign partner in the team.

1. *The 'foreign expert'.* The foreign teacher is the source of all knowledge and can do no wrong. This attitude has created several problems when it has existed in Koto-ku. Firstly, it establishes an imbalance in the relationship between the two teachers which is then reinforced by the structure and aims of the project. Secondly, it allows the Japanese teacher to relinquish any responsibility for the materials development, the teaching and any progressive development of the project as a whole. Thirdly, it makes it too easy for the CES teacher to assume that he or she is, in fact, the expert, and to then become the dominant partner in the team. Finally, the CES teachers may be lured into accepting this perception of themselves, to be unaware of the Japanese teachers' opinions about the material or teaching, and become insensitive to the relationship between the Japanese teacher and the students. In one sense the CES teachers are the 'foreign experts' but only to the same extent that the Japanese teachers are the 'native experts'. It is essential to keep this balance in mind.

2. *The 'walking tape-recorder'.* In this case the Japanese teacher may feel that the only thing the foreign partner can do is to act as a pronunciation model for the students, and a poor model, according to some, unless they happen to speak with the perfect 'Standard American or British' accents that can be heard on the cassettes that

TABLE 1. A COMPARISON OF DIFFERENT QUALITIES EXPECTED IN TEACHERS IN STATE LOWER SECONDARY SCHOOLS AND IN A PRIVATE LANGUAGE SCHOOL CATERING TO MOTIVATED ADULT STUDENTS

	State school	Private language school
1. The ability to translate the target text word-by-word and to explain the grammar and lexis in the students' own language	E	U
2. A detailed knowledge of English grammatical rules, lexical irregularities and obscure or rarely-used idioms	E	V
3. A detailed knowledge of examinations, examination techniques and assessment statistics	E	V/U
4. The ability to motivate students to work extremely hard on preparation for examinations	E	V/U
5. The ability to work in a team by adapting your own ideas to those of the established procedure	E	V
6. The ability to deal with student problems *in loco parentis* and to counsel students on personal problems	E	V
7. An extra-curricular interest and the willingness to develop this as a club activity for students	E	V
8. The ability to write new, effective and interesting teaching material, and whole courses, for use by other teachers	V/U	E/V
9. The ability to work in a team by contributing new ideas and suggesting improvements to established procedure	U	V
10. The ability to motivate students to work well together and enjoy the lessons	V/U	E

149

TABLE 1. *(cont.)*

	State school	Private language school
11. A detailed knowledge of pairwork resources, task-based activities, role plays, simulations, games for language learning and affective language learning resources	U	E
12. The ability to teach English through English to multilingual classes	U	E

Key
E = essential   V = valuable   U = unnecessary

accompany the textbooks, all other accents being less 'acceptable' or too difficult to understand. The CES teachers have come from a wide variety of linguistic backgrounds – England, with distinct accents ranging from Yorkshire, Derbyshire, West Country and the south of England, Scotland (Edinburgh), Eire (Dublin), Canada, Australia and New Zealand – and the only problems of comprehension occurred when the teachers wanted to speak at a more natural speed, whatever the accent. The 'walking tape-recorder' problem is more serious when the Japanese teachers believe that modelling the text for the students is all the foreign teachers *can* or *should* do in the classroom. At the very beginning of the project, the CES teachers felt some pressure of this kind as the Japanese teachers simply did not know what the CES teachers could do.

3. *The 'token foreigner'*. In this case the only justification that can be given for the presence of the foreign teacher in the Japanese school is that he or she is living 'proof' of the 'internationalisation' of Japan, or at least of one small part of it. Until the project began to be seen as valuable to both the Japanese teachers and students, this attitude was all too common in Koto-ku.

Attitude to the project

There was an assumption, at the very beginning of the project, that all the Japanese teachers involved in the project agreed with the aims of the project, thought that it was a good and necessary thing and actively wanted to take part in it. It was a rude surprise to find that this was very far from the case. In fact, at the end of the first year of the project, the

Japanese teachers complained strongly that the students' reading and writing skills were suffering. When the CES teachers commented that according to the aims of the project, they were only meant to concentrate on speaking and listening, it turned out that the Japanese teachers had not been informed of this fact. A fourth aim was immediately added to the original three: to improve the students' reading and writing abilities. Most of the Japanese teachers had not heard of the 'introduce new teaching methodology' aim either. Moreover, the teachers in all but nine of the schools had been unaware that they were going to have to team teach until about two weeks before it began! This is not entirely unbelievable, however, as it was more or less true for the CES teachers as well.

Even if the Japanese teachers *had* been aware of all the aims of the project, it is by no means certain that they would have agreed to team teach, and there is a persistent minority who would prefer not to. Unfortunately this minority argues a very logical case. The students have to take examinations and these examinations do not include speaking or listening skills, nor reading or writing exercises similar to the ones used in the project. The examinations are set on the contents of the textbook, and the grammatical structures and lexis it contains. All Japanese teachers feel that they do not have enough time to prepare the students well enough for the examinations, and accordingly that the team teaching project is taking away time from the essentials. This group of teachers also believes that the techniques and approaches they already use are successful, given the nature of the syllabus and examinations and, considering the overwhelming importance of the examinations, why should they change anything? They are polite, but genuinely believe that we are wasting their time, the students' time and a considerable amount of money as well. However, English language education in Japan *is* changing; the examination system is changing and, sooner or later, students will have to learn to speak and understand English. The approaches taken to the teaching of reading and writing skills will also undoubtedly change, and the project can be seen as a valuable prep-aration for all of these changes, with great potential for teachers and students alike. More and more Koto-ku teachers now view it in this light and the project is also attracting a considerable amount of attention from education specialists throughout Japan, including Mombusho, JALT (the Japan Association of Language Teachers), other professional teaching groups and boards of education in other wards and prefectures.

Language

Three of the 31 CES teachers have been able to speak Japanese at roughly the intermediate level. Most, however, start with no Japanese at all and end with very little. All the Japanese teachers can speak English, but there is great variation in ability. Japanese teachers, in general, are very insecure about their ability to communicate in English. There are situations in which it is difficult for the CES teachers and the Japanese teachers to communicate, and sometimes this is simply because the Japanese teacher's English ability is quite low. It is not enough to dismiss the problem like this, however, as there are other factors to consider. The language of teaching is highly specialised. The discussion of aims, objectives, activities, class management, function and grammar demands a highly specific lexis which is not easy to manipulate even for qualified and experienced EFL/ESL teachers who are native speakers of English. The 1988–89 Koto-ku session focussed on removing all the jargon from the lesson plans and looking closely in the workshops at any potentially confusing terminology that remained.

Other causes of difficulty for team teaching

TIME

All teachers want the team teaching to be a success, but not everyone has the time available for the lengthy discussions that can be necessary to ensure this. Japanese teachers are not paid overtime and part-time CES teachers must have overtime approved in advance. Teachers do have other commitments; many teachers are married with young families and however professionally motivated they are, no one is going to sacrifice his or her home life for the sake of a team teaching liaison meeting. Some teachers believe more strongly than others that unpaid overtime is an example of institutional exploitation rather than a reflection of personal commitment. CES teachers have a right to complain if they feel hard-done-by. Japanese teachers do not have this freedom and many feel bitter about it. Consequently making an innocent request for an extra meeting may be treading on thin ice.

DISCIPLINE

There are schools with a large number of 'problem students' and the issue of who is responsible for discipline in the classroom, and what form it should take, can add extra stress to team teaching. Attitudes towards discipline vary among the Japanese teachers, some take a 'do not give them any attention and they will stop it' approach, others deal with problems by talking *sotto voce* to the student(s) in question, some harangue the student in front of the class, some intimidate the students psychologically or physically. CES teachers also have different attitudes to discipline and it is only when the two teachers have completely different approaches that there may be problems.

STUDENT ATTITUDES

There are schools, or classes within schools, where the students are not academically motivated at all. Not all students like English and not all of those who do like English like the team-taught lessons. Koto-ku is a resettlement area and there are many students whose native language is not Japanese. These students are concentrated in a few schools and although special provision is made for them, they generally find it difficult to adapt to Japanese school life and find the English classes an extra problem. There are also several 'returnee' students whose parents have lived in English-speaking countries. Although it might be assumed that these students should find the English classes easier, they often have a very difficult time in school and do not want to 'stand out' any more than they already do by showing any special ability in English.

STAFFROOM ATMOSPHERE

Some Japanese schools do not have a good atmosphere in the staffroom. In several schools, the Japanese teachers disliked the atmosphere so strongly that they would barely speak in front of the other teachers. Sometimes the CES teachers would feel unwelcome, and sometimes they were. Some teachers resented the 'star' quality of the CES teachers, their freedom from the restrictions of the school environment or the fact that the timetable had been altered to accommodate them. Yet one of the major side benefits of the project has been to show that Japanese people and foreigners *can* work together as equals, that 'foreigners' are human and not at all like the few token 'foreign idols' seen on Japanese TV. The students watch the relationship between the Japanese teacher and the CES teacher closely and are very impressed to see the Japanese teacher speaking English, working with the CES teacher and having a good time. The project may well do some good for the internationalisation of Japan, unless the two teachers dislike each other and have a really bad time of team teaching: then the project may well do more harm than good in this respect. Usually the atmosphere in the staffrooms is very good and supportive. Many of the other teachers are delighted to meet the CES teacher and take the opportunity to try out their English.

Any one of the possible problems mentioned – personalities, lack of professional or personal respect, poor attitudes to team teaching, poor attitudes to the project itself, communication breakdowns, different assumptions about appropriate materials and methodology and an unwillingness to compromise, lack of time, discipline problems in the classroom, students who do not like English or students who do not enjoy the lessons, and a discouraging atmosphere in the staffroom, can easily cause a breakdown in the team teaching. There is no reason why there should only be one problem, either. A generous mixture of several

153

of these problems can make team teaching an unbearable experience. This all begs the question of whether or not the project is actually a success and how can we judge?

Evaluation

The students take mid-term and end-of-term exams. In the first two years of the project this created serious problems. The type of test items chosen, and the content of those items, should always reflect the style and content of the teaching, and this was not the case in the first two years. Originally, the Japanese teachers took complete responsibility for producing these examinations and except in very rare cases, did not produce examinations that reflected the new type of teaching. As a consequence the students' grades fell and this was seen as a failing of the project. Given the paramount importance of examinations in Japan, this seriously threatened to undermine the whole project. Eventually, however, as the project aims became more widely accepted and as the Japanese teachers took more responsibility for the materials production and teaching, the examinations started to reflect the teaching. By 1989–90, the CES teachers were actively involved in the writing of these examinations, helping to suggest test items and alternative approaches to testing, and producing listening scripts and tapes for those teachers who wanted to have listening as part of the examination. There are Japanese teachers however, who do not welcome suggestions for the examinations and feel that the examinations are completely their own responsibility. This may be an area for greater cooperation in the future, if the Japanese teachers as a group want the CES teachers to become even more actively involved. These examinations are prepared in each school and although the results are published within the school, they can only be used to discriminate between students in the same school. The results are interesting for the CES teachers because they can then see how students have responded to the team teaching. They are interesting for the Japanese teachers as they can compare the relative success of the students after different types of teaching – assuming the Japanese teacher uses a different methodology before and after the CES teacher's presence in the school.

Evaluation of the project as a whole in the 1988–89 and 1989–90 sessions took place in several ways:

1. At the end of the ten weeks of team teaching, every student was given a basic questionnaire. This aimed to find out what the students thought of the lessons, their language skills, the style of teaching and 'foreign culture'. This questionnaire was jointly produced by the

Japanese and CES teachers and both sides put considerable thought into the English and Japanese wording. It was only given out with the permission and support of the Japanese teacher. There were occasions when either the Japanese teacher or the CES teacher refused to give out the questionnaire and in such cases the team teaching had generally failed.

2. The Japanese and CES teachers were also asked to fill out questionnaires asking for comments and criticisms of the project. In the first few years of the project the Japanese teachers felt they could not openly criticise the CES teachers, the materials, the methodology or anything associated with the project and the exercise was relatively futile; this in itself demonstrated that there was not enough confidence, trust or communication between the two sides. At least 80 per cent of the Japanese teachers filled out these questionnaires, however, and the opportunity to put forward a comment, suggestion or criticism anonymously, was welcomed. Not all the comments were printed in the final report, however.

   These three components – the students' comments, the Japanese teachers' comments and the CES teachers' comments – were collated, edited and printed, and then given back to all 23 schools.

3. The Koto-ku Education Board writes an internal report on the project on an annual basis and any salient points are raised with the CES management.

4. The CES management prepares a similar report outlining any problems and suggestions for development which is used as the basis for discussion with the Koto-ku Education Board.

5. There is an end-of-session meeting between the coordinators from both sides where some of the more delicate issues are discussed – the ones that neither side wants to see on paper.

Evaluation of the project has to be open-ended as performance objectives have not been rigidly defined and so 'success' or 'failure' are both highly subjective. Most of the Japanese teachers had relatively low expectations of the project at the beginning and the results of the first two project-wide student evaluations have come as pleasant surprises for many. The English translation of the questionnaire given to the students in 1988–89 and 1989–90 is shown overleaf.

The students' responses seem to be positive, and there is quite an improvement from the first year to the second. This has in itself influenced the Japanese teachers' attitude to the project. The fact that a full-scale evaluation of the project in all schools took place at all gave the project a new validity to many teachers. The full report in the 1988–89 session compared each question by school and each school by question. The report showed which schools did 'best' and 'worst', which was

155

TABLE 2. QUESTIONNAIRE

	% yes		% no	
	88–89	89–90	88-89	89–90
1. Do you think your English has improved?	67	96	28	4
2. Do you think your speaking has improved?	63	78	32	21
3. Do you think your understanding of spoken English has improved?	73	86	22	14
4. Do you think your writing has improved?	57	67	38	32
5. Do you think your understanding of written English has improved?	61	76	33	22
6. Are you more interested in English?	63	79	31	20
7. Do you feel more confident about using English?	43	N/A	45	N/A
8. Would you like to continue to study English in this way?	74	88	21	12
9. Do you feel you understand more about foreign culture(s) and people?	56	69	38	29

illuminating in one sense as the schools with the best general academic records did not always show up as the best on the team teaching results, although generally they did. Teachers from schools at the 'lower' end generally seemed to be relieved that the students had responded as well as they did. The results vindicated the Japanese teachers' long-held suspicion that the students' writing ability was declining *relative* to their other skills and this suggested a need to reexamine the teaching material – or approach – with an aim to improving this situation. The students' response to question 7 about their confidence in using English came as a big disappointment until it was put into perspective: nearly all Japanese lower- and upper-secondary school students are extremely insecure about using English and the fact that *any* students responded 'yes' could be seen as a great success. Nonetheless, the Japanese teachers, on reflection, felt that the question was confusing – did it mean confidence in the classroom or outside? – and decided to drop the question from the questionnaire for the 1989–90 session. Nonetheless, figures of 96 per cent for question 1 and 88 per cent for question 8 are very impressive and would argue that both the way of teaching and the results of that teaching are successful in the students' opinion at least. In my view, this is the greatest vote of confidence the project could receive.

There are teachers from both sides, however, who do not think the evaluation process is justifiable in terms of the aims of evaluation, the process of evaluation or the final statistics. These teachers argue that self-evaluation is not a valid form of project evaluation, or that it is not constructive to compare schools, and that the final statistics are misleading. Unfortunately, they may be correct in some of the arguments, as there are problems with the statistics, for example:

1. in some schools the students were told to put a circle around either 'Yes' or 'No', and that they must complete all the questions;.
2. in some schools the students were told to put a circle around either 'Yes' or 'No', and that they could leave blank any questions they were not sure about;
3. in some schools the students were told to put a circle around either 'Yes' or 'No', or that they could put the circle *between* 'Yes' or 'No' to indicate 'Maybe';
4. in some schools the students were told to put a circle around either 'Yes' or 'No', or that they could put a double circle to indicate 'Yes, very much' or 'No, not at all';
5. in some schools the students were told to put a circle around either 'Yes' or 'No', a double circle to indicate 'Yes, very much' or 'No, not at all', a triangle to indicate 'Yes, but only a little' or 'No, but only a little', or that they could leave a question blank if they wanted to, or that they could write a comment, instead.

Obviously, it would be better for each school to administer the evaluation in the same way and the fact that this was not done calls into question the comparability of the statistics. It is also true that schools where the team teaching has not gone well do not want to administer the questionnaire at all. There may be a 'gradient of unwillingness', with only those schools that already know the team teaching was successful being totally prepared to administer the questionnaire. If teachers feel threatened by the results then the evaluation system has lost any positive influence it may have had. Whether or not student self-evaluation is a valid form of project evaluation is almost irrelevant: it is the responsibility of the Japanese and CES teachers to develop an evaluation system that both sides feel is appropriate or to decide not to have an evaluation system at all. It should be emphasised, however, that the 1988–89 and 1989–90 questionnaires were developed *jointly*, as was the decision to administer them. Some Japanese teachers, taking it for granted that the project is successful, have suggested additional or alternative questionnaires to try to find out why. In one school, the students were asked what type of activity they enjoyed most and what type of activity they found most valuable. This type of evaluation may be the future direction of any further student questionnaires. The argument that the evaluation system involves too much effort – which was heard from teachers on both sides – might suggest that a simplified version of the system may be introduced in the future.

Alongside the student questionnaire, both the Japanese and CES teachers filled out questionnaires asking for their opinions and comments. The overall tone was positive, as can be seen from the selection below.

1. Japanese teachers' comments

- I would like to suggest more cooperation throughout the year in making listening and speaking tests.
- The lesson plans were very effective, but there were so many stages and options that I couldn't do all of them.
- It would be better to have one lesson [instead of two] a week over a longer period.
- I liked the team teaching very much. The best thing about it was the clear and interesting lesson plans.
- I'd like to say that I appreciate that both you and we are trying very hard, but there are big problems: when should this program start? How many team teaching classes should we have a week? Should we pay so much attention to listening and speaking (even though) the entrance examinations (do not include them)? Anyway I have enjoyed the team teaching. Thank you for the wonderful opportunity.
- The teaching plans are wonderful and useful to me. If we have more English classes a week, I hope to continue the team teaching project.
- We have some problems in team teaching: one is to practise writing, and reading aloud.
- Please give us the printed lessons well in advance so there is enough time to prepare.

These comments compare with a report written in 1986 by one of the Japanese teachers on the pilot scheme:

> The overall teaching plan was not clear because of lack of communication between foreign teachers and Japanese teachers. Guidance in the aspect of writing was often neglected. The students do not necessarily understand the explanations by the British teachers. It took too much time for the students to under-stand the games. Some students did not have the confidence to ask questions and so did not enjoy the lessons. Some teaching material was found to be too difficult.

'Writing' is still mentioned as a problem in the questionnaires, but the other problems mentioned in 1986 no longer seem to be causes for concern and this shows that the project has improved and responded to the concerns of the Japanese teachers, although not perfectly.

2. CES teachers' comments:

a) Advantages:

- It gives the students a valuable opportunity to discover what communicating in a foreign language is all about, and that learning can be fun. It allows the Japanese teachers to use their English and shows them some new ideas about teaching. It gives the CES teacher an interesting challenge in materials writing, a chance to team teach, a chance to work in the state system with a solid back-up from the project.
- It helped to 'build bridges', allowed the Japanese teachers to meet foreigners (sometimes for the first time), and it helped to motivate the students. It enabled the Japanese teachers and CES teachers to learn a lot about themselves from each other. It also enabled the CES teachers to analyse their own attitudes and ideas about teaching.
- It gave me a lot of insights into Japanese schools and the opportunity to get to know some real Japanese teachers. Also the opportunity to teach 'real' English.

b) Disadvantages:

- There is not enough time. It will only be effective when a nationwide communicative syllabus is introduced so the current constraints (the textbook, the pace, the exams) are lifted.
- A feeling of frustration and helplessness in the face of the examination system which will probably undo any of the good we have done.
- Too much preparation time is needed. The Japanese teachers said they would revert to their old style because they haven't got enough time to prepare. At the beginning the students became aware of their level of incompetence and this led to a weakening of confidence – this would not be such a problem if the project were extended.

These comments show that these teachers felt that everyone gained from the experience of team teaching, but that the structural impediments of the education system meant that the project simply could not fulfil its potential. The Japanese teachers were also aware of this, but from the opposite perspective: how to reconcile the team teaching ideas and materials with the current course of study for first-year students and the all-important examination system. The two sides have obviously moved much closer since 1986, but they are still far apart and may always be so as long as the Japanese teachers' main duty is to 'process' the students through the textbook, through the course of study, through the school and through the examinations. If, however, the Mombusho communicative syllabus is introduced in 1995, then the value of the project may be more immediately apparent.

Conclusion

The Koto-ku project is a successful example of international cooperation in education. The project is not a total success in terms of its teaching aims but this is not perhaps surprising as the project has had to contend with several problems. The most difficult challenge has been to develop a way of teaching and a set of materials that both fulfil the aims of the project and also stay within the framework of the course of study for first-year lower secondary school students. The dominance and the nature of the university and upper-secondary school entrance examinations has placed severe restrictions on the classroom experience of teaching and learning English. However, the main issue facing the project is no longer the overall aims, organisation, approaches to team teaching, or materials, but the reaction of students and teachers – both CES and Japanese – to the team teaching and to the lessons in the classroom. The student questionnaires give reasonable proof that the students enjoy the lessons and the way of teaching, and that they believe their English is improving. The Japanese and CES teachers are aware of the limitations of the project but have, at least, developed a reasonably successful approach to working together in the classroom. The principle of 'flexible equality' has enabled teachers with differing personalities and ideas about how to team teach to define roles and responsibilities that are suitable for their own situation. The project has therefore managed to avoid the issue of the 'best' or 'correct' way to team teach. Above all, the project has benefited from the people who have worked on it – teachers with excellent ideas, who have genuinely enjoyed working together, who have been flexible enough to adapt to a new situation and who have been prepared to commit themselves fully to the project while they have been involved with it. The students have been a delight to work with and their enjoyment of the lessons has, perhaps, been the final justification for all the effort and compromise involved in producing material that both the Japanese and CES teachers find suitable. The project has eventually become accepted and respected by almost everyone involved in it, both for the teaching in the classroom and the cooperation between the CES and Japanese teachers. The project is different from other team teaching projects in Japan: it has different aims, different problems and a different definition of what constitutes successful team teaching. It is not meant to be a role model for other team teaching projects in Japan or elsewhere. Indeed, 'some elements that have proven successful in the Koto-ku Project may not necessarily be appropriate or transferable to other projects' (L. Stein 1989: 239). Nonetheless, everyone involved in the project believes that it is going in the right direction.

8 Some reflections on collaborative language teaching

Kathleen M. Bailey, Ted Dale and Benjamin Squire

Introduction

The purpose of this chapter is to discuss collaborative teaching in two ESL situations. After briefly considering team teaching, we will describe the context in which our collaborative teaching experiences have occurred, explaining the team processes used through the stages of planning, teaching and following up on the lessons offered. We will incorporate examples of team-taught lessons based on journal entries kept by Benjamin Squire as a practicum assignment. (See Bailey 1990 for a discussion of the use of such diary studies in teacher education.) Throughout this discussion we will highlight the advantages of collaborative teaching at each stage of the process. We will also raise some concerns about the disadvantages of a collaborative teaching arrangement, and make some suggestions about easing the process.

Nunan (this volume, page 1) suggests that:

> In language education, teachers, learners, researchers and curriculum specialists can collaborate for a number of reasons. They may wish to experiment with alternative ways of organising teaching and learning; they may be concerned with promoting a philosophy of cooperation rather than competition; they may wish to create an environment in which learners, teachers and researchers are teaching and learning from each other in an equitable way (a trend which is enhanced by the growing interest in action research); or they may wish to experiment with ways of incorporating principles of learner-centredness into their programs.

Some aspects of this description may be more familiar under the name of 'team teaching'. R. H. Johnson and Lobb have defined team teaching as follows: 'A teaching team is a group of two or more persons assigned to the same students at the same time for instructional purposes in a particular subject or combination of subjects' (1959: 59). We will see, however, that this more traditional definition is too narrow to encompass all the activities that may occur under the rubric of collaborative teaching.

162

Types of team teaching

Cunningham (1960: 22–3) has identified four general organizational patterns found in team teaching arrangements. These are reviewed briefly here:

1. *Team Leader Type*. In this arrangement one team member has a higher status than the others. He or she may well have a special title, such as 'Team Leader' or 'Chief Instructor'.
2. *Associate Type*. In this arrangement there is no designated leader. Leadership emerges as a result of interactions among the members of the team in a given situation, and decision-making power may be shared equally.
3. *Master Teacher / Beginning Teacher*. In this arrangement, team teaching is used to foster the acculturation of new teachers into the school or the profession. The beginning teacher may have much less decision-making power than the more experienced teacher.
4. *Coordinated Team Type*. In this arrangement there is no joint responsibility for a common group of learners, but there is joint planning by two or more teachers who are teaching the same curriculum to separate groups of learners.

Types 1–3 in this taxonomy refer to the extent to which responsibility and power are shared across the teaching team, or localized in one member of the team. The fourth type (the Coordinated Team) is distinguished not so much by the distribution of power and responsibility as by what specific group of learners is being served, since in Coordinated Team Teaching, teachers have responsibility for different sub-sets of a learner population. Note that R. H. Johnson and Lobb's definition (above) excludes the Coordinated Team Type as an instance of team teaching, but this type clearly fits within Nunan's description of collaborative teaching.

Variations on these types are found in many settings in language education. For example, the Team Leader type can be found in university language departments which employ teaching assistants, who may work under the supervision of a faculty member with primary responsibility for a particular course or level of instruction, or in teaching practica in which novice teachers are paired with more experienced cooperating teachers. (See Richards and Crookes 1988 for an overview of teaching practica in TESOL.) The practice of having a bilingual aide assisting a teacher with minority language students is an extreme form of the Team Leader type, and even the use of parent assistants in classrooms fits in this category. The Coordinated Team Type is not uncommon in university situations where several faculty members have responsibility for, say, different sections of an intermediate language course.

163

Each of Cunningham's four arrangements have been utilized, to varying degrees, in the collaborative teaching situations described below. As noted above, what distinguishes these various team teaching models is the extent to which power and responsibility are located in one individual or shared among the members of the team, while Nunan's use of the term 'collaborative teaching' emphasizes shared power and shared decision making. In the discussion that follows, we will point out that Cunningham's taxonomy seems somewhat rigid. What happens in practice is much more fluid and dynamic, depending on the local factors which influence the collaborating team.

Setting

The observations on team teaching reported here are based on two different team teaching experiences. Two of the authors (Kathi Bailey and Ted Dale) team taught one course over three different semesters prior to drafting this chapter. This course was an English class for non-native speakers enrolled as master's degree candidates (in the fields of international management, translation and interpretation, or international policy studies) at the Monterey Institute of International Studies. The course focusses on aural/oral fluency for academic purposes, so we deal with such target behaviors as note-taking in lecture settings, giving seminar presentations, asking and answering questions in classroom situations, and making panel presentations. In general the students have TOEFL scores of 550 or higher, but their listening skills and their speaking proficiency may vary considerably. They come from diverse countries, cultures, and native languages, with the majority of the students being Asian. According to six different sets of student evaluations (three of those based on team-taught versions of the course), most learners feel that the course increases their confidence and their fluency. (For a more detailed description of a similar course, see Hinofotis and Bailey 1978.)

The second team teaching situation discussed in this chapter started out as an example of the Master Teacher/Beginning Teacher arrangement. The data in this case are based on the student-teaching journal of one author (Benjamin Squire), working under the supervision of another (Kathi Bailey). This student-teaching experience took place in an eight-week multi-level ESL content course on learning styles, followed by an eight-week upper intermediate ESL content course on learning strategies. The students in these classes were from a variety of cultures and first language backgrounds, though once again the majority were Asian. The TOEFL scores of the students in these classes ranged from 410 to 550.

In both of these team teaching situations, the classes involved were scheduled in large rooms with movable central room dividers. This lucky circumstance allowed us a great deal of flexibility in occasionally dividing the students into two sections. It should be noted that team teaching in this way is no more costly, in terms of faculty salaries or space demands, than is staffing two entirely separate classes. Given our decision to collaborate, we could have used the pattern of having the two teachers present in the room at the same time with all the students at each session. Instead, we occasionally opted for a combination of joint teaching and jointly planned but separate teaching (following the Coordinated Team arrangement), making use of the movable room divider to create two separate spaces as needed.

In our experiences, the various models of team teaching can be much more flexibly utilized than Cunningham's taxonomy would suggest. For example, although the collaborative teaching relationship between Kathi and Benjamin started out being a clear-cut case of the Master Teacher / Beginning Teacher arrangement, it soon shifted into the Team Leader Type and then to the Associate Type. This shift is illustrated by Benjamin's journal entry on a day when the learning strategies class focussed on listening comprehension:

> Today it seemed like the sharing of the leadership role in the class was a lot more evenly delegated than it has been in the past. Even though we had planned it so that Kathi would be leading most of the activities, and I would just be her resource (e.g. when I went over my typical day's listening activities), I felt like I was in charge of more of the activities. When I was doing my listening spiel, she was working on their dictations, so rather than feeling like the 'resource', I felt like I was leading the class at that time. I think that was because she was focussed on something else, and even though she had introduced the task, she relinquished the leadership role . . .

On another occasion, when Benjamin was teaching the class and Kathi was observing him, the Master Teacher / Beginning Teacher roles were purposefully manipulated for the sake of an observation by the Master Teacher:

> I didn't really feel like Kathi was in the classroom as my co-teacher this time, since she was doing an observation (of me), although I suppose that could be an integral part of the Master Teacher / Beginning Teacher collaborative teaching model. I didn't really notice her or react to her very much as co-teacher this time, and I felt that I wanted to leave her alone as much as possible to do her observation. Normally, even if I'm teaching an activity on my own, I still feel that I can turn to her for input or any other type of interaction with the students as a part of the activity. This time, I didn't feel the freedom to do that.

Although some teams and some institutional settings may call for more rigid adherence to a given power structure, in these courses we were able to enjoy a great deal of flexibility in our collaboration.

Our intent in writing this chapter, then, is to describe the varied collaborative teaching experiences we have had. It is hoped that our ideas will encourage other language teachers to consider the possible benefits of collaborative teaching, and that it will also help them to avoid its pitfalls.

Procedures

It will be useful to examine our collaborative teaching experience in terms of what happens before, during and after the actual teaching event. At each of these stages, working together can be both extremely beneficial and somewhat frustrating. By describing our procedures in some detail we hope to suggest some ways of maximizing the benefits and minimizing the frustrations involved. While no cost-benefit analysis has been performed, it will be useful to keep this concept in mind as we discuss the advantages and disadvantages of collaborative teaching.

We should point out, however, that our reflections do not deal with the important issue of student achievement. After conducting a review of the available research literature on team teaching and academic achievement in general education, Armstrong (1977) concluded that there was little convincing evidence to show that team teaching led to significant increases in student gains. (See Nunan, this volume, page 6, for further discussion of Armstrong's points.) It is our belief, however, that collaborative language teaching offers benefits for both teachers and language learners, and we do have some preliminary data on the students' ideas, as well as other teachers' opinions about team teaching, which were gathered through the use of a questionnaire. We will turn to these findings after discussing our own experiences.

Pre-teaching collaboration

In each course our team teaching experience begins with syllabus planning. In the advanced oral communication course, the students are asked to complete a brief needs assessment form in which they rate the importance and the difficulty of several oral English tasks they will probably have to perform during their academic careers (e.g. giving seminar presentations, defending their ideas in English, interviewing for a job in English, etc.). We then plan the syllabus for the first half of the semester, utilizing the students' responses in the process. Thus, while our pre-teaching collaboration is largely of the Associate Type, it also involves some indirect collaboration with the students, who also have opportunities later in the term to make suggestions for topics and skills to cover during the last part of the semester. (See Budd and Wright, this volume, for a more detailed discussion of collaborative syllabus implementation.)

In the content course on learning styles and strategies, we first decided upon our goals for the class and then selected a textbook (Ellis and Sinclair 1989). We used the progression of the chapters in the book as a point of departure on which to base our syllabus. Later we agreed that there was a need to help the students learn to use the word processor, in order to help them with their assignments, so this topic was added to the syllabus.

Teamwork takes place at the level of weekly lesson planning as well as that of syllabus design. Even if only one teacher will be physically present in the classroom space, we have often had the feeling that 'two heads are better than one' when it comes to lesson planning. For instance, Benjamin wrote in his journal:

> For me personally, team teaching fits in very well with my working style. I'm not much of an idea person, but once given an idea, I feel that I have the ability to really take it and develop it into some-thing good. I have trouble working from scratch, so the teamwork of team teaching gives me the feedback that I need to get ideas, and to bounce my own development of ideas off someone else.

We each come to the planning sessions with ideas about the class, but in addition, we both get new ideas from talking to our partner.

In-class collaboration

Collaboration in the classroom can be either planned or unplanned. Team members may plan to interact in a particular way during a given lesson in order to demonstrate a point to the students. One team member may also spontaneously interject a comment during an activity that the other teacher is leading, in order to offer a salient example or to clarify a point.

Within any given class session, there are a variety of things that two teachers can do better than any one of us alone. For example, one day the students were given an information gap activity involving the con-struction of a three-dimensional structure using children's interlocking 'Lego' toys. The purpose of the activity was to give students a situation in which to practice clarification requests, confirmation checks and comprehension checks (Chaudron 1988). Before the students began the exercise, the two teachers demonstrated the task. Benjamin's journal entry states:

> While we were demonstrating the Lego exercise, I noticed that Kathi made a couple of her instructions deliberately ambiguous so that I would have to ask for clarification. I had already asked for clarification on a couple that I had really understood, in order to demonstrate the idea to the students, and I could tell that she was doing the same thing. It felt really good that we hadn't planned to do this beforehand, but just sort of automatically did it without having to discuss it. I felt like we were really working as the most highly effective team possible at that point because we were working together and following and understanding each other's cues without having to pre-plan it.

By definition, language is interactive. In a collaborative language teaching arrangement like this one, the learners are exposed to two (or more) proficient speakers interacting. This input includes examples of attention getting, turn-taking, negotiation for meaning, and disagreements in the target language. Although some of the interactions may be scripted dialogues or planned demonstrations, at least some will be spontaneous discourse, and will therefore be delivered more naturally than are most tape-recorded excerpts of interaction.

Other benefits of collaborative teaching have included the usefulness of having two models of the target language presented in class. For instance, some of our students have reacted favorably to having both a male speech model and a female speech model as teachers. While this benefit would not be an issue in same-sex teaching teams, we have found that some of our Japanese male students in particular are often concerned about whether or not they are learning 'women's English'. (This issue itself provides an interesting topic for in-class discussions.)

Collaborative language teaching can provide varied input, in terms of native speaker models, which would not be readily available otherwise without at least audio-recorded materials. Teaching teams can expose learners to varied regional dialects (British and American English, for example, or Castilian and Mexican Spanish), as well as to different cultural norms (rural versus urban attitudes), and even different points of view on controversial issues. On this point, Benjamin wrote a retrospective entry in his journal about a secondary school history class:

> These two teachers had decided to combine their classes, so the number of students was large, but they also had different teaching styles, and deliberately took different views in the study of history. It was nice not to just hear the official or remembered version of historical events, but also to hear the other side of the story. By taking different viewpoints, and even creating a sense of competition between themselves in the classroom, the teachers made the course interesting and fun.

In the present ESL context, an example of two different cultural perspectives arose in the learning strategies course when the two instructors were demonstrating a contact assignment, in order to prepare the student to conduct telephone interviews with native speakers of English about their holiday customs. In the demonstration the topic of traditional Jewish foods arose, which led to genuine information sharing between the two instructors.

When we are both present in the same teaching space, there are times when one of us can spontaneously contribute fresh ideas or pertinent illustrations to a lesson the other is leading. In cases where a student is confused and the teacher does not understand the source of confusion, the partner who was watching can frequently sort out the problem more easily than the partner who had primary teaching responsibility at the time. Teaching is such a demanding activity that we cannot always be fully aware of all that is happening while we are concentrating on the teaching. There are often times, for instance, when one of us will restate and clarify a point which the other has just made, if it does not seem to have been fully understood by the learners. In our experience, having a trusted teaching partner provides a resource to appeal to for examples, for clarification or an explanation, and for immediate feedback as to how the lesson is going. Benjamin's journal states:

> Today while Kathi lectured I felt pretty free to interject when I thought I could clarify something or give a salient example. There was, in fact, one point where I can remember doing just that.

To maintain the balance of power, it is important that such interjections be seen as beneficial by the teaching partner, and that the collaborative pattern of friendly interruption be practiced and welcomed by both.

Of course, the benefits of collaborative teaching are not limited to teacher-fronted instruction. In these courses we use groupwork a great deal. By structuring groups of three or four students, with each group consisting of learners from two or more native languages, we can increase the amount of talk-time and the types of speaking opportunities students get as compared to teacher-fronted lockstep instruction (instruction in which all students are working on the same task simultaneously) (see Long, Adams, McLean and Castaños 1976). Our preference is to set up a task for the learners and then let the students do the activity without much intervention. However, for those groups that get bogged down, establishing a lower student–teacher ratio (whether by the presence of two teachers in the same room, or by dividing the space and the students) provides greater opportunities for guidance, getting individual questions answered, and making one's own needs known.

Furthermore, with two instructors available, learners have a choice as to which teacher they seek out for help, perhaps matching their learning styles with our teaching styles. In the learning strategies course, after discussing learning styles, the students completed an activity designed to assess their own learning styles as being 'analytic', 'relaxed' or 'mixed' (Ellis and Sinclair 1989). Thereafter, on various occasions, we divided the room and offered two approaches to the same topic, an acquisition-oriented activity (e.g. a discussion) and a more analytic activity (e.g. the students listened to a tape of a native speaker and analyzed the reduced forms occurring in his speech), and let the students choose which type of activity best suited them.

Another practical benefit of having a divisible room (or two adjacent rooms) is that we can each develop two separate but coordinated one-hour lesson plans (following the Coordinated Team model). During the first hour of class, one teacher works with half the students and the other with the other half. Then we switch places and reteach the same lesson plan to a different group of learners. Using this strategy, we have enjoyed the opportunity to reteach the same lesson with different students, in order to try out improvements. In effect, with this arrangement we give ourselves an immediate second chance. For the students, this process allows contact with both of us at any given class meeting, as well as reducing the student–teacher ratio of the large class setting.

Having a teaching partner is also helpful in those inevitable moments when something goes wrong. If the videotape camera is not delivered on time, or the overhead projector bulb suddenly burns out, or three more photocopies of a worksheet are needed, one person can continue working with the students while the other tries to solve the technical problem.

Another purely practical point is that working in a collaborative teaching arrangement provides a built-in substitute who knows the students well, and who is, by definition, very familiar with the material covered to date. In cases where one of us cannot attend the class meeting for some reason, we still plan the lesson together and work jointly on whatever follow-up is needed. For instance, on a day when Kathi was gone, Benjamin taught a lesson which involved the students hearing tape-recorded instructions to Kathi's house. The students took notes as they listened to the instructions. Benjamin's journal states:

> The first activity, when I played the directions and they took notes, was the hardest . . . I let the students compare notes and listen again. After the second time around, one student said that he would probably find the house after a couple of days. Another said that he was going to call a taxi and let the cabbie listen to Kathi's tape . . . I then gave out the maps and several of them were able to trace the route from their notes. When I played the second half of the tape, with the more complicated directions, almost everyone was able to get it right. Even though Kathi wasn't there today, having her input for the planning stage was very helpful, and I didn't feel like I was teaching alone. This feeling was of course

intensified by the fact that she did more talking (on the tape) during the hour than I did.

If the students perceive that the collaborating partners are equal in power and responsibility, one partner's absence does not result in a substitute-like situation.

Post-lesson collaboration

Collaborative teaching also provides two perspectives on evaluation. There are benefits in this respect for the evaluation of both the learners' performance, and of the teachers' performance.

In reacting to learners' panel presentations, their individual speeches, or their written work, we have found that the two of us are a fairer team than one alone might be. In situations where two teachers work in the same physical space (e.g. when two teachers critique students' panel presentations) the students receive two independent sets of written comments from us. In evaluating the students' written work we discuss our grading and share in the marking of difficult papers. In fact, in this respect, collaborative teaching has forced us to make our grading criteria more explicit, first to one another and then to the language learners themselves. At the end of the course, we discuss each student's strengths, weaknesses, and improvement before assigning a final grade. At the very least, this process lends greater face validity to the marks we award, but the collaboration also helps us incorporate more information in the assessment process.

In terms of teacher evaluation, working collaboratively provides two perspectives for self-evaluation of our team teaching, as well as the other person's perspective on our individual work. This aspect of team teaching demands mutual trust and respect, but it has been a source of valuable professional development for us.

Reviewing a lesson together provides two points of view on the next most appropriate steps to be taken as a follow-up to that lesson. In addition, discussing a lesson with one another afterwards has often given us new ideas for what we might do differently the next time we cover similar material. For example, one day we split the learning strategies class so that Benjamin could teach the students to use a word-processing program. While he took half the group to the computer center, Kathi stayed in the classroom with the other half and worked on strategies for learning grammar. Benjamin's journal states:

> I really enjoy the fact that, being two teachers, we are able to act
> on the idea of giving our students options when we do different
> activities. The times we've done that, I really think that it's worked

171

out very well, both from our point of view and that of the students. Additionally, I think we could have gone even further with this sort of thing when I was teaching in the computer room. If we hadn't been tied to the idea of learner training and the grammar unit that we were working on, we could have taken the theme of computers even further and had the half of the students who weren't actually working on the computers doing something else in the classroom relating to computers. Additionally, when I first had the upper-level students in the computer center, Kathi could have been working with the lower-level ones on the vocabulary some more. This way the lower-level students may have gotten a little further with the WordPerfect lesson, possibly even as far as the upper-level students.

This entry from the journal provided a useful starting point for rethinking the next series of lessons.

A collaborative teaching set-up can also provide an ideal situation for practicing 'coaching'. Coaching is a process by which two teachers work together in a teaching team, but for the purposes of enhancing teacher development rather than pupil instruction *per se*. In a coaching arrangement, one partner watches while the other teaches, with the observer focussing on specific teaching behaviors selected in partnership with the teacher being observed (Joyce and Showers 1982, 1987; Showers 1985). Following the lesson, the two partners discuss the teaching event in terms of the key behavior. The process is then repeated with the roles switched: the former observer teaches a lesson, and the former teacher observes. Advocates of coaching say that it offers a non-threatening, iterative mechanism for promoting teacher development and innovation. A collaborative teaching arrangement, such as the one described here, can provide an ideal structure for beginning the coaching process.

Some concerns about collaborative teaching

Although there are a number of benefits to be gained from collaborative teaching, there are some pitfalls too. We will close this chapter by discussing some of the disadvantages we have encountered and then by suggesting ways to overcome or avoid these problem areas. We will also briefly review the opinions of other experienced team teachers. Their views were elicited through a questionnaire whose items were derived from the claims made in this chapter. (See Table 1, pages 175–6.)

Possible disadvantages

As noted above, the main feature which distinguishes the various models of team teaching is power – the extent to which it is shared or localized. For many teachers, giving up total decision-making and implementation power in their classrooms can be an uncomfortable experience.

Furthermore, collaborative teaching involves high front-end loading; that is, the amount of pre-teaching coordination involved in trying to collaborate on goal setting, syllabus design, and lesson planning may seem inordinate. Based on our experiences however, we believe that this demanding aspect of planning is minimized in second and subsequent collaborative efforts, especially when the same team offers the same course again.

Sometimes situations of shared responsibility can result in no one taking full responsibility. It is important for collaborative teaching partners to be very clear about who must accomplish what tasks and at what times. This issue is less likely to be a problem in the Team Leader model, given the clear leadership roles defined in that model, and more likely to be a source of difficulty in the Associate Team type, which – by definition – involves shared power and responsibility.

In our case, we have been working in a situation where our teaching goals are compatible, and we have agreed in advance to modify our syllabus each year on the basis of input from the learners. We suspect, however, that serious problems could arise in situations where the collaborating partners have different goals, incompatible approaches to teaching, or widely divergent teaching styles (see Shannon and Meath-Lang, this volume). There may also be instances in which two partners would suggest contradictory solutions to problems that arise.

Another issue has to do with who decides to implement a collaborative teaching arrangement, and once that decision is made, who determines the composition of the teaching partnerships. For instance, the Assistant English Teacher program in Japan was started by the Ministry of Education to give Japanese EFL students more access to native speakers of English. As a result, several young foreigners have been placed in the classrooms of Japanese EFL teachers, typically without the teacher's consent and with neither party receiving much training as to how to work in a teaching team. Anecdotal evidence suggests that the experienced non-native speaker teacher often feels threatened by the presence of the inexperienced native speaker in the classroom, and that, as a result, the native speaker's language skills are not fully utilized. (See Sturman, this volume, for a discussion of team teaching in Japan which involved much better communication.)

For these reasons, we believe that teachers themselves should make the decision, first, as to whether or not to enter into a collaborative teaching arrangement. Second, and perhaps more importantly, teachers themselves should decide who their teaching partner(s) will be. We feel that it is only in an atmosphere of trust and mutual respect that teaching partnerships can achieve their full potential.

Strategies for success

There are several steps that can be taken to increase the likelihood of a successful collaborative teaching experience. While these ideas will not necessarily solve all the problems that may arise, in our experience they have been helpful in minimizing disagreements.

1. First of all, to lessen power struggles, it is useful to *focus on goals rather than on personalities*. Particularly in situations where the teaching partners are amenable to using input from the learners (whether from formal needs assessments or from learners' informal suggestions), collaborating teachers should be able to determine the course goals first, and then decide how to achieve those goals. In cases where teaching styles or approaches to learning are quite different, focussing on the goals before deciding on specific teaching strategies can help orient the collaboration. Once the goals are agreed upon, different ideas as to how to accomplish those goals can be seen as alternative solutions, rather than as competing objectives. It is also helpful to recognize that new goals will emerge as the course evolves.

2. Another procedure for increasing the likelihood for successful collaboration is to *recognize one another's contributions*. Once the goals have been identified, each partner may accomplish those goals in very diverse ways. Simply recognizing that alternative solutions exist, can be tried, and may often work, makes the planning and the follow-up easier and smoother. (See Shannon and Meath-Lang, this volume, for a similar perspective.)

3. We have also found it useful to *set aside specific time for planning on a regular basis*. Initially at least, collaborative teaching can take more time in the planning stages than does individual teaching, since the process often involves time-consuming negotiations. A related point is that collaborating teams must allow enough time for disagreement as part of the planning and follow-up processes. It is helpful to agree to disagree, in advance of the event.

While we have benefited from team teaching, this type of collaboration may not be ideal for all teachers. In order to gather other teachers' opinions about the claims we have made in this chapter, we reprinted several of our assertions in the form of a simple questionnaire using the Likert scale format. Several language teachers were asked to describe a collaborative teaching experience they had had, and then to think about that experience in rating the items on the Likert scale. Their ratings in response to each statement were marked on a five-point scale (5 = strongly agree, 4 = agree, 3 = neutral, 2 = disagree, and 1 = strongly disagree). A total of sixty teachers, all of whom had had some experience with team teaching, responded to the questionnaire. The respondents were from the Monterey Institute of International Studies (n = 10), the Defense Language Institute (n = 20), the School for International Training (n = 7), and Temple University Japan (n = 23). The scale items, the mean ratings ($\bar{X}$) and the standard deviations (the measures of variance within the data) (S), and the number (N) of teachers responding to each item are given in Table 1. It is important to note that the reliability and validity of this instrument have not been established. Nevertheless we can see some patterns in the descriptive statistics. In general, the results

TABLE 1. TEACHERS' REACTIONS TO STATEMENTS ABOUT TEAM TEACHING

	$\bar{X}$	S	N
1. Only teachers themselves should decide whether or not to enter into a team teaching arrangement.	3.8	1.2	60
2. Planning together is the most valuable part of team teaching.	4.2	0.9	58
3. Team teaching works best if the partners' teaching styles match.	3.5	1.2	59
4. Working in class together is the most valuable part of team teaching.	3.4	1.1	59
5. My students seem to appreciate team teaching.	3.9	0.9	59
6. Team teaching is an effective way to teach languages.	3.9	0.9	60
7. Sometimes situations of shared responsibility result in no one taking full responsibility.	3.3	1.3	59
8. Serious problems could arise in situations where the collaborating teachers have widely divergent teaching styles.	3.8	1.1	60
9. It is helpful to agree to disagree in advance of entering a team teaching arrangement.	4.1	0.9	57
10. Having a partner helped to give me a new perspective on my teaching.	4.2	1.0	59
11. Having a partner was helpful in evaluating students.	4.0	1.1	59
12. Team teaching didn't seem to work for my students.	1.9	1.0	58
13. Having a partner gives me someone to appeal to for examples or clarification of explanations in class.	3.9	1.1	54
14. Our students seemed to like having a choice of which teacher to seek out for help.	3.6	1.0	57

TABLE 1. *(cont.)*

	$\bar{X}$	S	N
15. Working collaboratively provides two perspectives for self-evaluation of our team teaching.	3.9	1.0	56
16. Working collaboratively provides for evaluation of my individual work.	3.7	1.1	58
17. I have learned things about myself from working with a partner.	4.1	0.9	60
18. The amount of time necessary to collaborate on goal setting, syllabus design and lesson planning is more trouble than it's worth.	2.2	1.1	58
19. Team teaching is an effective means of teacher development.	4.0	0.9	60
20. Serious problems could arise in situations where the collaborating teachers have different goals.	4.3	0.9	59
21. Team teaching is more trouble than it's worth.	2.1	1.0	58
22. Only teachers themselves should decide who their teaching partners should be.	3.7	1.2	60
23. It is only in an atmosphere of trust and mutual respect that teacher partnerships can achieve their full potential.	4.6	0.7	59
24. In team teaching it is useful to focus on goals rather than personalities in order to lessen power struggles.	4.1	1.0	58
25. My partner's feedback after our lessons was not helpful.	2.2	1.2	55
26. Recognizing that alternative solutions exist makes planning and follow-up easier and smoother.	4.1	0.8	57
27. The benefits of team teaching far outweigh the effort involved.	3.8	1.0	59

of our survey served to reinforce the conclusions that we have drawn about the advantages and disadvantages of collaborative teaching.

Most subjects agreed with statements about the positive aspects of team teaching. The item that generated the strongest agreement was number 23, which stressed the importance of team teaching in an atmosphere of trust and mutual respect. It had the highest mean (4.6) and the lowest standard deviation (0.7). Another item which generated notable agreement was number 20, to the effect that serious problems could arise if the collaborating teachers have different goals (with a mean of 4.3 and a standard deviation of 0.9). Several items fall within the range of agreement (roughly 3.8 to 4.2) and others within the neutral area.

The respondents also tended to disagree with items which were negatively worded. The item which generated the greatest disagreement was number 12 ('Team teaching didn't seem to work for my students'). The mean of 1.9 ('Disagree') on this item suggests that teachers perceive team teaching as beneficial for the students – an observation which is encouraging but needs to be interpreted carefully, given our lack of student achievement data. Other items which generated disagreement were: number 21 ('Team teaching is more trouble than it's worth'), with a mean of 2.1; number 18 (regarding the amount of time involved in team teaching), and number 25 (about the partner's feedback being unhelpful), both of which had mean scores of 2.2 on the five-point scale.

Based upon these limited findings, as well as our own reflections on our collaborative teaching experiences, we believe that broader research in this area will reveal further advantages of team teaching. There are many possibilities for working with this topic in language classrooms, through action research, naturalistic inquiry or experimental research. (See Allwright and Bailey 1991: 40–5, for a discussion of these approaches to language classroom research, and Nunan 1989b, for some guidance on how to get started on teacher-initiated research projects.)

Postscript

In this chapter we have described our experiences working in a collaborative teaching partnership. While our experiences have been largely positive, we do not have any data as to the actual effect of our collaboration on the development of the students' oral English proficiency. We do, however, have the following comments from students who specifically mentioned team teaching in evaluating our courses:

- I enjoyed a lot (learning) from two teachers. I think two teacher is better than one teacher.
- I think two teachers is better in some class. We have more good idea. But sometimes I feel too [much] attention, [if] two teachers concentrate on what one student says.
- I think that having two teachers in class is good because every student can get the attention from the teachers.
- You two did very good job. But I can't accept doing the class two teachers, I mean other class. It was not serious. I don't think TESOL student is *real* teacher. [If] two teachers are teaching something. Who will control the class?

- Two teachers in a class is sometimes good and sometimes bad. There was no problem in this class. But at other class, both teacher didn't contact each other well maybe and they say different things. And we get confused!
- Two instructors in the same class, I think it's really helpful, especially when there are too many students. And they can take care for the whole class easily. I think it's really good!

Clearly more research is needed: (1) to document other teachers' experiences with collaborative teaching; (2) to determine students' attitudes toward team teaching; and (3) to assess what contributions, if any, collaborative teaching makes to the students' learning.

We hope, however, that this account of our experiences and ideas will be helpful to those who wish to try collaborative teaching. We believe the benefits (both for us and for the learners) far outweigh the initial extra effort involved. We have gained new ideas, improved our personal teaching repertoires, and been able to rely upon one another for support and assistance. To paraphrase Nunan (this volume), collaborative language teaching has provided us with an environment where teachers and learners can not only teach each other but can learn from each other as well.

Endnotes

This chapter was originally presented at the 1991 TESOL Convention in New York. The authors would like to thank Ruth Larimer and Leo van Lier for their constructive criticism of the manuscript. We are also grateful to the teachers who completed our questionnaire and to Diane Larsen-Freeman, Kawther Hakim, and Andrei Pashin for helping us to collect the data.

9 The power of observation: 'Make a wish, make a dream, imagine all the possibilities!'

Jerry G. Gebhard and Akiko Ueda-Motonaga

Introduction

The purpose of pre-service and in-service teacher supervision is often to evaluate the teacher's teaching, offer suggestions on the best way to teach, direct or guide the teacher, and model teaching behaviors. Although some teachers appreciate this directive supervisory approach, it does have limitations. The most outstanding limitation is that the supervisor's prescriptions about teaching force teachers to comply with what the supervisor thinks they should do in the classroom. As the decision making is mostly with the supervisor, the directive approach does not allow teachers to develop the skills they need to make informed decisions about how to teach.

An alternative way to approach supervision, as presented by Fanselow (1982, 1987, 1990), Fattorini and Oprandy (1989), Gebhard (1990a and b), and Gebhard, Gaitan and Oprandy (1990) is to provide teachers with opportunities to explore teaching. The aim of this approach is not to direct teachers as to how they should be teaching, but to work with them as they go through a process of discovery about teaching possibilities.

In this paper we present and illustrate the collaborative efforts of a supervisor and a teacher of Japanese to explore teaching possibilities. We begin with a description of the teaching setting. This is followed by discussion on how the teacher and supervisor approached the exploration of teaching in this setting, after which we show some of the things the Japanese teacher did. We then consider the collaborative nature of the exploration process. Finally, as a way to conclude, we give statements, in the Japanese teacher's own words, on what the teacher said she learned from engagement in the process of exploration.

The teaching setting

The course, Japanese II, was offered in the Critical Language Program at Indiana University of Pennsylvania. Seven undergraduate students participated in the class; all seven had studied Japanese I with the same teacher. The aim of the course was to teach students to use Japanese for communicative purposes on topics related to daily life. The class met three times a week for fourteen weeks, each session lasting one hour. Japanese was the medium of instruction.

The course text was *Japanese: The Spoken Language* (Jorden and Noda 1987) which included a book and audiotapes. Videotapes were also used. The class consisted of four main activities: core conversation performance, pattern drills, dialogue drills and situational drills. The teacher followed the text in a fairly routine way. At the beginning of the class, core conversations were performed by the students in pairs followed by pattern drills in which students practiced the structures introduced in the core conversations. After the students became familiar with the structures, they practiced short dialogues, and finally they practiced situational drills which focussed on longer dialogues in specific situations.

How the teacher and supervisor approached exploration

In order to begin exploration of teaching, the teacher and the supervisor decided to use Fanselow's (1987) *Breaking Rules: Generating and Exploring Alternatives in Language Teaching* as a guide to the discovery of teaching possibilities. The teacher selected episodes (chapters) to study. The supervisor, who had previous experience in the use of Fanselow's ideas (see Gebhard 1990a and b), also read these episodes, and the teacher and supervisor met once every two weeks for two hours to discuss the content of the episodes. During the initial meetings, the discussion centered on key ideas presented by Fanselow, and it was agreed that the goal of exploration is not to look for a 'better' way to teach, but to construct and reconstruct a detailed description of teaching based on awareness gained from systematic observation.

Also highlighted was the process through which exploration can be done. This process includes making audio or videotapes of interaction, making short transcriptions of selected sections from the tape, coding the transcriptions with FOCUS, an observation system developed by Fanselow (1977, 1987), studying the coding for patterns, interpreting what these patterns mean in relation to student learning, and making decisions about what to do in the classroom based on the patterns.

It is important to point out that the process we followed is discussed in much greater detail in Fanselow (1987, 1990) than we can give here. But, essentially, the process used by the teacher and supervisor to explore teaching and its consequences, as well as Fanselow's (1987) categories and coding labels (see explanation and scenes 1–3 below), were implemented as closely to his original work as possible.

The major categories of FOCUS which the teacher studied and used to code interaction allowed her to identify the *source and target* of communication (teacher, student, group, book, map, movie, etc.), the pedagogical purpose of communication or *move type* (structure, solicit, respond, react), the *mediums* used to communicate content (linguistic, nonlinguistic, paralinguistic, silence), the manner in which mediums are used to communicate content or *use* (attend to, present, characterize, reproduce, relate, set), and the areas of *content* that are communicated (study, life, procedure). Each of these major categories have minor categories, allowing for a very detailed description of interaction going on inside or outside classrooms.

As the teacher began to use FOCUS to code interaction, she paid attention only to the major categories (above). However, as she gained confidence in how to code through these major categories, she was able to consider some of the minor categories. For example, when the topic of discussion centered on the major category of *content* (life, study, procedure), the teacher became interested in learning more about the minor categories to code content-life. She discovered the minor category of *life-formula* (a formula in everyday life situations, such as when Americans say, 'How are you?' when they greet someone in the street or when Japanese say 'itadakimasu' before they eat). She also recognized the minor categories of *life-personal* (when the content is about the personal life of an individual) and *life-general* (when the content is common to groups of people, such as about how some Japanese families live or how some American teenagers date). (See Fanselow 1987 for a detailed description of these analytical terms.)

After coding the interaction in the short transcripts, the teacher and supervisor studied the coding to recognize patterns of interaction. An understanding of patterns is crucial to the process because it is through an analysis of the patterns of interaction that decisions can be made about what to do next in the classroom. In the next section examples of coding and patterns are presented (see scenes 1–3) within the framework of how the teacher worked through exploration of her teaching.

The teacher's exploration

The teacher began exploration by audiotaping her classes, selecting and transcribing short segments of interaction from the tapes, coding the interaction with FOCUS, and studying the coding for patterns. Scene 1 gives an example of a coded transcript taken from the Japanese class during a pattern practice drill. Participants in this segment of interaction include the teacher (T), the teacher's assistant (TA / Ms Tanaka), and two students (S1 / Mr Brown and S2 / Mr Smith). The exercise begins with the teacher pointing to a dictionary and asking the teaching assistant if it is her dictionary. The purpose was to model the structure for the students and to lead into practice of the pattern with the students.

Scene 1

			Source–Target	Move	Medium	Use	Content
	T:	Sore, Tanaka-san no jishyo desuka? [Is that your dictionary?]	t–ta	sol	l	pe	s
5	TA:	Ee, watashi no desu yo. [Yes, it's mine.]	ta–t	res	l	ps	s
	T:	Kore, Tanaka-san no jishyo desuka? [Is this Ms Tanaka's					
10		dictionary?]	t–s	sol	l	pe	s
	S1:	Hai, sore wa Tanaka-san no jishyo desu. [Yes, this is Ms Tanaka's					
15		dictionary.]	s–t	res	l	ps	s
	T:	Jyaa, Sumisu-san, Buraun-san ni kiite kudasai. [Then, Mr Smith, please ask					
20		Mr Brown.]	t–s	str	l	ps	p
	S1:	Sore, Tanaka-san no jishyo desu ka? [Is that Ms Tanaka's dictionary?]	s–s	sol	l	pe	s
25	S2:	Ee, Tanaka-san no desu. [Yes, that's Ms Tanaka's.]	s–s	res	l	ps	s

Key

t = teacher	pe = present elicit (asking
ta = teaching assistant	questions in which the
s = student	answer is already known)
sol = solicit	ps = present state (giving factual
res = response	information)
str = structure (organizing	s = study
interaction)	p = procedure
l = linguistic	

After studying the coding of this and other transcripts, she discovered certain patterns of interaction occurring over and over again in her classes. She found that she asks the majority of the questions and that students only ask questions (e.g. lines 21–2) when she tells them to ask (e.g. lines 16–18). She also discovered that she asks questions to which she already knows the answer, and that students simply repeat the same words she used when it is their turn to ask the question (e.g. lines 21–2). In addition, she found that in her classes the content is either study of language or procedure. She asked no questions which could be coded as content-life.

The next step in the teacher's exploration was to try something different which might give her insight into teaching behavior and its consequences. Based on the knowledge about patterns of interaction going on in her classroom and on her reading of Fanselow's *Breaking Rules*, the teacher decided to make a small change in her teaching, that of adding content-life questions, to see if this small addition might possibly change the pattern. In order to recognize if there was change, she audiotaped her class while asking content-life questions, transcribed parts of the class, and coded segments of the transcribed interaction. Scene 2 illustrates a short segment of her transcription and coding which is followed by a description of the patterns resulting from the initiated change. As will be discussed, she discovered an incidental consequence from adding a nonlinguistic medium, a map, to her lesson.

Scene 2

		Source–Target	Move	Medium	Use	Content
	T: Miraa-san wa, supuringu bureeku, domo ni ikimashita ka? [Mr Miller,					
5	where did you go during spring break?]	t–s	sol	l	pq	fp
	S1: Pittubaagu desu. [Pittsburgh.]	s–t	res	l	ps	fp
10	T: Pittubaagu no doko desu ka? [Where in Pittsburgh?]	t–s	sol	l	pq	fp
	T: (Takes out and looks at a map of Pittsburgh)	o–t	str	nl+l	a	p
15	C: (Students look at map)	o–c	str	nl+l	a	so

Scene 2 *(cont.)*

		Source–Target	Move	Medium	Use	Content
20	S1: Koko desu yo. Horumusu no chikaku desu yo. [Here. It's near Holms.]	s–t	res	nl+l	ps	so
25	T: Jyaa, daun taun wa doko desu ka? [Where is downtown?]	t–s	sol	nl+l	pq	so
30	S1: Monogarhera to Aregeni no aida. [Between Monogahela and Allegheny.]	s–t	res	nl=l	ps	so
	T: Hee, Koko desu ne. [Wow, here.]	t–s	rea	nl+l	ps	so
35	S2: Steeshon sukueaa doko desu ka? [Where is Station Square?]	s–c	sol	nl+l	pq	so
	S3: Koko. [Here.]	s–s	res	nl+l	ps	so
	S2: Ikimashita yo. [I went there.]	s–c	rea	l	ps	fp
40	C: Hee? [Really?]	c–s	rea	l	ps	fp
	S2: Omoshirokatta desu yo. [It was interesting.]	s–c	rea	l	ps	fp
45	S1: Totemo takai desu yo? [Things are expensive there?]	s–s	sol	l	pq	fg
	S2: Maa maa desu yo. [Not so expensive.]	s–s	res	l	ps	fg

Key

t = teacher	pq = present query (asking
s = student	questions to which the
o = other	answer is not known)
c = class	ps = present state (factual

sol = solicit	information)
res = response	a = attend (taking information in)
str = structure	fp = life personal
rea = reaction	p = procedure
l = linguistic (either in speech or print)	fg = life general
nl = nonlinguistic (things such as pictures, chairs, paper)	so = study other (study of content other than language itself)

The classroom interaction changed dramatically. Students solicited information from each other (e.g. lines 33–4, 44–5) and reacted to each others' comments (e.g. lines 38, 40). The teacher and students asked questions which they did not know the answers to before asking them (e.g. lines 9–10, 22–3, 33–4, 44–5). Such query was not evident in the interaction in the earlier class (scene 1).

What brought about this change in the interaction? The teacher's purpose was to ask content-life personal questions in order to see if the interaction would change in her class, and she did begin her lesson by asking two life-personal questions about where a student went on his spring break (e.g. lines 1–4 and 9–10). According to the teacher's analysis, this change was most likely a part of the reason why the interaction changed.

However, the teacher also used a map of Pittsburgh which she brought into class knowing that some of the students probably went to Pittsburgh over the spring vacation. This map, coded as both a linguistic (print) + nonlinguistic medium (lines 12–37), also had an apparent consequence (which the teacher was surprised to discover). The presence of the map allowed the interaction to shift from content-life personal (lines 1–10) to study-other (lines 15–37). In short, the teacher interpreted the combination of content-life personal solicits and the use of a nonlinguistic medium (the map) to be the reason for the emergence of student solicits and reactions. It is interesting that the teacher had not predicted that the use of the map would contribute to this change in pattern. This discovery was quite incidental, and is one of the reasons for doing exploration of teaching. As Fanselow (1987) points out, incidental learning can be as valuable as that which is planned. It can, indeed, make us appreciate the phrase 'expect the unexpected'.

From exploration the teacher had learned the power of small changes in teaching behavior, and she gained an apparent further interest in how life-personal content can become a part of the interaction in her class. In pursuit of this interest, she read Fanselow's (1987) and Nunan's (1988) ideas about looking outside the classroom to study what happens in the interaction between native speakers of the language being taught, in this case Japanese. In so doing she believed she could gain insight into how she could make changes in her teaching behavior so that her classroom

G

lessons could perhaps better prepare students for their 'real world challenges' (Johns 1985). Scene 3 illustrates a short segment of inter-action between native speakers of Japanese. Following this scene, there is a discussion of the patterns of interaction and what she found to be different about this interaction and that in her usual classroom teaching (scene 1). Participants in the conversation include Ms Suzuki (S) and Ms Yamamoto (Y).

Scene 3

		Source–Target	Move	Medium	Use	Content
5 10	S: Senshyuu wa kekkoo isogashikatta yo. Hitoga iroiro itte kite. Benkyoo shitakattan dakedo, honto damedane, asoko wa. [I was quite busy last week. Many friends came to see me. I wanted to study, but in that place, I can't.]	f–f	str	l	ps	fp
	Y: Ryoo? [The dorm?]	f–f	sol	l	pq	fp
	S: Ryoo. [The dorm.]	f–f	res	l	c	fp
	Y: Hee. [Ah.]	f–f	rea	l	ps	fp
15	S: Nakanakanee. Hitoga ooinyo. [There are so many people.]	f–f	rea	l	ps	fp
	Y: Hee. [Really.]	f–f	rea	l	ps	fp
20	S: Sugu asobinikuruto iuka . . . [They come often.]	f–f	rea	l	ps	fp
25	Y: Hee. Watashi wa ryoo ni sunda koto naikaranee. [Well, I've never lived in a dorm.]	f–f	rea	l	ps	fp
	S: Aah soo. [Oh.]	f–f	rea	l	ps	fp

Key
f = friend
str = structure
sol = solicit

l = linguistic
ps = present state
c = characterize

res = response	pq = present query
rea = reaction	fp = life personal

In scene 3, Ms Suzuki structured the communication by mentioning how busy she was last week (lines 1–2). Ms Yamamoto solicited, asking if Ms Suzuki was talking about her life in the dormitory (line 12). After Ms Suzuki responded (line 13), the rest of the conversation is all reaction to the response.

Through analysis of this and other segments of naturally occurring interaction, the teacher discovered that in authentic conversations between Japanese speakers much of the interaction, especially when the content is life-personal, has many reactions. When she compared this interaction to that of her usual classroom pattern (scene 1), she expressed concern that students were not really practicing the kind of interaction they would need in authentic conversations outside the class-room, especially that of being able to add reactions to others' reactions. Likewise, the idea that asking life-personal solicits, as she did in scene 2, as a way to possibly get students to react more in class was further reinforced.

The collaborative nature of the exploration process

So far we have considered a teaching setting, how a teacher and super-visor approached exploration of teaching in this setting, and the explorations of the teacher. Here we provide a discussion on the collaborative nature of the exploration process, including a brief history of the relationship between the teacher and supervisor, the tasks within the exploration process which called for teacher–supervisor collab-oration, and how the supervisor adjusted his behavior with the goal of making collaboration easier for the teacher.

At the start of the teacher's internship, the teacher and supervisor had known each other for nine months. The teacher had studied with the supervisor, as professor, in one graduate course, ESL Methodology, and was at that time taking Cross-cultural Communication with him. The teacher and supervisor also talked with each other informally during social events (in both American and Japanese contexts), and through both classroom experiences and informal gatherings, the teacher and supervisor learned about each other's abilities, interests, experience, and knowledge. For example, the teacher gained some understanding of the supervisor's approach to teacher education, especially the idea that learning to teach is a developmental process (Richards and Nunan 1990) which requires teachers to process and reprocess their knowledge about teaching through a variety of teacher education experiences (Gebhard

1990c; Gebhard, Gaitan and Oprandy 1990). Likewise, the supervisor had knowledge about the teacher's abilities as a student and interests as a teacher, especially her interest in learning more about her teaching behavior and its consequences on classroom interaction. In short, through previous knowledge, the teacher and supervisor had a base from which to build a working relationship during the internship experience, founded on a knowledge consistent with the goals of the internship, to explore teaching behaviors and their consequences.

However, although the goals of the internship were easily established, there was a need to establish procedures and tasks. At the start of the internship, the supervisor took on the responsibility to lead the teacher through the process of exploration and to set tasks for the teacher. These tasks were as follows:

1. Select and read episodes of Fanselow's (1987) *Breaking Rules*.
2. Summarize each episode. Write down questions about the content. Point out three things in each episode you liked.
3. Audiotape some of your teaching.
4. Transcribe short sections of the audiotape.
5. Code these sections with Fanselow's FOCUS.
6. Study the coding for patterns.
7. Give interpretations as to what these patterns possibly mean in relation to student learning. Bring in your knowledge about the teaching and learning process from your course work and reading.
8. Decide on a small change in teaching behavior which might break this pattern.
9. Implement this change, audiotape the lesson, transcribe, code, and study the coding for patterns. Compare the patterns before and after the small change.
10. Write a report on what you learned from your experience.

The types of tasks the supervisor set for the teacher suggest that he structured the teacher's experience in a highly systematic way as he led her through the exploration process. However, such tasks also gave the teacher freedom of choice. For example, she could select the episodes in Fanselow she wanted to read, make her own decisions about what classroom interaction to audiotape, as well as what part of this lesson to transcribe, code, and show to the supervisor. Likewise, the teacher had freedom to decide on what aspects of her teaching to change, and she could give her own interpretations of her teaching in relation to the possible impact it has on student learning.

The teacher was very receptive to this task-based approach, so much so that she began generating her own tasks by the end of the internship. For example, she decided on her own to tape-record naturally-occurring interaction between native speakers of Japanese to discover patterns in their interaction which might help her to glean insight into changes she would consider making in her own teaching.

An analysis of the supervisor's behaviors shows that he adjusted these according to the level of difficulty of the task and the attitude of the teacher toward the task. For example, when discussing the content of episodes in *Breaking Rules*, the supervisor frequently used open-ended discussion as a way to process Fanselow's ideas. He responded to the teacher's questions, as well as asked her questions, and reacted to her responses by elaborating and illustrating with examples from the teacher's own use of language.

The supervisor also used nondirective behaviors, especially when the teacher expressed her own interpretations of what patterns of communication mean in relation to student learning, although he also offered sources for her to read which addressed an aspect of teaching and learning in which she expressed interest. For example, he pointed out passages from Stevick's (1980) *Teaching Language: A Way and Ways* which address how teachers can maintain control while still offering students chances to initiate communication in the classroom, as well as Chaudron's (1988) *Second Language Classrooms: Research on Teaching and Learning* when her interest turned to what we know about the relationship between teaching behavior and learning outcomes.

When the supervisor was nondirective in his behavior, he used paraphrasing, in which he gave a 'recognized' version of what the teacher had said (Curran 1976, 1978) with the double purpose of working at better understanding what the teacher was saying and providing a 'mirror image' through which the teacher could reflect on her own ideas about teaching.

When the task seemed to be difficult for the teacher, such as deciding how to code communications which were ambiguous, the supervisor would be more directive, simply telling the teacher how he would code. Likewise, he adjusted his behavior by offering choices when the teacher was in a quandary. For example, the teacher was having difficulty deciding on what small change to make in her teaching to break the 'lockstep' pattern (scene 1). To limit the possibilities so that the decision could be easier for her, but still give her a choice, the supervisor offered three possibilities: (1) change the source/target of communication (group-work); (2) increase wait time after asking a question; and (3) change the content of the questions (from questions which focus on the study of language to questions which centre on students' lives or on the study of a subject other than language).

It is worth pointing out that the supervisor used elements of several models of supervisory behavior (e.g. directive, nondirective, suggestive) (Freeman 1982, 1990b; Gebhard 1990a; Gebhard and Malicka 1991) 'in the same sets of comments or conversations' (Fanselow 1990: 182).

189

In short, the supervisor changed his behavior to accommodate the teacher from moment to moment, depending on the type of task and degree of difficulty the teacher was having with that task.

Insights into teaching and exploration: what the teacher learned

In a written report, the teacher presented what she learned from going through a process of exploration, and she characterized what she learned in several ways, including a feeling of being freer to decide on activities to do in class, being more responsible for the activities she has students do, and an understanding of the importance of investigation and the power of observation. As a way to conclude, the teacher's comments, as she wrote them, are presented below.

> As I explore my teaching by describing – recording, transcribing and coding communications – rather than by seeking prescriptions and judgments from others, patterns are broken both consciously and unconsciously. I have sought alternatives in teaching and found them. After I found that I have alternatives, I felt freer and securer about deciding on activities for the students. Throughout the internship, I have learned how to see teaching more clearly and differently. In other words, I realized how much more I can do and noticed the unconscious patterns in my teaching.
>
> The aim of my course was for students to learn Japanese for communication in the real world. As Nunan (1988) points out, it is of vital importance to create as many links as possible between what happens in the classroom and what happens outside of it. Through investigation of interaction inside and outside classrooms, it is possible to know how to make such links. Through investigation I found that the classroom can be the real world.
>
> As a result of this internship I feel more responsible for the activities in class and know that I have more control over what goes on in my classroom. Stevick (1980) characterizes the teacher's role and the student's role in language learning by the terms 'teacher control' and 'student initiative'. 'Control' refers to structuring of classroom activities and the providing of constructive feedback on performance. 'Initiative' means decisions about who says what, to whom and when. Stevick stresses that 'control' and 'initiative' must be kept distinct and can be adjusted independently of each other; in the name of 'taking control', the teacher can be careful not to monopolize the 'student initiative'. Through observation and analysis of the interaction in my class, I have the power to gain a clearer understanding of how much initiative the students take and the means to know how I might

change the way I teach to make sure students have the opportunity to initiate.

During the internship I gained a new perspective of teaching and came to know something about the power of observation. Fanselow (1987) states that the breaking of rules is endless because the more we know about what we habitually and alternatively do, and the consequences of both, the more likely we are to want to continue to explore. Although my internship is over, I will continue observing and investigating classroom interaction to find what is going on in my teaching. I found an encouraging phrase in Fanselow's *Breaking Rules*, 'Make a wish, make a dream, imagine all the possibilities!'. I will make a wish, make a dream to see teaching clearly and differently, and imagine all the possibilities of teaching!

10 A teacher-research group in action

Sandra R. Schecter and Rafael Ramirez

During the past few years teacher research has become increasingly popular in North America both as a movement and as an emerging field.[1] Most of the activity has taken place within English education circles. In the 1970s, Lee Odell (1976, 1979) linked teacher research to writing research by presenting an agenda of writing research issues that presumably could be explored by teachers of writing.

Reports on research conducted by teachers are starting to find their way into print (Bissex and Bullock 1987; Goswami and Stillman 1987, 1988), as are pieces which provide guidance on how teacher research is actually to be carried out (Elliott 1981; Mohr and MacLean 1987; Myers 1985; Nixon 1981). Also recently appearing are conceptual pieces which attempt to characterize teacher research as a mode of inquiry and to establish its epistemological ground (Applebee 1987; Burton 1988; Cazden *et al.* 1988; Cochran-Smith and Lytle 1990; North 1987). Some of these pieces draw directly upon existing teacher-research projects, such as those sponsored by Bread Loaf and the Northern Virginia Writing Project. Cazden *et al.* (1988), for example, examines the foci, topics, and presentational form of 36 teacher-research accounts published in 1987, and speculates on the relationship and the 'commute' between teacher research and what she calls 'researcher research', with particular regard to writing.

In the literature, many claims are being made about the general efficacy of teacher research and its contributions to both the teaching profession and the individual development of teachers – that teachers involved in research become interested in and read the professional research literature, take leadership roles in their schools and influence decisions about school policy, contribute to professional knowledge on their own accord, become better classroom teachers (Atwell 1982, 1987; Newkirk and Atwell 1988; Richmond 1984). In addition, claims continue to be made by university-based researchers about the epistemological contributions of this type of inquiry (e.g. Applebee 1987; Cazden *et al.* 1988).

With all the speculation on the significance of teacher research and with all the design and implementation of teacher-research projects, however, there exists little in the way of formal study of the actual workings of teacher-research groups and the actual effects on teachers of the process of becoming researchers. We believe that both those involved in the teacher-research movement and those concerned with teacher research as a knowledge base would benefit from work that would describe, assess, and explain the effects of groups of teachers engaging in classroom inquiry under varying collaborative conditions. Accordingly, we undertook a two-year-long case study of one such well-supported teacher-research group affiliated with a prestigious US university.

Research questions and data sources

In this study, we were especially concerned with: (1) the kinds of support teachers need if they are to conduct classroom research, (2) the effects of becoming a researcher on teachers' views of classroom practice and of themselves as professionals, and (3) the kinds of knowledge teacher research can provide, and the ways in which teachers working as researchers represent and structure that knowledge in oral and written text. (See Appendix on pages 206–7 for specific research questions guiding the data collection.) In the study's first year, we addressed these concerns by focussing primarily on the group 'context', as it were; in the second year, we focussed on a number of participants who represented different perspectives on teacher research within this particular setting. These more detailed portraits were designed to yield 'thick' descriptions of the evolution of individual teachers' thinking about their professional identity and knowledge bases about literacy instruction in the course of ongoing classroom inquiry.

The following data bases were used to address the research questions: audio recordings and field notes taken during whole-group meetings, including audio recordings and field notes of smaller 'response-group' sessions during these meetings; all written materials distributed to participants; volunteered pieces from participants' journal entries; audio recordings of formal interviews with participants at various stages in their research processes; audio recordings and/or notes taken during informal conversations with the group facilitator and participants; participants' progress reports, including interim reports and end-of-year research reports; and in-house publications of participants' work.

In the remainder of this paper, we synthesize our findings, relying primarily on data collected during or ensuing from the first year of the study where the focus was on the group as a whole. Before so doing, however, we wish to stress the historically bounded character of the following account: these were the beginnings of what proved to be a dynamic and highly productive group in which participants addressed both the issues raised in this paper and others arising from the evolving context.

Orientation to 'the group'

The group comprised nineteen kindergarten through college teachers – most National Writing Project teacher-consultants, but several with no formal affiliation with the Project.[2] These teachers represented a broad spectrum, with many working in multi-ethnic classrooms and districts. Seven were elementary school teachers; three taught middle school; six high school; and three taught at college level. Two of the elementary school teachers were involved in Special Education programs. Of the middle school teachers, two taught Science and one History. All those at the high school and college levels taught English. The range of teaching experience was from two to twenty-three years, with the average being eleven. Most participants could be described as active members of their profession, belonging to several professional associations, sitting on various advisory boards, and attending conferences in their areas of interest regularly.

Participants found their way to the group through a number of channels. Five had been in the pilot seminar co-sponsored by the National Writing Project and the National Center for the Study of Writing the previous year, and were returning to extend and complete their research projects. Of the remaining fourteen, the largest number (six) were attracted by the Writing Project network, with some reading about the group in a Writing Project Newsletter, and others hearing about it either while participating in one of the Project's summer programs for educators or from a teacher-consultant they knew. Four found out about the program from colleagues at their school sites. Three, enthused by their experiences either in university courses they had taken or with university researchers conducting studies in their schools, sought out the seminar. One had read articles about teacher research, and found out how to hook up with a group in her geographical area at a professional conference she had attended.

The seminar met biweekly in a university classroom for approximately three hours, during which time participants engaged in a variety of activities designed to help them formulate and examine context-centered, pedagogical questions about writing. These questions were to emerge from the teachers' interests, observations, readings, and discussions with students and colleagues in the teacher-research group.

The actual seminar was made up of five segments, characterized by the following routines and participation formats, and occurring in the following order:

1. Participants begin to assemble around 5.30 p.m. – placing food items on tables at the front of the room – and socialize for approximately twenty minutes as other colleagues enter. They chat about events at the school site or district level, or in their personal lives.

2. The group leader begins the seminar by making and soliciting announcements about recent past and/or upcoming events related to teacher research or other professional activities for teachers. When appropriate, during this segment he also orchestrates plans for individual or group participation in future activities. The group leader's personal anecdotes – a misadventure on a canoe trip, experiences while facilitating writing-across-the-curriculum workshops for teachers in isolated locales – and jokes with local flavor pepper this warm-up segment.

3. One or several main activities ensue, each generally composed of a number of parts, separated by shifts in discourse routine and/or participation format. An example of one activity: (1) an invited guest presents a prepared topic; (2) toward the end of or following the presentation, individuals ask opinion and clarification questions to which the invited guest responds; (3) after the guest leaves, a whole-group discussion takes place on issues related to the presentation. A second example: (1) the group leader distributes an article or paper for participants to read during the seminar; (2) a period of individual reading follows; (3) when it 'feels right' to the group leader, participants are reconvened into the whole group or smaller response groups for discussion of issues arising from the reading. (Since there is no syllabus or schedule of events for the seminar, generally participants are not aware of the agenda for the main activity before it begins.)

4. A break of ten to fifteen minutes follows the main activity. During this period participants chat informally – sometimes about issues related to their research – and partake of the food and drink on the tables in the front of the room (although individuals feel free to snack during the other segments as well).

5. The group leader reconvenes the group and either introduces another main activity or asks participants to 'get into' their smaller response groups. These contain four or five permanently assigned participants, one of whom is designated 'group leader' at the start of the academic year. Response-group members share the contents of their most recent journal entries and/or discuss issues currently important in shaping their thinking about their research.

According to Mike, the group's leader, the format for the group 'came from the Marian Mohr model', which he wanted to 'experiment with to see what works and what doesn't work'.[3] In this regard, it is important to clarify that although many of the features of the group we observed did, in fact, correspond to those of 'the Marian Mohr model' – the group was teacher-led, response groups were assigned (rather than self-selected or rotational), participants were asked to maintain journals – it would be inaccurate to characterize the group as an exact copy of the

195

Mohr/MacLean group. It differed in several respects, perhaps the most significant being the absence of a syllabus showing a planned sequence of readings, assignments, and topics for discussion.

Mike perceived his primary business-at-hand to be guiding participants to an appreciation of the value of engaging in informed classroom observation and developing their thinking about their teaching practices by sharing their reflections with colleagues both orally and in writing. This goal, he believed, was most easily achieved by bringing teachers together to exchange ideas in a 'nonthreatening and nonintimidating' support-group environment. Such an environment, he further believed, was best created by being circumspect with respect to demands made on participants' extra-seminar time, flexible about expectations concerning task completion and deadlines, and ready to accept individual differences in work styles.

In pep talks Mike would remind the group frequently that 'the process is more important than the product'. 'Just remember, think process,' he would exhort. This concept, assumed as a basic working philosophy (although not necessarily shared) by all group members, was invoked frequently in participants' journal entries and contributions at group meetings.

Findings

1. SUPPORT TEACHERS' NEED FOR CLASSROOM RESEARCH

First, we would emphasize that because we intended this research to be useful both to the teacher-research group with which we were collaborating and to others forming across the country, we wanted to be sure to tap all available resources that could provide information about the kinds of collaborative conditions that teachers need in order to engage in informed observation. Therefore, in addition to making note of participants' contributions on this topic in the seminars, we also elicited information using a variety of interview techniques. We asked 'open' questions permitting participants to ruminate, and on different occasions we also asked 'closed' questions touching on as many areas as we could identify – time and scheduling, money, institutional and collegial support at the district and site levels, the structure and content of the seminar itself.

Although participants discussed their needs for support in all of the above areas, their two major concerns were: (1) 'being able to find a block of *time* to sit down and concentrate and do some writing', in the words of one teacher-researcher, and (2) the *structure and content of the group meetings*. This latter concern deserves additional comment, since in the first-year interviews over half of the participants' talk addressed this topic.

This large volume of talk can be at least partially explained by the tendency of participants' contributions to be the expression of debates they seemed to be carrying on internally, with the *same* participant elucidating the structural attributes of the seminar alternately as both strengths and weaknesses. In a typical conversation, for example, one participant complained that the group 'needs more structure . . . like handing something in . . . a sort of syllabus . . . maybe [having] some speakers a little earlier'; then, reversing direction, she said, seeming to remind herself, that a 'gentle approach is good' and that 'one of the reasons it works is because you're not getting all overwhelmed'.[4] In the same vein, a second participant, after expressing her preference for 'more formal deadlines' so that 'we would have felt accountable', does an about-face: 'On the other hand I like the flexibility too.' A third felt he could have used more formal feedback from the group leader and his response group, but in the end was not disappointed with the experience: 'This was something that was mine.'

One participant who by the end of the first year had not yet settled on a research topic, reminisced about how happy and productive he had felt doing a 'mini-research project' in a class on qualitative research he took with a local university professor. Although the class was 'open-ended' with respect to the type of research project he could undertake, it was also 'a lot more structured' than the teacher-research group, he explained. There were assigned readings representing 'models of different types of studies', firm deadlines for oral reports and submission of written work, and many opportunities for feedback from the instructor. Turning then to his experiences in the teacher-research group, the participant reported that at first:

> the relaxed attitude about getting going with your project appealed to me . . I've never been in a situation where you could just take your time like that . . . it excited me and I thought that's great, no pressure, just keep the journal . . . I thought you know whatever comes out of this I will really own. Will really be mine and I'll be you know proud of it. And happier about it.

Eventually, though, he had to admit to himself that: 'I didn't really respond that well to that . . . I wasn't as productive as I had been' [in the course with the university professor]. Nonetheless, he concluded his fifteen-minute-long monologue: 'I realize that's just part of the process.'

More than a few participants used imagery of disorientation in describing their experiences: 'generating a research agenda from scratch', in the words of one researcher. Much of the time, one participant said, she felt the group was 'operating in the dark'; later in the same interview she described her sense of being 'in a fog'. 'I have lots of questions and need some direction,' another participant wrote in her journal midway through the first year.

Many participants used the phrases 'more structure' and 'more organization' when referring to their perceived needs for: a syllabus with a logical progression; more judicious use of seminar time, including more focussed discussions; and regular feedback from the group leader and their response group. They also talked about the need for the seminar to be 'more formal', referring to features such as nonnegotiable deadlines for oral presentations and submission of written work, and written response to journal entries and drafts from the group facilitator and from Schecter who, in addition to conducting the meta-study, participated actively in the group.

Deadlines were especially important to participants because these milestones, they felt, 'catalyzed' their thinking and led to 'breakthroughs' in their research. One teacher-researcher reported in an end-of-year interview that the framing of her research problem and data-collection techniques (including ideas for more efficacious use of her journal entries as 'field notes') 'started to jell only in the last couple of weeks' before the deadline for her June report.

Before leaving this topic, we should mention that these findings were unanticipated. Most of the conceptual pieces we had read in preparation for this study focussed on released time, financial compensation, and the recalcitrance of the university research community *vis-à-vis* teacher inquiry when discussing the kinds of conditions teachers perceived as relevant to their productive engagement in classroom inquiry. We were, therefore, surprised to learn that the nature of the group process was as important an element as it turned out to be for the teachers involved in our study.

2. EFFECTS ON TEACHERS' VIEWS OF CLASSROOM PRACTICE AND THEMSELVES AS PROFESSIONALS

In conjunction with the findings on these issues, it is important to note that although participants' expectations varied – reflecting and sharing ideas with colleagues in a supportive environment, becoming familiar with classroom-oriented research methods that could be used to enhance teaching, using externally imposed timelines to keep to a writing schedule, association with the prestige of the university – comments describing these various expectations relate in some way or other to the theme of professional self-growth:

> – Forcing me to reflect on what I'm doing in my classroom.
> – I'd like to connect with other teachers to generate some fresh ideas.

- To become a better teacher of AP English; to have a further sense of focus in all my classes; to convince my district there are additional ways for teachers to improve . . .
- I really love the connection with [the university].
- I'd love to be able to work for a Ph.D. So this was the closest thing . . .
- I've been trying for years to make the time to keep a journal so I could reflect on each day's experience.
- One of the main reasons I joined the teacher-research project was because I needed that over my head to write.
- I'm interested in being able to try to explore a process . . . to learn the process of observing something and writing it up in some kind of way.

At the end of the first year, participants reported many positive effects of their experience on both their classroom practices and their views of themselves as professionals. In their responses to the open-ended question, 'Has the experience affected you as a teacher in any way?' they distinguished being part of the group process from the individual experience of engaging in a research project, and in the final analysis they had positive outcomes to report of both.

With regard to the group experience, almost all the participants appreciated the support function served by the group and the 'collegiality' of their peers: 'It's nice to come to a group that understood what you were going through.' Related to this theme were comments about the role of the group in countering teacher isolation, a problem participants previously saw as endemic to their profession.

Participants also appreciated the opportunities for reflection provided by the biweekly meetings and commended their colleagues as 'great resources for ideas'. Although a few would have preferred not to have had response groups and most would have preferred to have had some say about the composition of these smaller groups, most cited the response groups as the most important aspect of the teacher-research program: 'My response group is essential for me to keep on top of my project. Journal sharing, discussions, and networking have been important components of what we do in our group.'

One participant summed up his experience in the teacher-research seminar as follows:

> I love the sharing of problems, successes, goals, that I get with other teachers in the program. The log groups, especially, provide this, as well as more direct feedback in response to my particular difficulties. I love the energy I get from seeing/hearing other teachers' projects. These meetings make me think.

Several participants, expanding on this last observation, described the intellectual momentum provided by the collaborative experience: 'This class causes me to think about what I'm doing much more than I probably would otherwise . . . I usually have my brainy breakthroughs in thinking when I'm having [this] class. Or right after I've had a class. More than on my own.'

About their individual research odysseys, participants were almost unanimous in testifying that engaging in their own classroom-based research improved their teaching performances by making them more reflective practitioners. One participant reported that 'collecting data makes me ask good questions of kids who give me good answers, answers that help me improve as a teacher'. 'Teachers need to be researchers so that they get to look at what they are doing in the classroom,' one participant concluded, turning the issue on its head. This moral imperative for the profession is articulated by another participant as follows: 'Until teachers start reading research, doing research, they won't be a profession. If they're grounded on lesson plans, that's where they're going to stay.'

With regard to participants' claims that engaging in informed observation led to changes in their classroom practices, we understand that what people say and what they do may not necessarily constitute one and the same thing. Nonetheless, we find participants' testimonies revealing for what they tell us about the operative assumptions underlying this particular teacher-research group model. Like the expectations they articulated at the beginning of their research odysseys, participants' year-end testimonies about their changed behaviors are consistent with Rogerian concepts related to the goal of self-actualization. 'What it all boils down to,' one participant summed up, 'is looking at yourself as a teacher. I became a better teacher because of doing the teacher research.' Another participant expressed the same perspective, but in a more formal register: 'It's reflexive activity . . . that informs practice.'

Before moving on, we want to present one 'hard' piece of evidence testifying to participants' professional evolutions, and that is the interest that they appear to have developed in the work of other researchers – including university-based researchers – as the seminar progressed. Although most participants did not extensively review the literature related to their studies, all but two who submitted pieces to the in-house collection of working papers ensuing from this first year of the project read and appropriately cited other research in their respective areas. However, they did not begin their research by searching out this literature; rather, they consulted these works after they had determined either on their own or in consultation with a colleague that familiarity with these pieces might either stimulate their thinking at a crucial stage in their projects or help to 'validate [their] own perceptions'.

3. TEACHER-RESEARCHER KNOWLEDGE

In conjunction with our findings on this topic, some background information about participants' day-to-day experiences of being principal investigators on a research project is in order. First, reassurances about process being more important than product notwithstanding, many participants expressed concern about producing 'real research', as one teacher-researcher put it – research valuable both to the teaching profession and to the area of study. One participant wrote in his journal: 'I would like to contribute to the field in a significant manner.' A second, struggling with the articulation of her research problem, anguished: 'Why would anyone care?' A third, again in a journal entry, emphasized her concern with the final product: 'I have to admit the prospect of *publishing* was a *big lure* for me! I published one article once . . . and the euphoria lasted six months to a year.'

Also, after an initial show of bravado and in contradiction to the opinions expressed in some 'think pieces' to the effect that teachers already have all the expertise they need and can speak with authority from their classroom experiences (cf. Berthoff 1987), many participants expressed concern throughout with issues of 'method', 'proof', 'truth', and 'error' both as abstract concepts and as applied to their own work. 'I'm hyper over whether I'm doing everything the right way,' one participant fretted. Similarly, another reported on her state of progress: 'I'm ready to make it tighter. As a scientist I don't think it's super legit yet.' A third participant concluded near the end of the first year that 'the secret' of her study was classroom talk, but doubted she had the 'expertise' to undertake the indicated analyses; nor was she persuaded by the group leader's counsel to 'go ahead and write, background or no'. Several participants felt that their studies lacked sufficient rigor because they did not use sophisticated quantitative methods as did, they believed, university-based scholars.

As for the studies themselves: all eleven of the working papers included in the in-house publication treat classroom practice. All contain an explicit or implicit evaluative component, as the researchers sought to address the question 'What works in the classroom?' and to explain the relative success of different classroom practices. When the studies are categorized according to 'overall focus' and 'specific topic' (after Cazden *et al.* 1988), certain tendencies become evident. Eight of the papers test the effects of a specific pedagogical practice, while three have a more open-ended descriptive focus. Student writing is the explicit topic in nine of the papers, although the topic of writing is peripherally present in the other two. Considering foci and topics together, it becomes clear that nearly all of the researchers wanted to be able to assess closely the effects of specific pedagogical practices on students' writing.

With respect to rhetorical organization and the use of stylistic conventions, ten of the pieces included in the collection contain elements of narrative. Five are thoroughly narrative in their organization; of the remaining six, five are pastiche-like in organization, with elements of narrative combining with elements of formal – i.e. academic – and informal expository writing; one employs conventional academic exposition throughout. Interestingly, in six of the working papers containing narrative components, one finds two distinct narrative threads, the first telling the story of the research's progress – the road travelled by a student or a group of students in response to specific pedagogic interventions – and the second recounting the personal learning odyssey of the researcher him- or herself.

Now for the historic dichotomy between 'teacher-researcher knowledge' and 'university-researcher knowledge', to use two expedient phrases. Contrary to what several of the participants may have believed, the attributes distinguishing the group's working papers from articles found in academic journals have little relationship to mastery of elaborate experimental methodology. We found, however, several important differences.

First, in their write-ups university-based researchers must make a case that they are contributing to an established body of knowledge. To be able to do this they must demonstrate that they exercise deliberate control over the intellectual history of an issue by citing and synthesizing the relevant literature. The group of teacher-researchers we studied did not feel similarly constrained. Although, as previously mentioned, all but two of the eleven working papers' authors cited sources that had been useful to them as they sought to make sense of the phenomena they had observed, only one situated her problem within an established field of inquiry and none undertook or claimed to undertake systematic reviews of the existent research on their topics.

Second, in teacher research there exist as yet no recognized norms for reliability/validity judgements. Again with reference to the in-house publication, many (but by no means all) of the researchers considered personal experience sufficient grounds for asserting their claims. Others, however, in the face of this absence of norms, indicated that they felt the need for extreme epistemological caution in making claims about their data by using various strategies of triangulation, i.e. using data from more than one observer, source or technique, to test their hypotheses. Conversely, established norms for reliability/validity do exist within the university-researcher community. In this latter research context, experience is not considered a valid foundation (although it may be, in fact, the actual foundation) for the assertion of claims, and findings must be cast within a tradition of inquiry that admits designated kinds of data as evidence.

Third, not all of the teacher-researcher pieces we reviewed addressed a problem. The three which did not all asserted certain teaching methods to be successful, and went on to describe how these teaching methods are implemented as well as some positive outcomes of these methods as evidenced by either student performance or feedback. This is not to say that these three were the only pieces concerned with the benefits of certain classroom practices; as stated earlier, all the studies attempted to assess and draw conclusions with respect to effective classroom practice. It is to say, however, that for a minority of participants in our study research could be conducted outside of an articulated problem statement leading to a plan of action requiring consideration of at least two competing hypotheses concerning the benefits of the practices in question. Conversely, to be taken seriously, university research – in the natural and social sciences, at any rate, although not necessarily in the humanities – must contain a problem statement in which the researcher raises questions. This problem statement must be followed at some point by a plan of action in which the researcher demonstrates good faith in devising strategies for addressing these questions. Depending on the discipline and orientation, this good faith can be demonstrated in a variety of ways, but must entail consideration of competing interpretations of the data. (This is not to say that all university researchers embrace and elucidate the full complexity of the issues arising from their research, or even act in 'good faith' in attempting to do so, only that they feel constrained to demonstrate that they are behaving in the manner described.

Before leaving this topic, we should mention that in reports of preliminary findings from this study, we mentioned an additional dimension of difference between teacher research and university research, and that is the degree to which standardized rhetorical conventions are used. We noted that while university-based researchers (to be accepted into the academic fold, as it were) must demonstrate familiarity with the discourse conventions used by other researchers in their areas to frame the pertinent discussions, the teacher-researchers we studied did not feel similarly constrained. We arrived at this conclusion following analyses of oral and written accounts provided by group participants during the study's first year. In these accounts, we found rhetorical formats and stylistic conventions to vary across teacher-researchers and within similar topics. This finding did not surprise us; teacher research being relatively new to the American scene, we did not expect to see a pattern with respect to use of standardized stylistic conventions.

As time progressed, however, the market pressure – to borrow a concept from Bourdieu (1977) – in favor of the use of the double narrative, that is, a narrative of the research process interwoven with a narrative of self, in public forums grew stronger. Thus, for example, in an oral presentation on her project to the entire group early on in the second year, one researcher ran into trouble when she attempted to describe and explain in relatively detached language the manner in which the learning of a child previously labeled 'disabled' came to thrive when he was removed from the participant's own classroom and placed in a regular classroom with a 'whole language' teacher, i.e. one whose philosophy of language teaching is based on process writing, conferencing and a number of other techniques. Demanding to know 'But where are you in the research process?' participants refused to accept the researcher's account because it lacked reflexive testimony on the role of the self in the research process and the impact of the research process on the self. They asked: what role did her expertise in recognizing when and how to act in the better interests of the child play? What about the support function she served for the other teacher? In what ways did her own consciousness evolve as a result of engagement in the research process? It now appears to us that tacit valuation by the group of the use of certain expressive forms may well have influenced the rhetorical choices of authors of the pieces included in the in-house publication. However, at this point we cannot draw any confident conclusions regarding the existence of constraints governing the use of conventionalized rhetorical forms, and we look forward to reading more accounts of teacher-based classroom inquiry with a view to teacher research as an emergent genre.

Discussion

The investigation of the workings of teacher-research groups is still too incipient an enterprise for us to be able to, or even wish to, make definitive pronouncements based on the findings of our study. Instead, we prefer to discuss the potential benefits of this form of collaborative activity as suggested by the words and writing of participants in our project.

First, teacher research is clearly motivated to point us to a theory of practice, to a body of knowledge contributed by teachers that seeks to identify and define what actually and beneficially goes on in classrooms. Second, teacher research can exert pressure on that body of knowledge to be dynamic, generative, and responsive to the needs of students, as teachers engage with, challenge, and act upon their evolving understandings of subject matter, educational practice, and professional values through their daily classroom interactions. Third, beyond its epistemological contributions, teacher research has the potential to figure importantly in the evolution, or put more strongly, the shaping of teaching as a profession. For a number of participants in our study, in fact, who did not seek to publish their work in the in-house anthology or elsewhere, professional development proved the primary interest of the enterprise. But here we must be cautious to safeguard the notion of 'professionalization' from stereotypic top-down representations of 'staff development' in the form of programs instituted by school district officials or university types which teachers have no role in shaping. Participants in our group were unanimously firm on this point: teacher research has a contribution to make to the profession of teaching when and only when it is embedded in an institutional context where teachers are 'given the feeling that what they do is important', 'treated with respect', and maintain 'autonomy over the reflexive process'.

We would also like to take this opportunity to encourage other meta-studies of teacher-research groups. We see two advantages to these studies. First, because close observation of the workings of such groups can reveal the significance and value of teacher research as perceived by teachers, and it can also help pivotal actors in teacher-research projects to take appropriate actions. In our project, for example, the open relationship that existed between the various collaborators permitted the communication of preliminary findings in time to modify certain structural elements of the group environment for the subsequent year. As well, although in the maturation of this particular group professional self-actualization remained a principal motivation for participation, with critical awareness of this dynamic participants were able to express and act on their increasingly more strongly felt need to shift the goal orientation over somewhat to positive changes in their students' learning experiences.

Second, the study of a variety of teacher-research groups that differ in configuration and goals can provide a needed understanding of the spectra along which different groups may coexist and of the outcomes yielded by various combinations of points along these spectra. An appreciation of such spectra could generate useful hypotheses about, for example, how it is that the teacher-researchers in the project we have described undertook independent reviews of the literature relevant to their studies later in the research process than other groups working within a more traditional university-based framework. If the jumping-off point is the teacher's experience – as was the case with this group – there is no need to read at the outset; if, on the other hand, the jumping-off point is a body of academic knowledge, obviously it is in one's interest to become familiar with this corpus as soon as possible.

Similarly, it is understandable that – notwithstanding the increasingly sensitive and profound insights participants revealed about the learning strategies of their students – the teacher-researchers we worked with articulated the perceived benefits of teacher research primarily in terms of their own professional growth. The goal orientation of this group was self; through teachers' efforts to improve themselves as professionals, participants believed, students will learn better.

To these and other similar working hypotheses, we could begin to construct and then refine a list of spectra along which different teacher-research groups may be situated. The following examples are but a few which might be explored.

Degree of imposed structure on the research process

unstructured --highly circumscribed

Point of departure

teacher's expertise --body of research

Goal orientation

self ---other

Goals

teachers taking charge ---------------------------------students learning better

Audience

self --educational community

Thus, by studying groups with different configurations – different points of origin, different priorities, different structural features, and different directions – and hearing the voices of other teacher-researchers, we will come to better understand the range of contributions this form of intellectual practice can make to our notions of teaching as a profession and to our knowledge of the personal and environmental elements that influence learners' engagement with literacy.

Appendix

Specific research questions

KINDS OF SUPPORT

1. What do teachers say they need in the way of institutional (i.e. university and school district) and (teacher research) group support for this endeavour? What kinds of support do teachers actually receive?
2. What is the role relationship between the group leader and the other group members? (e.g. What are the [implicit and explicit] expectations of the group leader? How do group members understand these expectations? In what ways do these expectations evolve?)

EFFECTS ON VIEWS OF CLASSROOM PRACTICE AND PROFESSIONAL
ROLE (INCLUDING ADDITIONAL INFORMATION FROM FOUR CASE
STUDIES)

1. Why do teachers choose to engage in classroom inquiry?
2. Does being a researcher of one's own teaching produce role conflict?
   Conflict of interest? If so, what are the effects of these conflicts?
3. What changes, if any, come about in teachers' beliefs about practice
   and perceptions of their roles as a result of their involvement in their
   own research?
4. As the activity progresses, do teachers develop an interest in the
   research of university-based researchers? If so, what is the nature of
   this interest?

KNOWLEDGE TEACHER-RESEARCHERS PROVIDE

1. What kinds of questions do teachers ask? How do these questions
   emerge/evolve?
2. What kinds of evidence do teachers gather? What kinds of evidence
   do they feel they need to answer their questions?
3. What are the similarities and differences between the research of
   teachers and of university-based researchers?

Endnotes

[1] This chapter is based on research supported in part by a Presidential Grant for School
Improvement (PGSI) awarded by the University of California to the National Writing Project
in collaboration with the National Center for the Study of Writing. We thank Joan Cone,
Sarah Warshauer Freedman, Shawn Parkhurst, Mary Ann Smith and William Sweigart for
their helpful comments on earlier drafts. Most important, we thank our teacher-researcher
colleagues whose generous sharings have allowed us to grow both as teachers and as
researchers.

[2] The National Writing Project (NWP) is a US-based national program to improve student
writing by improving the teaching of writing. In this model of staff development, teachers
identified as exemplary by their colleagues meet in five-week summer institutes to exchange
successful teaching practices and learn to give demonstrations to groups of peers. Currently
there are 160 NWP sites at universities in 45 US states and six foreign countries.

[3] M. Mohr is co-director of the Northern Virginia Writing Project and co-author with
M. MacLean of *Working Together: A Guide for Teacher-research* (1989).

[4] To protect the anonymity of participants in the teacher-research group, sex pronouns are
randomly assigned to individual participants.

11 Putting a process syllabus into practice

Roger Budd and Tony Wright

The experiment: Roger Budd

The process syllabus

In his two-part article 'Contemporary paradigms in syllabus design' Breen (1987) outlines the rationale for a process-based syllabus for language learning. He argues that, as a way of meeting the current challenges facing syllabus design, its focus should be ' . . . upon *how* something is done rather than the mere provision of a plan of the knowledge of language as subject matter to be worked on . . . [It] also extends the focus upon procedures for learning to account for the actual social situation in which learning will take place' (*ibid*.: 160, 166). It goes further than a task-based syllabus 'in providing a bridge between content and methodology and in offering a means whereby the actual syllabus of a classroom group may be made more accessible to each of its members. The process syllabus focuses upon three processes: communicating, learning and the purposeful social activity of teaching and learning in the classroom' (*ibid*.: 166). Implicit in this argument is his assumption that a process-based syllabus will not only aid language learning but also reveal more about how language learning works. He summarises the main characteristics of such a syllabus as follows:

The model

THE LEVELS OR ELEMENTS OF A PROCESS SYLLABUS

Characteristics: *A plan* (or framework) of questions concerning the decisions which need to be made in classroom language learning. Decisions to be considered and jointly made by teacher and learners.

A bank of alternative procedures, activities, and (entailed) tasks to be chosen on the basis of decisions reached.

Each level or element relates to the others – a higher level entailing those below it. The Process syllabus in use involves *regular evaluation* and, thereby, a cyclic process through all levels – from 4 back to 1.

Level 1   DECISIONS FOR CLASSROOM LANGUAGE LEARNING

Relating to participation, procedure and subject matter

(Who does what with whom, on what content, with what resources, when, how, and why?)

Level 2   ALTERNATIVE WORKING PROCEDURES

To be chosen and agreed upon as the 'working contract' of the class (Changes over time)

PARTICULAR CONTENT SYLLABUS OF THE CLASSROOM GROUP

Outcome of decisions concerning WHAT is to be achieved and WHY (Changes over time)

Level 3   ALTERNATIVE ACTIVITIES

To be selected from on the basis of appropriateness to decisions made at levels 1 and 2

Level 4   ALTERNATIVE TASKS

To be selected and undertaken for the achievement of chosen activities. The *actual* teaching-learning work within the class

ON-GOING EVALUATION OF TASKS, ACTIVITIES, PROCEDURE AND CONTENT

Based on the *outcomes* (achievements and difficulties) from activities. Evaluation related to *initial decisions* made.

(From M. P. Breen, 'Contemporary paradigms in syllabus design'. *Language Teaching* 20: 2, 3.)

Roger Budd and Tony Wright

Purpose of the experiment

This chapter describes how this plan was used as a model to work from, and it attempts to evaluate to what extent the procedures and activities it generated could be considered successful in fulfilling the objectives of a process-based syllabus as outlined above. The approach is *hermeneutic* in character rather than *nomothetic* (see Ochsner 1979 for a fuller exposition of these two research methods) in the sense that it seeks to understand and interpret, rather than explain and predict. The essential differences between the two research methods can be summarised thus: in attempting to discover truth, a nomothetic approach relies, and places value, only on controlled experiment; reality (both human, psychological, as well as physical) is subject to discoverable laws; knowledge of reality is reducible to causation, because the world can be explained by controlled experiments and there is only one reality. A hermeneutic approach, on the other hand, believes in a methodological pluralism in its attempt to interpret knowledge of human realities, which can only be understood by personal interpretation, and thus recognises that there are many realities.

These varying realities are revealed through extracts from one of the learner diaries kept by the students,[1] extracts from the teacher's diary, with class task sheets, and brief descriptions of how the class reacted to and discussed the teacher's diary and class tasks. The justification for this is the belief that triangulating the data in this way provides a picture not only of the course of the experiment (seen from the 'outside') and the teacher's perceptions about such an approach and its application, but also of one of the learner's reactions and perceptions. This picture may produce more revealing insights about what goes on in a classroom, in particular about the interaction between the 'three syllabuses' (what the textbook purports to teach, how the teacher interprets this in the light of conditions in the class when the material is taught, and what the learner chooses to learn or not to learn when this material is presented – see Breen 1987). Relying on information provided by just one source (e.g. the teacher's diary) runs the risk of interpreting events in the light of *post hoc* rationalisation, and thus presenting an incomplete or falsified picture. Using information from differing sources may also prevent the teacher or researcher falling into the trap of assuming that the patterns of interaction he or she perceives as significant are perceived as equally significant by the learners.

Carrying out the experiment

The learner who kindly agreed to let her diary be used here was Japanese, newly arrived in the UK; she had been placed in an intermediate level class, along with eleven other students, mostly European of various nationalities, as well as two other Japanese and two Colombians. Most of them had enrolled with the intention of taking First Certificate English (FCE) at the end of the term in question. At the initial meeting, they were given the following awareness-raising task sheet.

Class discussion sheet 1: previous language learning experiences

Please answer the following questions as honestly as you can, then compare with what your partner has written.

Which language(s) have you learnt previously?
What level do you feel you have reached?
Did you learn formally (in a classroom), or informally?
How enjoyable did you find learning? Why/why not?
How aware were you of:
– 'making progress'?
– getting knowledge of how the language system worked?
How satisfying was the learning? Was there a match between what you felt you needed to learn, and what your teacher or your text-book felt you needed to learn?
Did you feel at any point that you no longer seemed to be learning as much as at the beginning?
Have you become more trusting, or less trusting, that the teacher knows what is best for learning?
Which of these three metaphors of language learning best describes your own experience of learning:
– 'the swimming pool': you are thrown into the deep end of the new language and have to learn to cope as best you can;
– 'the jungle': your teacher is your guide to explore the unknown new language with you;
– 'the gymnasium': you must do a series of regular exercises so as to make you fit enough to use the language outside.
Or would you prefer another metaphor to describe your experience of learning?
Which metaphor would you feel happiest working with during this term?

In constructing the questionnaire, I was very conscious of the likelihood of its level of language being too high for intermediate students, but also of the danger, in attempting to make the language more accessible, of oversimplifying and making over-wordy the ideas and concepts contained in the questionnaire. Indeed it was necessary to undertake considerable initial language work with the class in coming to an understanding of these ideas and concepts. This highlights the need to evolve a metalanguage accessible to both learners and teachers. Whole-group discussion revealed attitudes and experiences that one would intuitively expect, and that they had had a variety of successful and less successful language learning experiences. For example, most had learnt in a formal setting, some felt they had 'plateaued', many that learning itself was not very pleasurable but seeing the results was. It is, of course, very possible that there may have been an element of self-censorship in answering, say, the question about whether they had become more or less trusting about teachers' expertise, especially as the group was newly formed, and members did not yet know each other or the teacher well. The purpose of the questionnaire, however, was not to collect empirically verifiable data, but to act as a basis for exploration and discussion of the issues. None questioned why they were given this task, although several were intrigued by the questions on learning metaphors, and had no difficulty in thinking of classrooms in terms of metaphors: most had experienced 'the gymnasium', and wanted and/or expected to continue with it, although some hoped for the 'jungle'. Some of them expressed surprise that it seemed they would be given the opportunity of deciding how the class was going to work.

Keeping learner diaries (see Bailey in Richards and Nunan 1990) in order to reflect on their daily language-learning experiences had not yet been suggested to them, and it is therefore difficult to judge to what extent this task resulted in consciousness-raising. At the end of the session ('for homework') they were asked to think about the possibility of them deciding what they would do in the classes for the rest of the term. The following day they were given a needs analysis task (see class discussion sheet 2 below) to do individually and then collaboratively; this was followed by whole-group discussion on the feasibility of the group, rather than just the teacher, deciding on the planned syllabus for the term. The rationale for this was based on the belief that negotiating the syllabus would lead to consciousness-raising of learning processes within the learners themselves.[2]

Class discussion sheet 2: what shall we do this term?

When thinking about negotiating the syllabus together for this term, we need to discuss the following questions. Read through them and talk about them with a partner.

Should we use only authentic materials originally meant for native speakers of English, or should we rely mainly on materials specially produced for foreign learners, i.e. coursebooks and other EFL books to practise reading/listening etc.?
Should we try and plan a whole term's work, or should we make weekly decisions about what we want to do?
Should we spend an equal amount of time on all four skills – reading, writing, speaking and listening – or should we spend more

time on one or two of these skills?

Should we try and build a sequence of grammar points to be covered, or should we study whatever grammar happens to come up in the materials we study?

Will the classroom be the focus of activity, or will we aim to work much of the time outside the classroom, e.g. on projects?

Should classroom activities be mainly 'means to an end', for example doing grammar practice exercises so as then to be able to use the grammar in 'real-life' situations, or should they be 'ends in themselves', for example, recording interviews with people for a project?

Should ultimate responsibility for decisions about learning objectives, lesson content, and class organisation, etc., be with the teacher or the students?

We can learn about language, and we can learn to use language; should we try to do both, or concentrate on just one?

Do you think learning about language, and learning to use language are:
– complementary?
– intrinsically linked?
– contradictory?

Should we rely on the teacher to make evaluations of progress, or the students?

What should evaluations focus on?

Are there other questions you feel we need to consider?

Again, whole-group discussion revealed how intrinsically conservative (see Breen 1985) classrooms are. For example, there was the expected and accepted asymmetry of teacher–learner role relationships, and surprise and uncertainty at the possibility of shared decision making. In addition, Tomoko's diary for this day (see below) reveals her perception of the potential conflict between individual needs, and conventions of behaviour demanded by virtue of being in a group. As to how far these perceptions (and those in the rest of her diary) are particularly Japanese, is a moot point; further work could usefully be done exploring the different cultural perspectives of such learner reflections.

13 April 1988
Today's task: Make a list of all the major uses of English in my collective experience, in response to the question 'What do you need English for?'

At first it is necessary for us to get our ideas into shape. So I've not understood yet how the teacher leads the class, and what the teacher thinks we should do in the class.

But if the task should be done individually, we have to do our best individually. I can't agree with a person who starts chattering without deliberation. But then I need long, long time to get my ideas . . .

As a *quid pro quo* in persuading the students to keep learner diaries, it was also agreed that I should keep a diary; the first entry was given out to the students on the following day:

> 13.4.88
> *Below are the notes I made during this morning's class while you were doing the needs analysis task:*

> Have given out needs analysis sheet without much explanation and written on board:

> > TODAY'S TASK
> > Using the needs analysis sheet, work out a way to present me with the important information.

> I take a back seat – silence – individuals working on their own – a slightly tense atmosphere – Myriam and German start talking softly together – Myriam breaks general class silence by asking me for clarification of task as set out on sheet (not the later task as set out on board) which other students listen carefully to – at the moment no realisation that this has to be a jointly negotiated task (the rubric on needs sheet stresses *collective* presentation)
> - ask students later what metaphor describes this activity?
> - if I go round (however discreetly) looking over people's shoulders, murmuring approval etc., this will negate real pushing of responsibility over to them for learning
> - the group is very spread out, because of table layout – this probably hindering breaking out of individual into collective effort (point to bring up with students later)
> - when the need to start working collectively is realised, who will 'shuffle' themselves into organising/leading role?
> Yumi and Marzia starting to talk a little, seeking clarification from each other
> - Marzia, who might be expected to be an organiser, is looking round trying to decide whether to take initiative to release tension?
> - very difficult for me to hold back waiting for frustration/ impatience/irritation on students' part to reach such a level they they are forced to start working together
> - who will break first; me or them?
> - silently I have altered task rubric on board to ' . . . important collective[3] information'
> - does the effort and time students are spending individually filling out sheet mean (1) they are desperately putting off the time when they have to change from being private individuals to group participants? (2) they feel they will be evaluated on the quality of their written work on the sheets?
> - Marzia has started reading *Observer* magazine
> - I broke!

- students shared feelings of frustration – German said he desisted from pointing out this looked a silly task because he didn't know me well enough to know if I could accept criticism
- I pointed out crucial importance of physical layout of seating to encourage communication
- I appointed Deitrich to take organising role – they start exchanging personal experiences – Marzia taking lead, others sharing knowledge, and some very interesting things come out, e.g. need to widen cultural horizons, personal emotional development as reason for needing/using English, i.e. what they say seems to show such deep thought – maybe keeping them in suspense so long with seemingly not much happening was effective in getting them to come out with more than just superficial thoughts?

This provoked gasps of recognition from the students, that their perception of the purpose, the dynamics and the affective aspects of the previous day's class was essentially the same as the teacher's. Discussion of issues raised by the diary led to me abandoning completely my proposed lesson plan (of another task sheet to get them to further reflect on issues of culture and language); for they asserted (1) that, rather than a continuous debate about lesson content, they would prefer a coursebook; and (2) that they were quite happy to pass over responsibility for making decisions about class activities to the teacher, with the proviso that they would feel free to make suggestions as and when they wanted; this they did in all subsequent lessons, deciding which route to be taken through each unit of the coursebook (*Focus on First Certificate* by Sue O'Connell), and which exercises/activities they felt were unnecessary. Having to come to an agreement whether to do a particular exercise or activity brought out very clearly to each member the different learning goals, styles and perceived weaknesses of their fellow group members. The next diary entry:

15.4.88
I sense relief that we've started using a coursebook, i.e. that the class now feel more comfortable that it has settled down to previous expectations of how language learning should proceed. There was a point on Thursday when the group's suspension of scepticism about the proposed, more self-conscious and self-questioning way of working was about to collapse: they were losing patience about being asked to think so inquisitively into their own language learning styles / preferred ways of working and so on. Marzia's comment when presented with discussion sheet 2 summed it up: 'hope term hasn't passed before we decide what to do' (!) Yet I also sense that this first week spent consciousness-raising about language learning is appreciated, and that it is seen as useful; several students have started their diaries, and some

> interesting reflections are coming out, reflections they might not
> have articulated if they hadn't been pushed into being so self-
> conscious(?) We should follow these up – I'm sure they will be
> helpful to all of us. Taking a position, though, that students decide
> if they want their diaries to be private or public is not really
> allowing them a true choice; if they decide on a private diary they
> may suspect that it will be taken that they are being negative or
> critical or personal; if they agree to it being public, they may not
> reveal their innermost thoughts. On the other hand, has a language
> teacher any right to probe the psychological depths of his students?

By committing myself to keeping a diary, I find, even at this early stage,
that I am having to think hard about the value systems and presuppo-
sitions that have lain, up till now unarticulated, behind my everyday
teaching, encouraging me to be a more reflective practitioner.

As for the learners, it would appear that in the space of a few days the
group had proceeded through all the levels of Breen's work, albeit with
very conservative decisions made at level 2. Within a few days of
coming together as a group, an outside observer of a lesson would have
been hard put to say what distinguished this group from any other that
had not gone through this awareness-raising process and been offered
the chance of taking responsibility for managing classroom procedures
and content. The crucial difference, however, with this group was that it
was *they* who had decided on content and procedure, as opposed to a
more traditional group who had, by default or design, had similar
content and procedure imposed upon them. Moreover, it was remarked
by an outside observer making a video of this group after five weeks that
the feeling of group solidarity, cooperation and mutual support she
sensed led her to believe that they had been together as a group very
much longer.

Consideration, however, of Tomoko's diary entries below reveals
much more than the surface information available to an outside
observer, and illustrates many of Breen's (1987: 166–9) assertions about
the characteristics and rationale of a process-based syllabus.

> 15 April 1988
> Today's task: *First Certificate* p. 1–6 – Expand vocabulary –
> Choose the correct preposition – Relative clauses
> It is very difficult for me to read the sentences of questions.
> Because I don't know the words of grammar. If my English
> teachers in Japan had taught in English, I would have expanded
> my vocabulary more. No, no, I know it's my fault. By the way,
> why does the text have no answers? I must study this book on my
> own, because I don't take afternoon FCE classes. So if the teacher
> doesn't mind, I'd like to get answers and check up them and mine.

She appears to confirm Breen's assertion that there is a link between content and methodology, and that she is aware of it. She is conscious of the effect different ways of presenting information about language have on her understanding, and is also conscious of the need to find appropriate strategies for effective learning, as shown as well by her entry for 20 April (see below). On the other hand, the titles she gives to each of the lessons suggests she still sees language in terms of content and system; by the end of the course, her diary entries show she has a considerably more sophisticated view of language. The following entry shows that she is starting to realise that learning verbs only at the level of grammar is insufficient.

> 18 April 1988
> Today's task: *First Certificate* p. 7–11 – Vocabulary and definition
> – the present simple and the present continuous
> I didn't think that the verb form tells us so much about the
> situation.
> Also in Japanese, we can guess a lot of things behind the word
> which a speaker selects. I must understand the meaning that each
> verb style has correctly. Today I went to a bank. The clerk said
> something to me, but I couldn't understand. Sometimes I can hear
> what people say, but sometimes I can't. What is the difference?
> Speed? Because of my small vocabulary? I felt very shy . . .

In striving to communicate her thoughts on each day's proceedings, Tomoko is not only learning to communicate but also to be metacommunicative (see also her entries for 10 and 18 May). By reflecting on her language use outside class, she is encouraged to see that to regard language solely in terms of content and system is not the answer. The affective element in language learning is very powerful for her: she felt 'very shy' and can't see why she has this difficulty in communicating.

> 19 April 1988
> Today's task: *First Certificate* p. 7, p. 11–14 – Game – Directed
> writing – Vocabulary review
> I'm surprised that I see the students from other countries some-
> times complain about the way of working. They are volitional [*sic*]
> to learn, aren't they? . . . It is more important for me to consider
> and decide how I'm going to learn English than what I learn about
> English.

The diary gives her the opportunity to articulate her realisation of the importance of developing learning strategies and the need to decide which are best for her. The following entry also shows how the process of decision making about content and procedure is in itself a communicative activity.

H

Roger Budd and Tony Wright

> 20 April 1988
> Today's task: *First Certificate* p. 9 – Hearing
> It is very difficult for me to hear some conversations and under-
> stand their contents. If I read the questions first, it becomes easier,
> but while I continue to hear, I'm forgetting the previous things. I'm
> very happy when I can understand what people say, so in order to
> improve my skill of listening, I bought a radio! (but cheapest one
> that was made in China . . .) I hope I would be a good listener as
> soon as possible.

She is taking control of her learning, making her own needs diagnosis.

> 21 April 1988
> Today's task: *First Certificate* p. 11 & 12 – Listening – Phrasal
> verbs (workshop)
> As I said yesterday, listening is a weak point for me. All day long, I
> try to catch person's words with making the whole body 'ears'. I'm
> very tired every day . . . Phrasal verb is, I think, also one type of
> verb. We must learn them by heart and try to use over and over
> again. It is useful to say in a voice, and then we would be able to
> remember them in their rhythm.

A comparison of her diary entry for 21 April with mine for the same day
neatly illustrates the 'three syllabuses' phenomenon:

> I proposed a grid system for learning 'phrasal verbs' as possibly
> helpful, although qualified it with observations about its disadvan-
> tages, naively thinking that students would make, or be able to
> make, an informed decision. Of course they won't, and can't be
> expected to: the teacher–student relationship is unequal, at least in
> terms of the students' perception that it is only natural to rely on
> teacher for advice about language learning. By pointing out the
> disadvantages, I had made the decision for them.

In other words, what the teacher thought was the most significant aspect
of the day's lesson was not at all shared by the learner. My diary entry
continues:

> Students seem to like working collaboratively on, for example,
> grammar exercises; except for Valérie, who perfectly reasonably
> said she preferred working on them individually. I think however
> that German, who happened to be sitting next to her, and would
> have been her partner on today's task, felt she was being a bit
> antisocial towards him. This is one of the many fleeting glimpses
> one gets about how the group is forming in social terms; how
> much right does one have to bring it into the open? how useful is
> it? maybe useful in terms of provoking class discussion.

In fact the learners were intrigued by my observation about Valérie and
German, and they agreed it had been like this. The teacher's role is more
than just instructional, or managerial, or as a source of knowledge: he

218

or she is inevitably a social member of the group, sensitive to social conventions about what is appropriate and what is not appropriate to communicate when one is a member of a social group (see Wright 1987).

The learners' difficulty in coming to terms with a non-directive teacher's role is evident in the following diary extract:

> 22 April 1988
> Today's task: *First Certificate* p. 15, p. 21 – Lead-in 1 – Grammar (past)
> The thing, which I feel everyday, is that the person who decides a today's menu is not our teacher, but a student! Is this a typical style of education in Europe? In Japan, a teacher always leads his class, and his students take a passive position. We do our home-work because our teacher tells us to do that. So this is an interesting difference between Europeans and us. Their eagerness for study attracts my attention everyday.

She appears still to be coming to terms, some time after the group decisions were made, with all the implications of decisions made about procedure. She notes, for example, how very different the teacher–learner role relationship is from previous experience in Japan; she keeps an open mind about this, and is prepared to see advantage in it. This entry was written whilst I was away and the class was being taken for a few days by Tony Wright. It is interesting to see that her being reflective does not stop when she has a new teacher.

> 25 April 1988
> Today's task: *First Certificate* p. 27–31 – Listening – Vocabulary – Informal letters
> Hello Roger! Although I had worked for three years, I had never written formal letters. Through today's class and the option class 'Commerce', I knew how to write letters in English a little bit. I'm looking forward to writing to the friends from the other countries whom I could meet during this term.

> 29 April 1988
> Today's task: *First Certificate* p. 46, p. 48, p. 45 – Vocabulary review – Grammar (*must, have to*)
> Is there a difference between *must* and *have to*? I've not studied accurate difference, only about the tense. It is very important to study language at the place where it is used. Because we can find a delicate meaning every word has – sometimes they have a same meaning when they are translated into Japanese – from a turn of expression given by native speakers.

The entry for 29 April reveals the danger of trying to ascribe linguistic performance in class as evidence of learning: she was able to successfully do the exercises practising *must* and *have to*, thus giving the impression of successful learning. Her diary shows her to be still very unsure. This difficulty with *must* and *have to* did in fact lead to an ongoing evaluation of content (level 4 of the working model). The group decided to construct a questionnaire on usage of these two verbs and administered it to some native speakers; this showed that the coursebook had arbitrarily oversimplified common usage, and led the group to trying to construct their own rules for use, to take account of the much 'fuzzier' picture of use L1 speakers seem to have.

> 10 May 1988
> Today's task: *First Certificate* p. 73, 77 – Listening – Grammar (future)
> Today's focus on grammar is 'future'. I know only *be going to*, and *will*, but didn't know the different meaning between them. In addition, 'present continuous', 'present simple', 'future simple', 'will be going to' . . . they express at least what is going to happen in future, but meanings that they have are various . . . It's surprising!

Here the learner is developing a very much more sophisticated and sensitive view of language than perhaps authors of EFL coursebooks give intermediate learners credit for. In the next extract she also demonstrates awareness of the complex interplay of language and culture.

> 18 May 1988
> Today's task: *First Certificate* p. 178–181 – Exam practice
> I think languages are composed with culture, history, and various backgrounds. In regard to jobs, people whose linguistic skills are excellent, but who have never tried to understand the country where the language is spoken, would never obtain good results. Because he can keep in touch with the foreigner only in their conversation, but never enter into his feelings. I know English better because of living in England, and it might be impossible when I was in Japan.

   In her next entry, she is aware of the conflict between individual learning needs and constraints of group membership, i.e. she is conscious of the social, as well as the cognitive and methodological, dimensions of the learning environment (see also her entry for 19 April).

> 23 May 1988
> Today's task: *First Certificate* p. 98, 104 – Formal letters – Describing objects – Vocabulary – Odd man out
> Today's lesson was filmed on the video. The advantage of our class is that we have many opportunities to tell teachers what we want to learn, and what we don't understand now. On the other hand, the students sometimes ask teachers about what they have already learned, or what they can study by themselves easily. I think we had better distinguish between the things that we should ask

teachers and those that we shouldn't in the class. The lesson is for the whole class, not only for you.

Conclusions

Before the experiment was undertaken, I was doubtful about the feasibility of adopting this process-based syllabus with a class designated to sit FCE at the end of the term. Would the demands of the exam be perceived by the students as imposing too powerful an external constraint on experimentation? Would this approach only be workable where risk was acceptable? In fact, this problem did not arise, precisely *because* such an approach takes cognizance of the fact that a teacher working from a required syllabus inevitably interprets it for appropriacy to his or her learners, and learners inevitably reinterpret it to their own needs. Once a comfortable *modus operandi* had been established by the group, they were clear that further, continual, renegotiation of method or content was not *per se* an essential element of the process in this situation; it is possible that, had they not had the prominently extrinsic motivation of FCE as the goal to be reached at the end of this time of experiment, reevaluation and renegotiation may have been more lengthy or more often initiated. The important thing was that the learners had the opportunity and responsibility for deciding on their preferred ways of working.

Trying to evaluate the success or otherwise of the experiment presents certain problems. The only objective measure is whether the learners passed FCE at the end, since this was the purpose for which they enrolled in the class. In fact, they did all pass. This, however, is a superficially *instrumental* view of the experiment, and fails to capture what both learners and teacher felt it had achieved. The only source for this type of knowledge, of course, is reactions and reflections of learners and teacher, as well as of the outside observer quoted earlier. These are subjective and impressionistic, and fail to fall into neat categories that any objective measure would require. On a deeper, *experiential* level, the outside observer's perception of the affective and social changes this approach generated has already been noted; Tomoko's diary entries for 18 May, and 14 and 15 June also highlight the experiential dimension by which the experiment can be judged. She sees language as more than simply linguistic content to be learned; for her it is a means of achieving intellectual and emotional enrichment.

> 14 June 1988
> Today's task: Quiz
> My friends finished their exam today, and most of them are going back to their countries after this term. It is only two months since I've met them first, but after three days we are parting from each

221

other. I will miss them very much, so I would like to write to them
as much as possible, and cherish our friendship beyond the sea
from now on, too!

15 June 1988
Today's task: Poem
I really look up to poets. How do they choose their words? I'm
quite unimaginative, and this is a typical Japanese characteristic.
When we are given some subjects we will do a good job on them.
However, if we are given only a white paper, we won't know what
to do with it. What we can do is just importing the wonderful
objects of art from other countries, and making money by using
them.

It has already been stated that Breen (1987: 160) considers that one of
the three processes a process syllabus should focus on is the 'purposeful
social activity of teaching and learning *in the classroom*' (my italics).
Tomoko's diary, written after my class, away from the classroom, and
as an individual reflecting privately on her language learning experiences, suggests that this is just as necessary for successful learning to take
place as what goes on in the classroom during lesson time. Maybe we
should extend our metaphor for 'the classroom' to mean more than just
the four walls, and the activities going on there (a social and physical
reality), to the processes generated in the mind, a psychological reality as
well. The learner is encouraged to become just as much the 'reflective
practitioner' as the teacher. And, if we accept this extended meaning of
'the classroom', the dichotomy between 'language of the classroom' and
'language in the real world' becomes spurious.

Consideration, then, of the diaries, as well as introspections during
and after the experiment by the teacher, leads to the belief that the
experiment revealed the characteristics of a process-based syllabus that
Breen has outlined as it encouraged the learners:

- to learn about learning, to learn better, and
- to increase their awareness about language, and about self, and hence
  about learning;
- to develop, as a result, metacommunicative as well as communicative
  skills;
- to confront, and come to terms with, the conflicts between
  individual needs and group needs, both in social, procedural terms as
  well as linguistic, content terms;
- to recognise that content and method are inextricably linked, and
- to recognise the decision-making tasks themselves as genuine communicative activity.

In seeking to understand the workings of a language class, one should, in my view, continually keep in mind Barthes's assertion that one should not pretend to be able to ascertain the 'truth' of any phenomenon, but simply to 'construct intelligibility', and seek to develop the conceptual frameworks helpful in gaining this intelligibility. That so many of Breen's assertions about the characteristics of a process-based syllabus found expression during this experiment suggests that they are useful conceptual frameworks.

Reflections: Tony Wright

Personal contribution in the classroom

I was fortunate enough to participate in the experiment both as a teacher and as an outside observer and colleague. My own direct contribution to the experiment lasted one week – the third week of their course. I took the group for their first session of the day for five days. I was well aware of the approach being taken and had discussed it with Roger on several occasions prior to my work with the group. We did not agree any specific strategy while I was with the class, however, other than that I should try to maintain the collaborative process in his absence.

Working with the group

My reactions after working with the group on the first morning were mixed. I had naively expected a group keen to discuss course content and reflect on learning processes. Instead, I found a group watchful and even evasive. Had I got the approach wrong? The group was far more 'suggestible' than I had thought they would be; they accepted my final judgements on the desirability of doing suggested exercises and seemed ill-at-ease with the negotiated approach. This was all in direct contrast to the optimistic picture that Roger had painted for me.

In fact, I felt that the group had manoeuvred me into the position of 'final arbiter' regarding both content and process. I decided to be less direct with the approach after this initial encounter and for the rest of the week kept the negotiating process at the level of content only, discussing which exercises from the coursebook we would try, and offering a choice of grammar and vocabulary points for the class to work with. The group appeared to enjoy working collectively, in sub-groups and in pairs, and so I ignored the overt negotiation of process beyond the group's stating preferences for pair or groupwork. I became more and more aware of the fact that I might be interfering in the relationship that had been established between the group and Roger on a personal level and made a decision to keep the relationship I had with them at a 'business' level. It made sense in view of my position as 'supply' teacher. My diary entry of 21 April expresses this:

> Deliberate policy not to focus too heavily on the sub-text of the course that R. has taken. That's something being negotiated with Roger. I'm minding the shop and wouldn't want to go too heavily into the sort of relationship that he's fostering in my few days.

I noted at the end of my week with the class that I did not envy Roger's task in having to reestablish contact with them. I sincerely hoped that I had not interfered in what was so evidently a contract on the process between him and the group that only he could fulfil in the long run.

Tasks

Among the many observations regarding the work of the group I could record, one is particularly worthy of mention in view of the nature of the process syllabus. The group were very keen on both metalinguistic and metacognitive exploration. An example of this was evidenced when we decided to examine phrasal verbs: the exercise (see Appendix on page 229) proved very productive and revealing in assisting them in the problem of tackling what was for them a difficult area of English. I noted the following:

> 21/4/88
> The unconscious raising of metalanguage *through* activities, and examining learning strategies with the group is very productive. This language seems to come out better during activities than being directly addressed.

The approach that Roger had deliberately adopted was evidently succeeding in the sorts of activity described. I felt optimistic about this, even after only a few days with the class. The process appeared to be having an effect in raising consciousness about the learning process itself.

Collaboration – what does it involve?

From my own point of view, this brief insight into the workings of a process syllabus in action has led me to reflect on several issues raised by the experience.

Change in role relationships

Collaboration affords the opportunity to overtly discuss and reflect upon a wide range of teaching and learning processes and activities. This sort of discussion goes on informally in every educational institution, usually between teacher and teacher, or learner and learner. The shift of emphasis that a process approach demands creates a new dialogue between teacher and learner. Traditional role relationships (see Wright 1987) are brought into question by the very possibility of such a dialogue. The apparent reluctance of the learners to become involved is almost certainly an outcome of the conflict that a shift in role relationships brings about. Learners are unlikely to give up the security that results from a more traditional relationship with their teacher. Furthermore, the change of attitude on the part of both teachers and learners required to take full advantage of the new opportunities afforded by dialogue is likely to take time. On reflection, my decision to keep the relationship I had with the class on a 'business' level for the short time I was with them, and not to force the issue of diary-keeping or discussion of the process was probably justified.

Threat to the privacy of the classroom

An interesting problem emerges from the previous issue. The class would probably not have perceived (and had certainly not been informed) that Roger and I were working closely. After all, how many teachers do? It would have run counter to their own experience of teaching and learning. Thus, the group were justified in being suspicious of me in the first session – here was I trying to be like *their* teacher. And I wasn't! Was I invading private territory? Their special relationship? No wonder they clammed up, if this was the case.

The experience of discovering the 'privateness' of a teacher–learner group relationship has caused me to reflect on the problem of 'sharing' classrooms with colleagues. What surprises me is the surprise on discovering the privacy. We do not normally realise how quickly and how deeply private a learning group's relationships become, because we are involved personally. The privilege of participation enabled me to glimpse this privateness anew. Classrooms may be even more 'private' than I had thought. I wonder if the experience would have been different if we had worked as a team, together in the class from the outset? Does the process approach described by Roger lead to an even closer teacher–learner relationship than a conventional approach? It would appear to be extremely paradoxical if it did – it is supposed to give rise to learner autonomy (see Dickinson 1987). It is, however, worth noting that the initial agenda for activity is set by the teacher – see Roger's questionnaires which set up the priorities. What is important is that the process syllabus involves the learners in contributing to the decision-making process. Rejection of the teacher's agenda, which to some extent occurred later in the experiment, was an important outcome, made possible by the initial process, I feel.

Collaboration is communication

If teachers and learners develop closer relationships while pursuing learning in a collaborative manner, we, as teachers and learners, need to consider how we communicate. After all, in collaborative ventures, the participants are taking risks by revealing motives, feelings and thoughts; they are investing a great deal of trust in each other, primarily because the teaching/learning contract is open to discussion. The principal problem, and yet the most vital element in the strategy must be to establish lines of communication between teacher and teacher, teacher and learner, learner and learner. This happens anyway, but usually in a haphazard manner. Shared diary-keeping as illustrated by Roger is a useful channel – it can be private if participants require it to be so, a reading exercise rather than open discussion. There are other, more open ways of sharing experience, however. Edge (1989) offers a range of structured and semi-structured means of sharing experiences openly and face to face. If we are serious about changing the teacher–learner relationship, we need to be able to support ourselves as teachers and our learners in balanced and reflective ways (see Schon 1983 for a rationale for the 'reflective approach' to teaching, for example).

The processes set in train by collaboration appear additionally to offer the prospect of developing a language for describing and interpreting classroom life which is accessible to its participants, for them to further their own development as a learning group. The way forward would appear to be to describe the process of teaching and learning *as we, the participants, see it, rather than using outsiders' perceptions unless we need them* – and initially to avoid over-conceptualisation and abstraction. Thus teachers and learners may develop a language that is initially accessible only to themselves and obscure to outsiders. Admittedly, the initial privacy of this language may create barriers to external comprehension (see, for example, the problems of research into classroom language, epitomised by Walker and Adelman's 1976 account) but by sharing our accounts of classroom experiences with learners and fellow teachers, we may be able to take the first steps towards creating a common descriptive language for the classroom. What matters at this moment in time is that the language which evolves is shared by its immediate users, and that this mutual investment is seen as a priority.

Collaboration requires different skills for the teacher

What about collaboration between teachers? I wonder whether the process we have described would have been enriched by my continuing a relationship with the group, or whether it would have been impeded? My brief contribution sheds only a little light on a complex set of processes and yet I sense that previous collaborations between myself and Roger made it easier to discuss the experiment with him and to try to continue with it in his absence. Unlike the majority of our colleagues, I found myself in broad sympathy with the experiment and did not feel it at all unusual that a class should be working with these principles. On the other hand, the whole notion of negotiating course content and process was, with one or two exceptions, treated with some degree of scepticism by colleagues. This leads me to consider the notion of developing this type of collaboration as part of teacher development, for it is only through the experience of sharing deeper levels of awareness and values that we can come to understand both the theory and practice of new approaches (see Edge 1989). Collaboration itself may involve reflection on one's value systems in relation to teaching, and I sense that the comparative isolation suffered by Roger while pursuing the experiment was due, in no small measure, to a lack of shared experience or knowledge of either the theory or practice of the process syllabus with other colleagues prior to the experiment.

The loneliness of the innovator can be overcome through mutual support. As I have remarked, collaboration is not a new phenomenon – talking about it is. As teachers, we need to develop our skills at discussing and reflecting upon our experiences. An approach to teacher development which is reflective ('thinking about') (see Handal and Lauvås 1987 and Wallace 1990), and reflexive (one which acts on reflections, building them into practice, see Hammersley and Atkinson 1983), and in which we actively take control of the processes of change and development, sharing the risks, would appear to be elements of an emerging 'collaboration culture'. Such a culture has its own means of research (see McNiff 1988 for an account of action research which matches the procedures described in the main text of this paper) and a commitment to mutual support. Such cultures may develop spontaneously in institutions. The question is whether they are to be encouraged to grow.

Collaboration, as innovation, needs to be organised

Innovation and change may be perceived as threatening; practitioners who pursue change may be seen as pretentious. Sharing these experiences and perceptions in teacher development sessions would seem to offer one way out of the impasse. It is interesting to note that other teachers who took the group did not appear to attempt to negotiate the process, thus reinforcing the group's idea that this was something that only they and their class teacher were undertaking.

While individual teachers may be able to manage the process of innovation internally, as it were, and elicit the full cooperation of their group, they need support. Innovations need publicity and debate within institutions. White (1987) has remarked on some of the dangers of 'unmanaged' innovation. Collaboration, of the type described in this chapter, is innovative, but should not be above evaluation. Management, as an external agency in the process, may be best equipped to initiate evaluation. But without information or communication – teachers and learners are in their private world of the classroom – the outcome is unlikely to be worthwhile. The classroom extends beyond the metaphor of 'four walls and a blackboard' – Tomoko's diary entries show that conclusively. I wonder how far teachers are prepared to change their metaphors of the classroom and to create new organisational relationships? Our experience has given us a glimpse of the rich potential such innovations afford.

Endnotes

1 I am extremely grateful to Tomoko Kurihara for now allowing me to quote from her diary – particularly as she was under the impression when she was keeping the diary that it was to be private. Such shabby trickery on the teacher's part perhaps meant, however, that, had she known all along it was to be public, she would have been more liable to self-censorship.

2 There is, of course, a paradox here: the teacher had decided that the content and procedures for the term were going to be negotiated – which was non-negotiable! This is unavoidable, given that however 'equal', open or free teachers try to make the teacher–learner relationship, they always have ultimate power – an inevitable characteristic of the 'culture' of the classroom.

3 It is interesting to note how Tomoko shows in her diary entry that she had misunderstood the teacher's intended meaning of 'collectively'.

Appendix

What is a phrasal verb?

1. What grammatical differences and similarities can you see between the verbs in the following sentences?

   a) My brother shouted at me.
   b) I picked her up at half past three.
   c) I couldn't look at Jules for fear of laughing.

2. Try to divide the sentences that follow into two groups according to the properties of the verbs in them. Try to formulate your reasons for dividing them as you have done.

   a) They left their best player out of the team.
   b) He's getting on well with his brother.
   c) I don't approve of loutish behaviour.
   d) In many countries, young men are called up at the age of eighteen.
   e) The motorist ran over the dog.
   f) You can get a book out of the library.
   g) He's knocking about with a weird crowd.
   h) I was fitted out with the best equipment money could buy.
   i) They did away with the old styles.
   j) He's going to burn out unless he takes it easy.

3. Are there any rules which might be useful?

   Look at the rules which follow and try to use them with the verbs in Exercise 2 above.

   Prepositional verbs

   i) The preposition in a prepositional verb comes before the prepositional object.
   ii) If the object is a pronoun, it must follow the preposition in a prepositional verb.
   iii) An adverb can be placed between the verb and the preposition in a prepositional verb.
   iv) A prepositional verb accepts a relative pronoun, e.g. *whom* after the preposition when a *yes/no* question is formed.
   v) Prepositional verbs can be made passive, but phrasal verbs cannot.

4. Are phrasal verbs really just items of vocabulary? Thus learning them is nothing stranger than learning any other vocabulary items.

What are the best ways of organising vocabulary learning? Can vocabulary learning be organised, or is it hit-and-miss?

12 Toward a collaborative approach to curriculum development: a case study

David Nunan

The 'curriculum' of a given institution or language program can be looked at from different perspectives. On the one hand, it can be seen as a statement of intent, the 'what should be' of a language program as set out in syllabus outlines, sets of objectives, and various other planning documents. Another perspective is that of the curriculum as 'reality', that is, in terms of what actually goes on from moment to moment in the language classroom (Nunan 1988).

Recognition of the fact that there is no simple one-to-one relationship between intention and reality has promoted interest in classroom research in recent years (see Chaudron 1988, and van Lier 1988, for comprehensive reviews of classroom research from quite different perspectives). This work on classroom research has underlined the complexity of language learning and teaching and has provided insights into why there are mismatches between what is planned, what actually gets taught, and what learners learn. Additional insights have been provided from second language acquisition research, which has demonstrated that mismatches between the various curriculum perspectives can be accounted for, among other things, by speech-processing constraints, i.e. constraints imposed by the limits of short-term memory on the ability to produce target language forms (see, for example, Pienemann 1985).

In addition to a range of diverse and sometimes contradictory views on the nature of language and language learning, curriculum developers need to take account of and respond to data coming from classroom researchers, second language acquisition researchers, test and evaluation specialists, funding authorities, learners, teachers, and so on. They need to incorporate these into a design that is consonant with the political, social, cultural, and historical contexts in which the language programs will be implemented.

Most curriculum proposals can be ranged on a 'control continuum', with fully centralised curricula at one extreme and decentralised curricula at the other. The history of education systems can be seen as an interplay between forces representing centralisation and decentralis-

This chapter is an updated version of a paper which first appeared in *TESOL Quarterly 23* (1), 1989.

ation. For example, in the twenty years following the Second World War, many school systems were based on the centre–periphery model, wherein, in Schwab's graphic phrase, curricula were 'decided in Moscow and telegraphed to the provinces' (1983: 240). This was followed by a period in which various forms of school-based curriculum development were experimented with. (See also Richards' (1987) distinction between bottom-up and top-down approaches to the language curriculum.)

The interplay between centralised and decentralised forms of curriculum development is reflected in language curriculum development. During the 1970s, a number of developments prompted experiments with various forms of school-based curricula. Changing views on the nature of language, particularly the development of communicative language teaching in its various guises, with its implication of differentiated curricula for different learner types, the work of the Council of Europe with its behavioural approach to syllabus design, Munby's (1978) needs-based approach, the application of competency-based education to second language learning, and, in Britain, the Graded Levels of Achievement in Foreign Language Learning (Clark 1987; Clark and Hamilton 1984) all promoted the cause of decentralised language curriculum development.

School-based models accord greater power and control to the classroom practitioner in the curriculum development process than do more centralised models. This article describes an experiment that has employed such an approach, an experiment in which the practitioner has been accorded a central role in the curriculum development process and in which the renewal of the curriculum reflects a collaborative effort between teachers and curriculum developers.

Background

The Australian Adult (Im)migrant Education Program (AMEP) is a large, federally funded English language education program for immigrants and refugees. Some 1,500 teachers provide instruction in 300 language centres across the country. Annual enrolments total 130,000.

Until the early 1980s, the AMEP curriculum followed a classical centre–periphery model. Course materials were centrally produced by a team of curriculum writers and disseminated to the various language centres around the country. The course materials, which were, in effect, covert teacher-training instruments as well as the embodiment of the chosen curriculum model, were intended for all learners undertaking AMEP courses, irrespective of their needs, previous learning experiences, and so on.

The fragmentation of client groups, which was accelerated during the

David Nunan

late 1970s and early 1980s by a large influx of Southeast Asian refugees, drove home the message that a single curriculum cannot hope to cater to a huge and diverse group of learners. Influenced by the work of the Council of Europe (see, for example, Holec 1981; Richterich 1972, 1983; Richterich and Chancerel 1978), the AMEP embraced a needs-based philosophy in which a centralised model was abandoned and in which curriculum activity was encouraged at the local level. However, it is worth noting that although the funding authority (the Federal Department of Immigration and Ethnic Affairs) was happy to promote a reformulation at the level of pedagogy, it retained a centralised approach to program management and administration.

In order to facilitate and assist school-based curriculum development, a teaching and research unit, the National Curriculum Resource Centre (NCRC), was established in 1984. Philosophically, the Centre was committed to localised curriculum development and focussed its energies on establishing processes and structures to support local initiatives.

As a federally funded program, the AMEP was subject in 1985–86 to a ministerial committee of review. The committee noted the difficulties teachers were having in implementing the school-based curriculum and recommended the establishment of a curriculum 'task force' consisting of three curriculum experts. This group's brief would be to develop a curriculum model and produce a set of guidelines for its successful implementation (Campbell 1986). The danger of such an initiative was that it could lead to a return to a centralised approach to curriculum design.

As the body responsible for curriculum issues, the NCRC was asked to manage the task force, in accordance with Campbell's (1986) recommendation. However, it wanted to do so without returning to a centralised curriculum model. In order to determine what the teachers thought, a detailed ethnographic study of the AMEP professional workforce was undertaken (see Nunan 1987 for a detailed account of this study, its methodology and results). Over half of the 1,500 teachers in the AMEP were surveyed and interviewed.

The most striking result of the study was the affirmation by teachers of the localised approach to curriculum development. However, almost all teachers called for greater support. From several hundred oral and written submissions, eighteen principal problem areas emerged. These are listed in rank order in Table 1.

The study revealed that problems with the chosen curriculum model could not be seen solely in pedagogic terms but that they had administrative, managerial, and organisational roots. In many centres in which the virtues of localised curriculum development were acknowledged by classroom practitioners, program administrators continued to behave as though they still belonged to a centralised system. In one centre, for

232

TABLE 1. REASONS FOR LACK OF CURRICULUM CONTINUITY

Rank	Item
1	Lack of curriculum guidelines or models
2	The philosophy and nature of the Program
3	Lack of skills or experience on the part of the teachers
4	Lack of time for consultation and communication
5	Lack of information about students' previous courses
7	Lack of appropriate administrative support
7	Problems caused by students (e.g. irregular attendance)
7	Heterogeneous groups and diverse learner types
9	Courses too short
10	Lack of support resources
11	Rapid changes in TESOL theory and practice
12	Lack of appropriate teaching materials
13	Lack of appropriate assessment procedures
14	Lack of information for learners about courses
15.5	Lack of funding
15.5	High teacher turnover
17	Lack of information and induction for new teachers
18	Class sizes too large

example, teachers were prevented from organising flexible learner groupings that were responsive to learner needs because the administration would not provide the required number of roll books and learner logs.

From the study, it was clear that the great majority of teachers endorsed a bottom-up, school-based approach to curriculum renewal despite the fact that it made their job more complex and difficult. A minority of teachers felt that curriculum issues should not be their responsibility and said they would be happy to implement a curriculum produced by outside experts. Whether they would be satisfied, in the event of such a curriculum being produced, is a matter for conjecture.

All teachers wanted greater support as they planned, implemented, and evaluated their programs. The major issue was how this support might be provided. In the short term, many centres established professional support networks and 'program band' meetings (meetings between teachers working with similar learner types). Although these networks and meetings provided teachers with collegial support (Shaw and Dowsett 1986), this support was not sufficient for most classroom practitioners.

In the end, the solution that emerged in lieu of the curriculum task force was the establishment of a network of teacher-based curriculum projects under the rubric of the AMEP National Curriculum Project (NCP). The establishment of this project is described below.

The National Curriculum Project

The NCP was given a limited lifespan (eighteen months) and a limited budget (an amount equivalent to what would have been required to employ three task force consultants for eighteen months, had the original Campbell (1986) recommendations been carried out according to the letter of the law). The project coordinators developed a four-stage strategy for implementing the NCP.

Stage 1: School-based curriculum documentation

It was decided to use most of the available funds to underwrite projects in which teachers documented curriculum planning, implementation, and evaluation activities and carried out a number of classroom research projects. Teachers were required to bid for funds by submitting a curriculum-funding proposal. In formulating their proposals, teachers were assisted by local curriculum advisers and support staff. The following information was required on curriculum funding proposals.

1. Curriculum process to be documented
2. Location
3. Starting and terminating date
4. Total and distribution of teaching hours
5. Teaching plans
6. Student profile
7. Learning objectives
8. Rationale for documenting this curriculum process
9. Description of documentation to be provided
10. Other relevant information

Teachers were funded for 10 per cent of total teaching time of the learning arrangement. Thus, a bid to document a 300-hour course would, if successful, attract 30 hours of funding.

Exactly 100 proposals for funding were submitted by individual teachers and small teacher teams. Figure 1 and Table 2 show the range and diversity of proposals. The former provides a breakdown of all proposals according to their principal curriculum focus, and the latter provides a more detailed illustration of the actual proposals received from one state.

The submissions received (Figure 1 and Table 2) provide insights into those curriculum areas and issues that were preoccupying teachers, as

---

**Curriculum Documentation Proposals From
Adult Migrant Education Services (Victoria)**

---

1. Distance-learning materials for Spanish speakers
2. Use of computerised information for class placement
3. Development of learning objectives from proficiency-rating scales
4. Provision of collegial support for teachers with similar learner types
5. Use of withdrawal support classes for learners with special needs
6. Development of access skills (job/study skills for disadvantaged migrant / refugee young adults)
7. Documentation of the work of bilingual support, bridging course, computer-assisted learning and learning objectives working parties
8. Use of (Spanish) L1 in the language program
9. Interviewing procedures for diagnosis and placement
10. The curriculum/administrative interface
11. Provision of in-service curriculum support
12. Development of independent learning strategies
13. How to deal with mixed-proficiency groups
14. Strategies for teachers to influence the organisation and management of a learning centre
15. Counselling and student referral
16. Refugee youth program
17. The interface between language centres and centres for technical and further education
18. Strategies for encouraging the development of oral interaction skills in older adolescent students with interrupted schooling
19. Diagnosis and placement of students in special literacy classes
20. Bilingual strategies for developing advanced writing skills
21. A model for ongoing course evaluation
22. Exercises for developing morphosyntax
23. Negotiation of the curriculum with unemployed migrants
24. Use of bilingual assistance in the language class
25. Development of strategies for low-level literacy programs

Figure 1

TABLE 2. TOTAL NUMBER OF SUBMISSIONS CATEGORISED ACCORDING
TO PRINCIPAL CURRICULUM FOCUS

Curriculum focus	No. of submissions
Activities/task types	18
Independent learning strategies	16
Learning arrangement case studies	16
Formative evaluation	7
Learning arrangement materials	6
Objective setting	6
Prelearning arrangement needs analysis	5
Morphosyntactic sequencing	5
Teaching sequences	4
Summative evaluation	4
Teacher/learner needs analysis	3
Learning activity course outline/design	3
Use of the learner's first language	2
Team teaching	2
Self-access centre case study	1
Administrative/curriculum interface	1
Professional development	1

well as those that, by their omissions, were not so highly rated. Not
unexpectedly, the greatest number of submissions related to the development of task and activity types. The work done within the AMEP in
the last few years on learning styles and strategies was also reflected in
the number of proposals received for this area. It is also worth noting the
comparative lack of interest by teachers in summative assessment and
evaluation – areas of intense interest to those funding the AMEP!

The project coordinators had two objectives in mind in providing
small grants to many projects, rather than giving all the available funding to the best of the submissions. The first objective was a process one.
It was believed that the act of systematically working through and
documenting curriculum processes would be a form of curriculum
consciousness-raising for teachers, would help obviate the grass-roots
distrust of the concept of curriculum revealed by the Nunan (1987)
study, and would act as a self-directed learning experience, providing
those involved with practical skills in curriculum renewal. Given the fact
that almost one-third of the national workforce of 1,500 teachers was
directly involved in one project or another, it was believed that this in
itself would assist in alleviating some of the problems associated with
localised curriculum development.

The second objective was product oriented. The NCP was to provide
curriculum resources that could be collated and disseminated back into

the Program for centres to exploit in their curriculum planning, implementation, and evaluation. In other words, the AMEP curriculum was to be derived from representative samples of practice from within the classroom itself.

To provide teachers with a common vocabulary to assist them in documenting their curriculum processes and to facilitate the collation of what would inevitably be a massive amount of data, a set of guidelines was drawn up and distributed to teachers taking part in the NCP. However, it was not mandatory for teachers to submit data along the lines suggested in the guidelines. In several cases the nature of the curriculum processes being documented made it undesirable to follow the format suggested by the guidelines. The guidelines addressed the following areas:

1. Principles of adult learning
2. Goals for learners in the 0–2 proficiency range as determined by the Australian Second Language Proficiency Rating (ASLPR) Scale (Ingram 1984)
3. Objective setting and sample objectives for learners in the ASLPR Scale range 0–2
4. Sample activity types for learners in the ASLPR Scale range 0–2
5. Selection of experiential content
6. Sequencing of learning tasks
7. Development of learning strategies and skills
8. Learner assessment and program evaluation
9. A practical framework for learner-centred curriculum development
10. Use of second language acquisition research to grade morphosyntax

Stage 2: Data analysis

The second stage of the NCP was to analyse and categorise the enormous amount of data resulting from stage 1. Two experienced teachers were released from their regularly assigned positions to temporary duty with the NCRC to sort and categorise the data and, in consultation with the project coordinators, to create a data base that would allow for the ready retrieval of data. The data base was created on a Macintosh computer using Filemaker Plus, a powerful, flexible, and easy-to-use software package that allows large amounts of text to be stored in a number of specially-created information categories.

The project teachers created nineteen categories as follows:

1. Project code number
2. Location of project
3. Title of project given by teacher/team responsible for the project

    4. Project authors
    5. Class type (13 class types were identified, and each project was assigned to one or more of these)
    6. Proficiency range as measured by the ASLPR Scale (Ingram 1984)
    7. Age range
    8. Pace (whether the project targeted slow-, medium-, or fast-track learners)
    9. Ethnicity (principal ethnicity of learners)
    10. Length of residence in an English-speaking country
    11. Educational background
    12. Sex mix
    13. Occupations
    14. Learning arrangement (e.g. community class, individualised learning, small-group approach, team teaching)
    15. Duration of course
    16. Intensity (e.g. whether full/part-time, number of hours per week)
    17. Whether the project was tested or was a plan or proposal
    18. Evaluation (each project was given an evaluative rating as to its potential utility as a curriculum planning tool)
    19. Content (what the documentation actually provided in terms of needs analysis, student profiles, course outline, description of methodology, description of learning styles, lesson plans, materials/references, diary of activities, assessment, evaluation)

Table 3, which presents one of the data-base records, illustrates the coding of information.

Individuals can gain access to relevant records by specifying a need relating to one or more of the information categories. For example, information on the project listed in Table 3 would be called up by a request for data on part-time courses for factory workers, by a request for data on courses with a social/communication orientation for intermediate proficiency, mixed-ethnicity groups, and so on.

In addition to the curriculum documentation data that were fed directly into the data base, a number of projects yielded valuable and interesting data that did not fit the data base. A brief description of one such project will demonstrate the value of collaborative, classroom research between teachers, researchers, and curriculum specialists.

In this particular project, the teacher concerned had become interested in the second language acquisition research on speech processing and learnability, particularly the testable hypotheses yielded by the research of Pienemann and Johnston (see, for example, Johnston 1985; Pienemann 1985; Pienemann and Johnston 1987). In setting up the project, she was assisted by a curriculum adviser with expertise in second language acquisition research and research methods.

TABLE 3. SAMPLE RECORD FROM DATA BASE

Information category	Data
1. Code	SAPA
2. Location	[Deleted]
3. Title	Part-time, ongoing course
4. Authors	[Name deleted]
5. Class type	General, social/communicative interaction for learners in the ASLPR Scale 1− to 1+ range
6. Proficiency	ASLPR Scale 1− to 1+
7. Age range	20–50
8. Pace	Medium
9. Ethnicity	Mixed
10. Length of residence	6 months–7 years
11. Education	Mixed: 3–14 years formal education
12. Sex mix	21 male, 11 female
13. Occupations	16 factory workers, 6 unemployed, 10 not in workforce
14. Learning arrangements	Classroom, one teacher
15. Duration	9 weeks
16. Intensity	Part-time, 4 hours/week
17. Tested	Yes
18. Evaluation	Likely to be of intermediate utility
19. Content	Course outline, lesson plans, materials/references, activity evaluation, course assessment

The aims of the project were: (1) to test the predictions made by the Pienemann–Johnston model for one syntactic area (question formation), noting any variability across task types; (2) to document the practical ramifications for teaching methodology, syllabus, and materials development of attempting to take learnability into account in day-to-day teaching; and (3) to document a range of activity types and teaching materials that could be used in a course centred around asking questions and to identify any notable gaps.

Using semi-structured elicitation procedures, the teacher collected speech data from a sample of learners before the course and assigned them to a developmental stage according to the syntactic assessment procedure developed by Pienemann and Johnston (1987). Classroom instruction was then focussed on those question forms that the learnability hypothesis predicted would be learnable according to learners' development stages. Speech data were collected from learner performance on classroom tasks and post-course data were then collected using pre-course procedures for selecting and sequencing course content and learning tasks. These were analysed and checked against the predictions of the learnability hypothesis.

239

Although space does not permit a detailed analysis and critique of this particular project, this brief description does illustrate one way in which a collaborative approach between classroom practitioner and curriculum adviser can yield classroom data that, potentially at least, can be utilised in subsequent curriculum development.

Stage 3: Creation of curriculum frameworks

During stage 3, a number of senior teachers from within the AMEP were temporarily released to the NCRC to write curriculum frameworks derived from the data yielded during stages 1 and 2.

They carried out this work under the guidance of a steering group that consisted of the project coordinators and three outside curriculum consultants. Eleven frameworks, written for a range of class/learner types (see Table 4), were written and tested. (Sample extracts from one of the frameworks can be found in the Appendix on pages 245–53.)

TABLE 4. CLASS/LEARNER TYPES FOR WHICH CURRICULUM FRAMEWORKS WERE WRITTEN

ASLPR Scale proficiency level	*Class/learner type*
0 to 1−	Indo-Chinese; cultural focus
0 to 1−	Slow; elderly; reading/writing focus
0 to 1−	Young; fast-track; survival
1− to 1+	Young; fast-track; educational focus
1− to 1+	General; social/communicative interaction
1 to 2	Job-seeking; work experience focus
1+	Social interaction focus
1+	Media focus
1+ to 2	Education/study skills focus
1+ to 2	Long-term residents (stabilised learners); reading/writing focus
1+ to 2	Linked skills (bridging)[1]
1+ to 2	Particular; professional skills focus
0 to 2	Mixed ability

The frameworks were written in such a way as to enable teachers working, either individually or in small groups, to systematise the planning, monitoring, and evaluation of their programs. They are thus intended as teacher development tools as much as curriculum planning tools. This reflects the notion that in school-based curriculum systems, curriculum development becomes largely a matter of teacher development. The following principles underlie the frameworks:

1. The teacher has a key role to play in curriculum development, particularly in systems such as the AMEP, in which courses are meant to be responsive to learner needs.
2. Curriculum guidelines and frameworks should be flexible enough to allow teachers to work from a variety of different starting points in planning courses. Frameworks are devised so that teachers can start with resources (materials, coursebooks, etc.), learning tasks, communicative skills, or lists of learning outcomes. They are intended to facilitate planning for courses with either grammatical, functional, or notional focuses.
3. Existence of a framework does not imply that courses derived from it will be identical. It is recognised that each course is unique, being shaped by interaction and negotiation between learners and teacher.

Although frameworks differ somewhat from one another, each contains the following information and resources:

1. An introduction and statement of underlying principles
2. A description of how the framework might be used
3. A description of the learner type for whom the framework is written
4. A statement of appropriate goals for the target group
5. A set of principles underlying the framework
6. Models and examples of alternative methods of program planning
7. Sets of syllabus-planning checklists (these include topics, tasks, objectives, functions, notions, morphosyntax, vocabulary, settings, learning styles, and strategies appropriate for the designated group)
8. Sample teaching units
9. Assessment and evaluation resources

Stage 4: Evaluating the project

Ultimately the value of the NCP will be determined by the extent to which it makes a difference to curriculum development at the school level. This is one of the central questions to be answered by the formal evaluation of the Project.

At the outset of the NCP, an evaluator was appointed who, though outside the AMEP, had undertaken curriculum research within the Program and was therefore familiar with its history, politics, and aspirations. In keeping with the essentially collaborative flavour of the NCP, it was decided that a process- rather than a product-oriented approach should be taken toward the evaluation. To this end, the evaluator was provided with access to all the documentation relevant to the Project, including the transcripts of meetings – between one of the project coordinators and teachers and administrators – that gave shape to the NCP (described in Nunan 1987). He was also invited to attend as participant observer at project management and consultation meetings. As a result, the evaluator was able to provide information and insights that were used formatively during the course of the NCP itself (for example, he was influential in encouraging a more process-oriented approach to the curriculum frameworks). A final, summative evaluation was undertaken in spring 1990, by which time the frameworks had been comprehensively tested and introduced into the Program. In 1991, a Teachers' Guide, based partly on data from the evaluation, was produced to assist teachers in using the frameworks.

In a project of this sort, it would be desirable to undertake a product-oriented evaluation, that is, to conduct pre- and post-project assessments to determine the efficacy of the intervention in terms of learning outcomes. In the current situation, however, this has not been possible because the NCRC has no mandate to assess students, this being the sole responsibility of the state and territory education departments that are actually responsible for program delivery.

Discussion

Numerous problems and difficulties arose in initiating and implementing the NCP. In the beginning, there was resistance from the funding authority, which wanted a return to a centre–periphery curriculum model. There was also a certain amount of resistance and suspicion from some state program managers and administrators (although, it must be said, that there was also a great deal of support). In addition, many teachers mistrusted the intentions of the project coordinators.

Once initial submissions were received, another major problem emerged: many of the most experienced and talented teachers within the Program had not bothered to apply for funding. Presumably this was because these teachers had few problems in developing their own curriculum and saw little point in providing assistance to teachers who were having problems.

During stage 2, the data analysis stage, it became apparent that the data were uneven in terms of quality. Some of the projects resulted in high-quality information that could be fed directly into the curriculum frameworks, whereas others provided very little usable data at all. During stage 3, it was therefore necessary to censor, cull, and reformulate a great deal of data.

With the wisdom of hindsight, it is possible to identify ways in which a project such as the NCP could be carried out differently next time around. In particular, the democratic impulse to involve as many teachers as possible would probably be tempered by the need to obtain the cooperation of those teachers who have the most experience and skill in curriculum development.

Greater care would also be taken in identifying learner groups and class types, although decisions made on educational grounds can be preempted by political and demographic factors. In the case of the NCP, changing patterns of immigration and government policy have, since the initiation of the Project, changed the profile of AMEP clients and made largely redundant several of the curriculum frameworks.

Given the instability of learner types, it becomes extremely important for a learner-centred, school-based curriculum model to be reinforced at the local level with key teachers who have the skills and knowledge necessary to help their peers to plan, implement, and evaluate a range of programs that can be readily adapted to changing client groups. It would certainly be educationally indefensible to return to a more centralised approach.

Conclusion

The localised, school-based approach to the language curriculum outlined in this article attempts to model the curriculum on instances of successful practice and is therefore tied closely to the classroom. Such curriculum development requires a collaborative approach between the different stakeholders in the educational enterprise, including teachers, researchers, curriculum specialists, and program managers and administrators.

The AMEP National Curriculum Project, an ambitious attempt at curriculum renewal involving many teachers, administrators, and curriculum personnel, is an example of such an approach. This Project bears similarities to a number of other attempts at school-based curriculum renewal, most particularly and recently to the Graded Levels of Achievement in Foreign Language Learning in Britain and the Australian Language Levels Project (both of which are described in some detail in Clark 1987). The following characterisation aptly summarises the essential spirit of localised curriculum development:

> The two most important factors in school-focused curriculum renewal are the quality of relationships between participants and the sharing of responsibility. Education is about people, whether it be teacher education or pupil education, and the most valuable contribution that a project leader can make is to ensure that the diverse strengths, energies and personalities of those involved are harnessed and forged together harmoniously. For this to occur, a democratic framework of shared responsibilities is essential, rather

David Nunan

> than a simple hierarchical structure. The sort of accountability that
> seems to work best in curriculum renewal is not managerial . . .
> but rather one of mutual responsibility.
>
> (Clark 1987: 136)

Endnotes

[1] = courses in which language and content from other subject areas (usually technical, such as electrical trades) are taught in an integrated fashion.

Appendix

Teaching approach

This framework is based on the following principles:

☐ The goals and objectives of the course should be determined on the basis of the learners' needs and should be apparent to both teachers and learners. Learning tasks should be linked to objectives, i.e. the relationship between what learners do in class, and what they should be able to do after instruction should be clear.

☐ Authentic samples of language will be presented as far as possible. Task complexity rather than linguistic complexity will be adjusted to the level of the learner.

☐ Learners will be encouraged to develop an awareness of how language learning takes places and how they can be involved in achieving their language learning objectives.

☐ There will be a focus on the development of learning skills and skills in learning-how-to-learn. As adults, learners should be encouraged to develop independent learning skills.

☐ Learners will be encouraged to practise their developing language skills in the real world outside the classroom.

☐ Learners will be encouraged to be involved in assessing their language ability in relation to learning objectives.

☐ As learning is an organic rather than a linear process, tasks and language items will be recycled and represented. It is not assumed that learners will master a particular linguistic element or aspect of language after a single exposure.

☐ Learners learn at different rates and in different ways. As far as possible, these differences should be accommodated.

☐ Learners learn best in a caring, supportive environment.

☐ While tasks will generally focus learners on comprehending, producing and interacting in meaningful contexts, learners will also be given the opportunity of focusing on English as a linguistic system. Here, we are thinking of a process-rather than a product-oriented view of language. This view has been described as follows: *Given all that we presently know about language, how it is learned, and how it can be taught, the 'grammatical' part of a 'grammatical syllabus' . . . specifies how . . . language content . . . is to be exploited . . . Language acquisition is not a linear progression, but a cyclic one, or even a metamorphic one. That is, the learner is constantly engaged in reanalysing data, reformulating hypotheses, recasting generalisations etc.* (Rutherford 1987: 159)

> **Are these principles appropriate for your learners?**
>
> **Using the above list as a guide, write your own set of principles.**
>
> **How might you inform your students of these principles?**

David Nunan

Using the framework

It is hoped that, wherever possible, this framework can be used by *teachers working collaboratively*. This may mean, for example, co-planning arrangements, team teaching or Program Band groups. Individual teachers may also use the framework, but it would be useful to have support networks or curriculum personnel to tap into.

The framework is a starting point to help you decide what to teach and when. Aspects of the curriculum process are necessarily represented throughout the document in a linear sequence. This is not really what happens in practice. In practice, the process might look something like this.

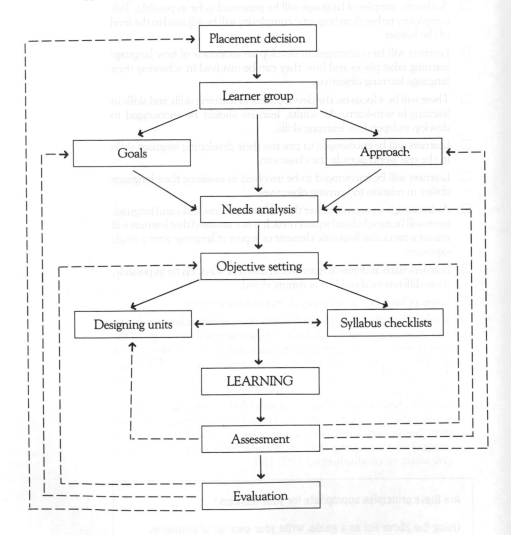

Action plan — one way of using the framework

☐ Look at the diagram on page 4.
Look quickly through the framework to get a rough idea of its contents and organisation. From your first impression, does this seem to be a reasonable sequence of steps for considering the curriculum process?

☐ You will probably have come into the curriculum process after placement decisions have been made. If so, read the section on **Grouping Learners** (p.7) and list the characteristics of your learners.

☐ Read the section on **Goals** (p.9) and work out goals for your group of learners.

☐ Read the **Teaching Approach** (p.3) and consider your own approach. Discuss new ideas with your colleagues.

☐ Read **Specifying Objectives** (p.10) and choose an appropriate means for getting input from your learners.

☐ Read **An Approach to Listing Objectives** (p.15) and draw up a list of possible objectives for your first units of work, based on the results of your needs analysis.

☐ Syllabus Planning: Read **Designing Units of Work** (p.17). Choose an approach that makes sense to you and decide on a method of recording your planning decisions. Plan your first unit or couple of units. As you proceed through your course, you can adjust your method of planning and recording.

☐ Syllabus Checklists: These can be used as a resource or as a means of recording. Each checklist includes things which are seen as potentially teachable to students in the identified range. The checklists are open sets; you should add and amend items as you feel the need, and the loose leaf format of the framework has been designed to facilitate this.

☐ Although presented as a last step in the process, Assessment and Evaluation go on throughout the whole course and affect everything. Read this section (p.40) and decide how you will incorporate them into your course and when it would be appropriate.

David Nunan

Instrument for Needs Analysis: Survey for class use in English

Name:..

What do you want to study?

1. **What is most important for you to study in this course?**
   (Number these from 1 - 4)

   _____ Listening   _____ Speaking

   _____ Reading   _____ Writing

2. **Do you have any problems speaking English**

   — with neighbours and friends .... YES / NO

   — at your children's school .... YES / NO

   — in shops .... YES / NO

   — in banks .... YES / NO

   — in the Post Office .... YES / NO

   — at work .... YES / NO

   — in offices (e.g. Social Security) .... YES / NO

   — when you are buying bus or train tickets .... YES / NO

   — in hospitals or with the doctor or dentist .... YES / NO

   — on the telephone .... YES / NO

   — in other places .... YES / NO

   (Where? ....)

3. **Would you like to understand people better**

   — on the TV .... YES / NO

   — on the radio .... YES / NO

4. **When do you need to speak English? (Who to?)**

   ....
   ....
   ....

5. **Are you happy with your reading and writing?** ....

6. **What would you like to be able to do at the end of this course that you can't do now?**

   ....
   ....

248

Goals

The next step in the process is to develop course goals from the learner goals stated in the learner profiles. The term 'goals' is generally used within the AMEP to refer to the broad, general purposes for which the language is being learned.

Primary goal

From the information set out above, we can see that all of these learners have the same broad purpose which can probably be described as 'general, communicative interaction'.

The primary goal for such a group would be:
☐ to communicate socially and transactionally in English

This can be elaborated as follows:
☐ to begin to develop and maintain interpersonal relationships through the exchange of social pleasantries, the sharing of ideas, opinions, feelings etc. in English;

☐ to use English for obtaining foods, services and information;

☐ to use newspapers, radio and television to obtain the information and for exposure to samples of authenic Australian language;

☐ to understand the social and cultural nature of living and working in Australia, and to use relevant public and private facilities.

Secondary Goals

In addition, we would probably want to give learners an insight into the nature of English and the way it works, to encourage them to practice their English out of class and to develop skills in learning how to learn. Our goals would also therefore include:
☐ to develop a systematic understanding of the English language;

☐ to practise English outside the classroom;

☐ to develop learning skills in order to continue learning outside the AMEP.

Are these goals appropriate for the learners you will be teaching?

Using the above list as a guide, drawn up your own set of goals.

Think of ways in which you can inform the students of these goals.

J

Select a Topic, a real world task, a structure or whatever you have chosen as your starting point (see pp.29-31)

Specify Objectives (see pages 29-31)
For each objective, *consider the situations* where this competence would be useful to the learners. If you have difficulty thinking of more than one situation, you might question the priority of this objective in the course.

Consider the language elements involved in achieving each objective, in terms of functions, structures or whatever you like to use (see checklists).
If we consider the nature of the communication which takes place within the situations listed, we will become aware of the language our learners need to develop.

Consider the skills and strategies involved in achieving each objective in real world situations.

↓

Select/Create Activities & Resources (for each objective) using Input Data (p.37)
If we consider the skills and strategies required in these situations in the real world, we can present activities in class which help our learners to go through the same mental processes. It is not necessary to re-create the real world situation in the classroom (as in a role play), but rather, to devise activities which require the same skills and the same language: in this way, we can simulate the type of interaction which occurs in the real world.
We may, at times, choose to use other macroskills as a means to that end (e.g. Reading could be used as a tool for achieving a spoken objective as it allows time to reflect on and internalise language).
Make sure you include activities aimed at developing learning strategies (see p.34)

Consider the Unit
a) in terms of its internal integrity — are there any gaps?
☐ Develop any related extensions (e.g. further work on a structure, vocabulary expansion, pronunciation, etc.)
☐ Link objectives within the Unit by recycling language, materials, etc.)

b) as a part of the overall course
☐ Link this Unit with others (preceding and following) by selecting language, materials, activities, etc for recycling.
☐ Make a note of these points as personal reminders for planning future Units

Is this a procedure you would use?

How would yours differ?

UNIT: Unit One — Socialising

Objective(s)	Language elements	Skills/Strategies	Activities & Resources	Comments
Learners will be able to ask for and provide basic personal information in social situations. SITUATIONS: ● meeting friends of family ● meeting family of friends ● getting to know neighbours ● getting to know people in interest groups (eg. church, children's school, etc)	Asking for personal information. **Giving personal information** I.D. QUESTIONS: – simple present – formulaic 'Wh' questions (including, 'Where do you come from?/live?', 'How long have you been in Aust.?', 'What's your occupation?', etc.) RESPONSES TO I.D. QUESTIONS – short answers – longer answers using formula & simple present	LISTENING Predicting . . . Listening for the gist . . . Listening for information . . . (and providing info) (Intensive) Listening for . . . speech models SPEAKING Pronunciation . . . Oral practice – accuracy . . . Oral practice – fluency . . .	AUSTRALIAN MODELS IN . . . LIFELINES-DIALOGUE UNIT 2 – provide suitable language for filmstrip (without having heard soundtrack) – retelling the basic story around the class – Information-gap activity (Lifelines General Listening U.1/2 – Listening grid) – 'Blankety Blanks' (competitive cloze of dialogue-oral) §# 1 – stress & intonation work on questions & responses 'Jazz Chants' Personal Q.s – matching Question & Answer cards – class surveys §# 2 – small group Q & A sessions, swapping personal info for teams competition. (Record each group for input data for 'accuracy' activities later)	– This recycles 'Using appropriate greetings' & 'Introducing a 3rd person') – other listening activities which develop this strategy (eg. sequencing pictures to follow aural story) – other listening activities which develop this strategy (eg. Starting to Listen, U.3 & 12) – vocab extension (other occupations & nationalities) – Other activities in which learners have to recognise questions (by structure, key words & intonation) in samples of authentic speech – §# 1 – *Extension:* reading and writing (form-filling acts. **Recycle in Medicare forms, Joining the Library, Opening a bank account etc. **Recycle in 'Families' talking about a family member § *Learning Strategies:* §# 1 – techniques for memorising §# 2 – recognising patterns in language

A complete pro forma (showing an objective developed into classroom activities)

David Nunan

Functions (A Basic Checklist)

Polite phrases & phatic communion ✔
Attracting attention ☐
Greeting and leave-taking ☐
Talking about health, the weather etc ☐

Personal information
Introducing oneself & others ☐
Asking for and giving personal facts ☐
Talking about likes and dislikes ☐
Talking about one's family ☐
Describing people, places and things ☐
Talking about one's past life ☐
Talking about possessions ☐

Interpersonal communication
Inviting ☐
Accepting and refusing an invitation ☐
Offering ☐
Accepting and refusing an offer ☐
Arranging to meet someone ☐
Making suggestions ☐
Asking for and offering help ☐
Apologising ☐
Asking for and giving reasons ☐
Expressing sympathy ☐
Talking about health and feelings ☐
Talking about present activities ☐
Talking on the telephone ☐
Complaining ☐
Asking for repetition or clarification ☐
Asking for things ☐
Talking about frequency ☐

Information about the outside world
Asking for and telling the time ☐
Asking for goods, services and information ☐
Asking and talking about cost ☐
Asking and talking about location ☐
Asking and talking about facilities ☐
Asking for directions ☐
Following instructions ☐
Comparing things ☐
Describing events ☐

Notions*

Identification	☐	Money and numbers	☐
Questions	☐	Food	☐
Relationships	☐	Quantity	☐
Home	☐	Entertainment	☐
Possession	☐	The Telephone	☐
Space	☐	Health	☐
Location	☐	Ability	☐
Direction	☐	Crime	☐
The Past	☐	The News	☐
Comparison	☐	Work	☐

* For an approach to teaching according to Notions, see Leo Jones' 'Notions in English' CUP

Grammar: add to the examples we have provided

		✔
Adjectives		
Predicative	asleep, alive, well	☐
Attributive	young, tall, blue, modern, nice, terrible	☐
Possessive	my, your, his, here, our, their	☐
Adverbs		
Frequency	always, sometimes, never	☐
Place	here, there	☐
Time	tonight, tomorrow, yesterday, last week	☐
Intensifiers	very, too, enough	☐
Articles	indefinite, definite	☐
'Be'	am, is, are, was, were, will be	☐
Existential	it, there	☐
Modals	can (ability and permission)	☐
	will (polite request), must	☐
Comparisons	adjectives . . . er and more . . . than	☐
Superlatives	adjectives . . . est and the most . . .	☐
Conjunctions	and, but, or	☐
Nouns	count, mass, plurals, possessives	☐
Numbers	cardinal, ordinal	☐
Prepositions	for, to, with, from, by	☐
Place	in, on, under, at, on top of, next to, beside, between, in front of, behind, opposite	☐
Time	at, by, from . . . to, on, in	☐
Pronouns		
Demonstrative	this, that, these, those	☐
Subject	I, you, he, she, it, we, they	☐
Object	me, you, him, her, it, us, them	☐
Possessive	mine, yours, his, hers, ours, theirs	☐
Questions		
Marked by intonation	He's coming at **five**?	☐
Yes/No questions	Do/Does? Did . . .? Are/Is . . .? Have/Has . . .?	☐
Wh questions	who, what, where, when, how much, how many, how long, how old, how do you spell, which, whose, why	☐
Tenses		
Simple present	used with feelings, descriptions, likes, habits, customs	☐
Present continuous	asking for/giving an explanation about a situation (What's happening? What are you doing?)	☐
Simple past	both irregular & regular	☐
Simple future	will	☐
Future of intention	going to	☐
'Have'	have, has (plus 'got' with attributes, possessions and illnesses), had, will have	☐

Sample extracts from D. Nunan (ed.), *New Arrivals: Initial–Elementary Proficiency. A Curriculum Framework for Adult Second Language Learners.* 1989. Sydney: National Centre for English Language Teaching and Research.

References

Allwright, D., and K. M. Bailey. 1991. *Focus on the Language Classroom: An Introduction to Classroom Research for Language Teachers.* Cambridge: Cambridge University Press.

Applebee, A. N. 1987. Teachers and the process of research. *Research in the Teaching of English 21:* 5–7.

Applebee, A. N., and J. A. Langer. 1983. Instructional scaffolding: reading and writing as natural language activities. *Language in Arts 60*(2): 168–75.

Armstrong, D. 1977. Team teaching and academic achievement. *Review of Educational Research 47*(1): 65–86.

Asher, J. 1982. *Learning Another Language through Actions: the Complete Teacher's Guidebook.* 2nd ed. Los Gatos, Ca.: Sky Oaks Productions.

Atwell, N. M. 1982. Class-based writing research: teachers learn from students. *English Journal 71:* 84–7.

1987. *In the Middle: Writing, Reading and Learning with Adolescents.* Montclair, N. J.: Boynton/Cook.

Bailey, K. M. 1990. The use of diary studies in teacher education programs. In J. C. Richards and D. Nunan (eds.), *Second Language Teacher Education.* New York: Cambridge University Press.

Bassano, S., and M. A. Christison. 1988. Cooperative learning in the ESL classroom. *TESOL Newsletter 22*(2).

Bateson, M. C. 1984. *With a Daughter's Eye.* New York: William Morrow.

Bazerman, C. 1980. A relationship between reading and writing: the conversational model. *College English 41:* 656–61.

Beasley, B., and L. Riordan. 1981. The classroom teacher as researcher. *English in Australia 55.*

Bedley, G. 1985. *The Big R: Responsibility. Encouraging and Cultivating Responsible Behavior.* Irvine, California: People-Wise Publications.

Beebe, L. M. 1983. Risk-taking and the language learner. In H. Seliger and M. Long (eds.), *Classroom-oriented Research in Second Language Acquisition.* Rowley, Mass.: Newbury House.

Beggs, D. (ed.). 1964. *Team Teaching: Bold New Venture.* Bloomington: Indiana University Press.

Bejarano, Y. 1987. A cooperative small-group methodology in the language classroom. *TESOL Quarterly 21*(3).

Berthoff, A. 1987. The teacher as researcher. In D. Goswami and P. R. Stilman (eds.), *Reclaiming the Classroom: Teacher Research as an Agency for Change.* Portsmouth, N.H.: Boynton/Cook.

Bissex, G. L., and R. H. Bullock. 1987. *Seeing for Ourselves: Case-study Research by Teachers of Writing.* Portsmouth, N.H.: Heinemann.

References

Bogdan, R., and S. Biklen. 1982. *Qualitative Research for Education: An Introduction to Theory and Methods*. Boston: Allyn and Bacon Inc.

Bourdieu, P. 1977. The economics of linguistic exchanges. *Social Sciences Information* 16(6): 645–68.

Brandes, D., and P. Ginnis. 1986. *A Guide to Student-centred Learning*. Oxford: Basil Blackwell.

Brandt, R. 1987. On cooperation in schools: a conversation with David and Roger Johnson. *Educational Leadership 45*: 3, 14–19.

(ed.), 1989. Coaching and staff development. Readings from *Educational Leadership*. Alexandria, Va.: Association for Supervision and Curriculum Development.

Breen, M. P. 1985. The social context of language learning: a neglected situation? *Studies in Second Language Acquisition 7* (2): 135–58.

1987. Contemporary paradigms in syllabus design. *Language Teaching 20*: 2, 3.

Brown, G. 1989. Making sense: the interaction of linguistic expression and contextual information. *Applied Linguistics 10*: 1, 97–108.

Brown, P., and J. Slutzky. 1986. Communication: the missing link in the delivery of technical education. *Teaching English to Deaf and Second Language Learners 4*: 25–8.

Bruffee, K. 1984. Collaborative learning and the 'Conversation of mankind'. *College English* 46(7): 635–52.

Bruner, J. 1983a. *In Search of Mind: Essays in Autobiography*. New York: Harper & Row.

1983b. *Child's Talk*. New York: W. W. Norton & Co.

Burke, K. 1935. *Permanence and Change*. New York: New Republic Press.

Burton, F. R. 1988. Reflections on Strickland's 'Toward the Extended Professional', *Language Arts*, Dec. 1988: 765–8.

Campbell, J. 1986. *Towards Active Voice: Report of the Committee of Review of the Adult Migrant Education Program*. Canberra: Department of Immigration and Ethnic Affairs.

Carr, W., and S. Kemmis. 1986. *Becoming Critical: Knowing through Action Research*. Victoria, Australia: Deakin University Press.

Carrell, P. 1988. SLA and classroom instruction: reading. *Annual Review of Applied Linguistics 9*: 223–42.

Carter, K., and W. Doyle. 1987. Teachers' knowledge structures and comprehension processes. In J. Calderhead (ed.), *Exploring Teachers' Thinking*. London: Cassell Publications.

Cazden, C. 1988. *Classroom Discourse: the Language of Learning and Teaching*. Portsmouth, N.H.: Heinemann.

Cazden, C., J. Diamondstone and P. Naso. 1988. Relationship between teacher research and researcher research on writing instruction. Paper presented to American Educational Research Association, New Orleans.

Chamot, A. 1987. The learning strategies of ESL students. In A. Wenden and J. Rubin (eds.), *Learner Strategies in Language Learning*. Englewood Cliffs, N.J.: Prentice-Hall.

Chaudron, C. 1988. *Second Language Classrooms: Research on Teaching and Learning*. New York: Cambridge University Press.

Childs, C., and P. Greenfield. 1982. Informal modes of learning and teaching: the case of Zinacenteco weaving. In N. Warren (ed.), *Advances in Cross-Cultural Psychology*, vol. II. London: Academic Press.

Clark, J. L. 1987. *Curriculum Renewal in School Foreign Language Learning*. Oxford: Oxford University Press.

Clark, J. L., and J. Hamilton. 1984. *Syllabus Guidelines: Parts 1, 2 and 3: A Graded Communicative Approach Towards School Foreign Language Learning*. London: Centre for Information on Language Teaching and Research.

Cochran-Smith, M., and S. L. Lytle. 1990. Research on teaching and teacher research: the issues that divide. *Educational Researcher 19*(2): 2–11.

Cohen, E. G. 1986. *Designing Group Work: Strategies for the Heterogeneous Classroom*. New York: Teachers College Press.

Cole, M. 1985. The zone of proximal development: where culture and cognition create each other. In J. Wertsch (ed.), *Culture, Communication and Cognition: Vygotskian Perspectives*. Cambridge: Cambridge University Press.

Cooper, M. 1986. The ecology of writing. *College English 48* (4): 364–75.

Cooper, M., and M. Holzman. 1989. *Writing as Social Action*. Portsmouth, N.H.: Heinemann.

Crookes, G. 1986. *Task Classification: A Cross-disciplinary Review*. University of Hawaii at Manoa: Center for Second Language Classroom Research.

Cunningham, L. L. 1960. Team teaching: where do we stand? *Administrator's Notebook 8*: 1–4.

Curran, C. 1976. *Counselling-Learning in Second Languages*. Apple River, Ill.: Apple River Press.

1978. *Understanding: A Necessary Ingredient in Human Belonging*. Apple River, Ill.: Apple River Press.

Davis, N. 1975. Printing and the people. In *Society and Culture in Early Modern France*. Stanford, Cal.: Stanford University Press.

DeKeyser, R. 1988. Communicative Processes and Strategies. *Annual Review of Applied Linguistics (1988) 9*: 108–21.

Dewey, J. 1938. *Experience and Education*. Collier Books Edition in 1963. New York: Collier Macmillan Publishers.

Dickinson, L. 1987. *Self-instruction in Language Learning*. Cambridge: Cambridge University Press.

Doheny-Farina, S. 1986. Writing in an emerging organization. *Written Communication 3*(2): 158–85.

Doyle, W. 1983. Academic Work. *Review of Educational Research 53*(2): 159–99.

Edge, J. 1989. *Cooperative Development*. English Language Research Paper, University of Birmingham.

Edwards, D., and N. Mercer. 1987. *Common Knowledge*. New York: Methuen.

Elbow, P. 1973. *Writing without Teachers*. New York: Oxford University Press.

Elliott, J. 1981. Foreword. In J. Nixon (ed.), *A Teachers' Guide to Action Research: Evaluation, Enquiry and Development in the Classroom*. London: Grant McIntyre.

References

Ellis, G., and B. Sinclair. 1989. *Learning to Learn English: A Course in Learner Training*. Cambridge: Cambridge University Press.

Erber, N. P. 1988. *Communication Therapy of Hearing Impaired Adults*. Abbotsford: Clavis Publishing.

Færch, C., and G. Kasper. 1983. Plans and strategies in foreign language communication. In C. Færch and G. Kasper (eds.), *Strategies in Interlanguage Communication*. London: Longman.

Færch, C. 1986. Rules of thumb and other teacher-formulated rules in the foreign language classroom. In G. Kasper (ed.), *Learning, Teaching and Communication in the Foreign Language Classroom*. Aarhus: University Press.

Faigley, L. 1985. Nonacademic writing: the social perspective. In L. Odell and D. Goswami (eds.), *Writing in Nonacademic Settings*. New York: Guilford Press.

Fanselow, J. F. 1977. Beyond Rashomon: conceptualizing and observing the teaching act. *TESOL Quarterly 11*(1): 17–41.

1982. 'What kind of flower is that?': a contrasting model for critiquing lessons. In H. Eichheim and A. Maley (eds.), *Papers from Goethe Institute–British Council Seminar on Classroom Observation*. Paris: Goethe Institute.

1987. *Breaking Rules: Generating and Exploring Alternatives in Language Teaching*. White Plains, N.Y.: Longman.

1990. 'Let's see': contrasting conversations about teaching. In J. C. Richards and D. Nunan (eds.), *Second Language Teacher Education*. New York: Cambridge University Press. (Reprinted from *TESOL Quarterly 22*.)

Fattorini, S., and R. Oprandy. 1989. Promoting professional development through teacher investigations and other activities. Paper presented at the 23rd TESOL Convention, San Antonio, Texas.

Fine, M. 1987. Silencing in public schools. *Language Arts 64* (2): 154–74.

Flatley, M. E. 1982. A comparative analysis of the written communication of managers at various organizational levels in the private sector. *Journal of Business Communication 19*(3): 35–40.

Flower, L., and J. Hayes. 1981. A cognitive process theory of writing. *College Composition and Communication 32*(4): 365–87.

Forman, J., and P. Spector. 1980. A multidisciplinary approach to teaching English. *American Annals of the Deaf 125*: 400–5.

Freeman, D. 1982. Observing teachers: three approaches to in-service training and development. *TESOL Quarterly 16*: 21–8.

1989. Teacher training, development and decision making: a model for teaching and related strategies for language teacher education. *TESOL Quarterly 23*(1): 27–45.

1990a. 'Thoughtful work': reconceptualizing the research literature on teacher thinking. Qualifying paper: Graduate School of Education: Harvard University.

1990b. Intervening in practice teaching. In J. C. Richards and D. Nunan (eds.), *Second Language Teacher Education*. New York: Cambridge University Press.

258

1991. 'The same things done differently': a study of the development of four foreign language teachers' conceptions of practice through an in-service teacher education program. Doctoral dissertation: Graduate School of Education, Harvard University.

Freire, P. 1970. *Pedagogy of the Oppressed*. New York: Herder & Herder.

Gass, S., and E. M. Varonis. 1985. Task variation and nonnative/nonnative negotiation of meaning. In S. Gass and C. Madden (eds.), *Input in Second Language Acquisition*. Rowley, Mass.: Newbury House.

Gebhard, J. G. 1990a. Models of supervision: choices. In J. C. Richards and D. Nunan (eds.), *Second Language Teacher Education*. New York: Cambridge University Press.

1990b. Freeing the teacher: a supervisory process. *Foreign Language Annals* 23: 517–25.

1990c. Interaction in a language teaching practicum. In J. Richards and D. Nunan (eds.), *Second Language Teacher Education*. New York: Cambridge University Press.

Gebhard, J. G., S. Gaitan and R. Oprandy. 1990. Beyond prescription: the student-teacher as investigator. In J. C. Richards and D. Nunan (eds.), *Second Language Teacher Education*. New York: Cambridge University Press. (Reprinted from *Foreign Language Annals 20*, 1987.)

Gebhard, J. G., and A. Malicka. 1991. Creative behavior in teacher supervision. *Prospect* 6(3): 40–9.

Glasser, W. 1986. *Control Theory in the Classroom*. New York: Harper & Row.

Goldberg, J. P., and M. B. Bordman. 1974. English language instruction for the Hearing Impaired: an adaptation of ESL methodology. *TESOL Quarterly* 8: 263–70.

Good, T., and J. Brophy. 1987. *Looking in Classrooms*. New York: Harper & Row.

Goody, J. 1977. *The Domestication of the Savage Mind*. Cambridge: Cambridge University Press.

Goswami, D., and P. R. Stillman (eds.). 1987. *Reclaiming the Classroom: Teacher Research as an Agency for Change*. Montclair, N.J.: Boynton/Cook.

1988. Learning from children: teachers do research. *The Harvard Education Letter* 4: 1–5.

Graff, H. 1981. *Literacy and Social Development in the West: A Reader*. Cambridge: Cambridge University Press.

Grimmett, P., and G. Erickson (eds.). 1988. *Reflection in Teacher Education*. New York: Teachers College Press.

Halliday, M. A. K. 1975. *Learning How to Mean*. New York: Elsevier North-Holland Inc.

1985. *An Introduction to Functional Grammar*. London: Edward Arnold.

Halliday, M. A. K., and R. Hasan. 1985. *Language, Context and Text*. Victoria, Australia: Deakin University Press.

Halpern, J. W. 1985. An electronic odyssey. In L. Odell and D. Goswami (eds.), *Writing in Nonacademic Settings*. New York: Guilford Press.

References

Hammersley, M., and P. Atkinson. 1983. *Ethnography: Principles in Practice*. London: Tavistock Press.

Handal, G., and P. Lauvås. 1987. *Promoting Reflective Teaching: Supervision in Action*. Buckingham, England: Open University Press.

Hanslovsky, G., S. Mayer and H. Wagner. 1969. *Why Team Teaching?* Columbus: Charles E. Merrill Publishing Co.

Hanssen, E. (with L. Mangiola). Forthcoming. *Children of Promise: Language-based Learning with Students of Diverse Linguistic and Cultural Backgrounds*. Washington, D.C.: National Education Association, Center for the Study of Writing, and American Educational Research Association.

Harwood, J. T. 1982. Freshman English ten years after: writing in the world. *College Composition and Communication 33*: 281–3.

Heath, S. Brice. 1983. *Ways with Words: Language, Life and Work in Communities and Classrooms*. Cambridge: Cambridge University Press.

Heath, S. Brice (with A. Branscombe). 1985. Intelligent writing in an audience community: teacher, students, and researcher. In S. W. Freedman (ed.), *The Acquisition of Written Language: Revision and Response*. Norwood, N.J.: Ablex Publishing Co.

1986. The book as narrative prop in language acquisition. In B. Schieffelin and P. Gilmore (eds.), *The Acquisition of Literacy: Ethnographic Perspectives*. Norwood, N.J.: Ablex Publishing Co.

Heath, S. Brice, and C. Thomas. 1984. The achievement of preschool literacy for mother and child. In H. Goeman, A. Oberg and F. Smith (eds.), *Awakening to Literacy*. Exeter, N.H.: Heinemann.

Hinofotis, F. B., and K. M. Bailey. 1978. Course development: oral communication for advanced university ESL students. In J. Povey (ed.), *Workpapers in Teaching English as a Second Language*, vol. XII. Los Angeles, University of California (ESL Section).

Holec, H. 1981. *Anatomy and Foreign Language Learning*. Oxford: Pergamon Press.

1987. The learner as manager: managing learning or managing to learn? In A. Wenden and J. Rubin (eds.), *Learner Strategies in Language Learning*. Englewood Cliffs, N.J.: Prentice-Hall.

Hunkins, F. P. 1980. *Curriculum Development: Program Improvement*. Columbus, Ohio: Charles E. Merrill Publishing Co.

Ingram. D. 1984. *The Australian Second Language Proficiency Rating Scale*. Canberra: Department of Immigration and Ethnic Affairs.

Johns, A. M. 1985. Some principles of materials design from the world around us. *TESOL Newsletter 19*: 1–2.

Johnson, D. W., *et al.* 1988. *Cooperation in the Classroom*. Edina, Mn.: Interaction Book Company.

1990. *Circles of Learning. Cooperation in the Classroom*. 3rd ed. Edina, Mn.: Interaction Book Company.

Johnson, D. W., and R. T. Johnson. 1987. *Learning Together and Alone*. Englewood Cliffs, N.J.: Prentice-Hall.

1989. *Cooperation and Competition. Theory and Research*. Edina, Mn.: Interaction Book Company.

Johnson, R. H., and M. D. Lobb. 1959. Jefferson County, Colorado completes three-year study of staffing, changing class-size, programming and scheduling. *National Association of Secondary School Principals Bulletin 43*: 57–78.

Johnston, M. 1985. *Syntactic and Morphological Progressions in Learner English*. Canberra: Department of Immigration and Ethnic Affairs.

Jones, L. 1979. *Notions in English*. Cambridge: Cambridge University Press.

Jorden, E. H., and M. Noda. 1987. *Japanese: The Spoken Language*. Hartford: Yale University Press.

Joyce, B. (ed.). 1990. Changing school culture through staff development. *The 1990 ASCD Yearbook*. Alexandria, Va.: Association for Supervision and Curriculum Development.

Joyce, B., and B. Showers, 1982. The coaching of teaching. *Educational Leadership 40*: 4–10.

1987. Low-cost arrangements for peer-coaching. *Journal of Staff Development 8*(1): 22–4.

1988. *Student Achievement through Staff Development*. Harlow: Longman.

Kagan, S. 1986. Cooperative learning and sociocultural factors in schooling. In *Beyond Language: Social and Cultural Factors in Schooling Language Minority Students*. Bilingual Education Office, California State Department of Education, Sacramento, California. Los Angeles: Evaluation, Dissemination and Assessment Center, California State University, Los Angeles.

1989. *Cooperative Learning. Resources for Teachers*. Riverside, Ca.: University of California, Riverside.

Kelly, G. A. 1955. *A Theory of Personality. The Psychology of Personal Constructs*. New York: Norton and Company.

Kemmis, S., and R. McTaggart (eds.). 1987. *The Action Research Planner*. 3rd ed. Geelong, Australia: Deakin University Press.

Kirk, J., and M. Miller. 1986. *Reliability and Validity in Qualitative Research*. Newbury Park, Ca.: Sage Publications.

Kohonen, V. 1987. Towards experiential learning of elementary English. A theoretical outline of an English and Finnish teaching experiment in elementary learning. *University of Tampere: Reports from the Department of Teacher Training in Tampere A 8*. Tampere, Finland.

1989. *Experiential Language Learning: Towards Second Language Learning as Learner Education*. University of California, Santa Cruz: Bilingual Research Group #89–04.

Kolb, D. 1984. *Experiential Learning. Experience as the Source of Learning and Development*. Englewood Cliffs, N.J.: Prentice-Hall.

Krashen, S. 1982. *Principles and Practice in Second Language Acquisition*. Oxford: Pergamon Press.

1987. Applications of psycholinguistic research to the classroom. In J. C. Richards and M. H. Long (eds.), *Methodology in TESOL*. Rowley, Mass.: Newbury House.

Langston, C. and M. Maxwell. 1988. Holistic judgment of texts by Deaf and ESL students. *Sign Language Studies 60*: 295–312.

Larsen-Freeman, D. H., and M. H. Long. 1991. *An Introduction to Second Language Acquisition Research*. Harlow: Longman.

References

Lave, J. 1978. Tailored learning: education and cognitive skills among tribal craftsmen in West Africa. Unpublished manuscript. University of California, Irvine.

Legutke, M. 1988. *Lebendiger englischunterricht*. Bochum: Kamp.

Lemke, J. 1985. *Using Language in the Classroom*. Victoria, Australia: Deakin University Press.

Levi, P. 1989. *Other People's Trades*. New York: Summit Books.

Littlewood, W. 1981. *Communicative Language Teaching*. Cambridge: Cambridge University Press.

Long, M. H. 1981. Input, interaction and second language acquisition. In H. Winitz (ed.) Native Language and Foreign Language Acquisition. *Annals of the New York Academy of Science*, 379.

   1989. Task, group and task-group interactions. *University of Hawaii Working Papers in ESL 8*(2): 1–26.

Long, M. H., L. Adams, M. McLean and F. Castaños. 1976. Doing things with words: verbal interaction in lockstep and small group classroom situations. In J. F. Fanselow and R. Crymes (eds.), *On TESOL '76*. Washington, D.C.: TESOL.

Long, M. H., and G. Crookes. Undated. Units of analysis in syllabus design. Unpublished manuscript. Manoa: University of Hawaii.

Long, M. H., and P. A. Porter. 1985. Group work, interlanguage talk and second language acquisition. *TESOL Quarterly 19*(2): 207–28.

Marx, R. W., and J. Walsh. 1988. Learning from academic tasks. *The Elementary School Journal 88*(3): 207–19.

Maxwell, M. M. 1979. A model for curriculum development at the middle and upper school levels in programs for the Deaf. *American Annals of the Deaf 124*: 425–32.

Mayor, A. 1988. *Open Season*. New York: Putnam.

McLaughlin, B. 1987. *Theories of Second Language Learning*. London: Edward Arnold.

McNiff, J. 1988. *Action Research: Principles and Practice*. Basingstoke, England: Macmillan Education Ltd.

Meath-Lang, B., and Albertini, J. 1983. English for Specific Purposes in the clinical setting: applications for Hearing Impaired language learners. *Journal of the Academy of Rehabilitative Audiology 16*: 271–82.

Miller, J. 1988. *The Holistic Curriculum*. Toronto: OISE Press.

Ministry of Education, Japan. 1983. Course of study for lower secondary schools in Japan. Printing Bureau, Ministry of Finance, Japan.

Mohan, B., and S. Helmer. 1988. Context and second language development. *Applied Linguistics 9*(3): 275–92.

Mohr, M. M., and M. S. MacLean. 1987. *Working Together: A Guide for Teacher-research*. Urbana, Ill.: National Council of Teachers of English.

Morrow, K. 1981. Principles of communicative methodology. In K. Johnson and K. Morrow (eds.), *Communication in the Classroom*. Harlow: Longman.

Munby, J. 1978. *Communicative Syllabus Design*. Cambridge: Cambridge University Press.

Murray, D. E. In preparation. *Conversation for Action: The Computer Terminal as Medium of Communication*. The Hague, Holland: John Benjamin.

Myers, M. 1985. *The Teacher-researcher: How to Study Writing in the Classroom*. Urbana, Ill.: National Council of Teachers of English.

Newkirk, T., and N. Atwell. 1988. *Understanding Writing: Ways of Observing, Learning and Teaching*. 2nd ed. Portsmouth, N.H.: Heinemann.

Newport, E. 1988. Constraints on learning and their role in language acquisition: studies in the acquisition of American Sign Language. *Language Services 10*: 147–72.

Nixon, J. (ed.). 1981. *A Teacher's Guide to Action Research: Evaluation, Enquiry and Development in the Classroom*. London: Grant McIntyre.

North, S. M. 1987. *The Making of Knowledge in Composition: Portrait of An Emerging Field*. Montclair, N.J.: Boynton/Cook.

Nunan, D. 1987. *The Teacher as Curriculum Developer*. Adelaide: National Curriculum Resource Centre.

1988. *The Learner-Centred Curriculum*. Cambridge: Cambridge University Press.

1989a. *Designing Tasks for the Communicative Classroom*. Cambridge: Cambridge University Press.

1989b. *Understanding Language Classrooms: A Guide for Teacher Initiated Action*. London: Prentice-Hall.

1989c. *New Arrivals: Initial-Elementary Proficiency. A Curriculum Framework for Adult Second Language Learners*. Sydney: National Centre for English Language Teaching and Research.

Nystrand, M. 1982. Rhetoric's 'audience' and linguistics' 'speech community': implications for understanding writing, reading and text. In M. Nystrand (ed.), *What Writers Know: The Language, Process, and Structure of Written Discourse*. New York: Academic Press.

O'Brien, T. 1989. Some thoughts on treasure-keeping. *Phi Delta Kappan 70*(5): 360–5.

Ochs, E. 1988. *Culture and Language Development*. Cambridge: Cambridge University Press.

Ochsner, R. 1979. A poetics of second language acquisition. *Language Learning 29*: 1.

O'Connell, S. 1987. *Focus on First Certificate*. London: Collins.

Odell, L. 1976. Classroom teachers as researchers. *English Journal 65*: 106–11.

1979. Teachers of composition and needed research in discourse theory. *College Composition and Communication 30*: 39–45.

1985. Beyond the text: relations between writing and social context. In L. Odell and D. Goswami (eds.), *Writing in Nonacademic Settings*. New York: Guilford Press.

Olson, D. 1981. Writing: the divorce of the author from the text. In B. M. Kroll and R. J. Vann (eds.), *Exploring Speaking–Writing Relationships: Connections and Contrasts*. Urbana, Ill.: National Council of Teachers of English.

1984. 'See! jumping!' Some oral language antecedents of literacy. In H. Goelman, A. Oberg and F. Smith (eds.), *Awakening to Literacy*. Exeter, N.H.: Heinemann.

References

O'Malley, M. 1987. The effects of training in the use of learning strategies on acquiring English as a second language. In A. Wenden and J. Rubin (eds.), *Learner Strategies in Language Learning*. Englewood Cliffs, N.J.: Prentice-Hall.

O' Malley, M., and A. Chamot. 1990. *Learning Strategies in Second Language Acquisition*. Cambridge: Cambridge University Press.

Ong, W. J. 1982. *Quality and Literacy: The Technologizing of the Word*. London: Methuen.

Padden, C., and T. Humphries. 1988. *Deaf in America: Voices from a Culture*. Cambridge, Mass.: Harvard University Press.

Paradis, J., D. Dobrin and R. Miller. 1985. Writing at EXXON ITD: notes on the writing environment of an R & D organization. In L. Odell and D. Goswami (eds.), *Writing in Nonacademic Settings*. New York: Guilford Press.

Peterson, N., and D. Bownas. 1982. Skills, task structure and performance acquisition. In M. Dunnette and E. Fleishman (eds.), *Human Performance and Productivity*. Hillsdale, N.J.: Erlbaum.

Pica, T., and C. Doughty. 1985. Input and interaction in the communicative language classroom: a comparison of teacher-fronted and group activities. In S. Gass and E. M. Varonis (eds.), *Input in Second Language Acquisition*. Rowley, Mass.: Newbury House.

　1986. 'Information gap' tasks: do they facilitate second language acquisition? *TESOL Quarterly* 20(2): 305–25.

Pienemann, M. 1985. Learnability and syllabus construction. In K. Hyltenstam and M. Pienemann (eds.), *Modelling and Assessing Second Language Acquisition*. Clevedon, England: Multilingual Matters.

Pienemann, M., and M. Johnston. 1987. Factors influencing the development of second language proficiency. In D. Nunan (ed.), *Applying Second Language Acquisition Research*. Adelaide: National Curriculum Resource Centre.

Pinar, W. P. 1975. The analysis of educational experience. In W. P. Pinar (ed.), *Curriculum Theorizing: The Reconceptualists*. Berkeley: McCutchan.

Pring, R. 1984. *Personal and Social Education in the Curriculum*. London: Hodder and Stoughton.

Richards, J. C. 1987. Beyond methods: alternative approaches to instructional design in language teaching. *Prospect* 3: 11–30.

Richards, J. C., and G. Crookes. 1988. The practicum in TESOL. *TESOL Quarterly* 22(1): 9–27.

Richards, J. C., and D. Nunan (eds.). 1990. *Second Language Teacher Education*. New York: Cambridge University Press.

Richmond, J. 1984. Setting up for learning in a cold climate. In M. Meek and J. Miller (eds.), *Changing English: Essays for Harold Rosen*. London: Heinemann.

Richterich, R. 1972. *A Model for the Definition of Language Needs*. Strasbourg: Council of Europe.

　(ed.). 1983. *Case Studies in Identifying Language Needs*. Oxford: Pergamon Press.

Richterich, R., and J. L. Chancerel. 1978. *Identifying the Needs of Adults Learning a Foreign Language.* Oxford: Pergamon Press.

Riley, P. 1984. Coming to terms: negotiation and intercultural communication. *Mélanges Pedagogiques.* CRAPEL, Université de Nancy II 1984, 117–40.

Rogers, C. 1975. The interpersonal relationship in the facilitation of learning. In D. Read and S. Simon (eds.), *Humanistic Education Sourcebook.* Englewood Cliffs, N.J.: Prentice-Hall.

Rosenblatt, L. M. 1976. *Literature as Exploration.* New York: Modern Language Association.

Rosenthal, R., and L. Jacobson. 1968. *Pygmalion in the Classroom.* New York: Holt, Rinehart & Winston.

Rosenthal, R., and D. B. Rubin. 1978. Interpersonal expectancy effects: the first 345 studies. *The Behavioral and Brain Sciences 3*: 377–415.

Rutherford, S. 1988. The culture of American Deaf people. *Sign Language Studies 59*: 129–47.

Rutherford, W. E. 1987. *Second Language Grammar: Learning and Teaching.* Harlow: Longman.

Rutherford, W. L. 1975. *Team Teaching – How Do Teachers Use It?* University of Texas at Austin Research and Development Center for Teacher Education, Austin, Texas.

Salmon, P. 1988. *Psychology for Teachers.* London: Hutchinson.

Schieffelin, B. B., and E. Ochs. 1986. Language socialization. *Annual Review of Anthropology 15*: 163–91.

Schmidt, M. F. 1981. Needs assessment in English for Specific Purposes: the case study. In L. Selinker, E. Tarone and V. Hanzelli (eds.), *English for Academic and Technical Purposes.* Rowley, Mass.: Newbury House.

Schon, H. 1983. *The Reflective Practitioner: How Professionals Think in Action.* London: Temple Smith.

Schwab, C. 1983. The practical 4: something for curriculum professors to do. *Curriculum Enquiry 14*: 239–65.

Selzer, J. 1983. The composing processes of an engineer. *College Composition and Communication 34*: 178–87.

Shannon, N., and M. McMahon. 1989. Students, teachers, authors: co-creators of a text. Paper presented at the Convention of American Instructors of the Deaf, San Diego, California.

Sharan, S. *et al.* 1984. *Cooperative Learning in the Classroom: Research in Desegregated Schools.* Hillsdale, N.J.: Erlbaum.

Shaw, J., and G. Dowsett. 1986. *The Evaluation Process in the Adult Migrant Education Program.* Adelaide: National Curriculum Resource Centre.

Shaw, P. 1986. Learning in groups. Keynote speech, Steinbeck Chapter CATESOL Mini-conference, Monterey Peninsula College, Ca., October 25.

Showers, B. 1985. Teachers coaching teacher. *Educational Leadership 42*(7): 43–8.

Singer, I. J. 1964. What team teaching really is. In D. Beggs (ed.), *Team Teaching: Bold New Venture.* Bloomington: Indiana University Press.

Slavin, R. E. 1983. *Cooperative Learning.* New York: Longman.

   1987. Cooperative learning and the cooperative school. *Educational Leadership 45*: 3, 7–13.

References

Snow, C., and C. Ferguson (eds.). 1977. *Talking to Children: Language Input and Acquisition.* New York: Cambridge University Press.

Snow, C., and B. A. Goldfield. 1983. Turn the page please: situation-specific language acquisition. *Journal of Child Language 10*: 551–69.

Snow, C., and A. Ninio. 1986. The contracts of literacy. In W. H. Teal and E. Sulzby (eds.), *Emergent Literacy.* Norwood, N.J.: Ablex Publishing Co.

Spretnak, C. M. 1982. A survey of the frequency and importance of technical communication in an engineering career. *The Technical Writing Teacher 9*: 133–6.

Stein, L. 1989. Some comments on 'Team teaching in Japan: the Koto-ku Project'. *JALT Journal 11*(2): 239–44.

Stein, N. 1982. What's in a story?: interpreting interpretations of story grammars. *Discourse Processes 5*(2): 319–35.

Stern, H. H. 1983. *Fundamental Concepts of Language Teaching.* Oxford: Oxford University Press.

Sternberg, R. 1985. General intellectual ability. In R. Sternberg (ed.), *Human Abilities.* New York: W. H. Freeman.

Stevens, R. J., N. A. Madden, R. E. Slavin, and A. M. Farnish. 1987. Cooperative integrated reading and composition: two field experiments. *Reading Research Quarterly 22*(4).

Stevens, R. J., R. E. Slavin, and A. M. Farnish. 1991. The effects of cooperative learning and direct instruction in reading comprehension strategies on main idea identification. *Journal of Educational Psychology*, March.

Stevick, E. 1980. *Teaching Language: A Way and Ways.* Rowley, Mass.: Newbury House.

Stewart, D., and A. Hollifield. 1988. A model for team teaching using American Sign Language and English. *Perspectives for Teachers of the Hearing Impaired 6*: 315–18.

Swain, M. 1985. Communicative competence: some roles of comprehensible input and comprehensible output in its development. In S. Gass and C. Madden (eds.), *Input in Second Language Acquisition.* Rowley, Mass.: Newbury House.

Swisher, M. V. 1989. The language learning situation of Deaf students. *TESOL Quarterly 23*: 239–57.

Tannen, D. 1984. *Conversational Style: Analyzing Talk Among Friends.* Norwood, N. J.: Ablex Publishing Co.

Todd, R. 1981. Methodology: the hidden context of situation in studies of talk. In C. Adelman (ed.), *Uttering, Muttering: Collecting, Using and Reporting Talk for Social and Educational Research.* London: Grant, McIntyre.

van Lier, L. 1988. *The Classroom and the Language Learner.* London: Longman.

Vann, R. J. 1981. Bridging the gap between oral and written communication in EFL. In B. Kroll and R. J. Vann (eds.), *Exploring Speaking–Writing Relationships.* Urbana, Ill.: National Council of Teachers of English.

Walker, R., and C. Adelman. 1976. Strawberries. In M. Stubbs and S. Delamont (eds.), *Explorations in Classroom Observation.* New York: Wiley.

Wallace, M. 1990. *Training Foreign Language Teachers: A Reflective Approach*. Cambridge: Cambridge University Press.

Wenden, A. Undated. A curricular framework for promoting learner autonomy. Unpublished manuscript, York College, City University of New York.

—— Undated. Metacognition: an expanded view on the cognitive abilities of L2 learners. Unpublished manuscript, York College, City University of New York.

—— 1987. Incorporating learner training in the classroom. In A. Wenden and J. Rubin (eds.), *Learner Strategies in Language Learning*. Englewood Cliffs, N.J.: Prentice-Hall.

Wesche, M. B., and D. Ready. 1985. Foreigner talk in the classroom. In S. Gass and C. Madden (eds.), *Input in Second Language Acquisition*. Rowley, Mass.: Newbury House.

White, R. 1987. Managing innovation. *ELT Journal 41*: 3.

Willing, K. 1988. *Learning Styles in Adult Migrant Education*. Sydney: National Centre for English Language Teaching and Research.

Wragg, T. 1984. Education for the twenty-first century. In C. Harber *et al.* (eds.), *Alternative Educational Futures*. New York: Holt, Rinehart & Winston.

Wright, T. 1987. *Roles of Teachers and Learners*. Oxford: Oxford University Press.

Young, R. 1988. Input and interaction. *Annual Review of Applied Linguistics (1988) 9*: 122-34.

Zamel, V. 1985. Responding to student writing. *TESOL Quarterly 19*(1): 79–101.

Zeichner, K. 1987. Teaching student teachers to reflect. *Harvard Educational Review 57*: 23–48.

Index

Subject index

action research *see* teacher research
AMEP (Adult Migrant Education
　　Program) 231–2

case study 89–96
classroom
　　authority 58, 60, 64, 66–8
　　control 58, 60, 63, 64, 66–8
　　management 4
　　research 56–80
　　interaction 57, 65–76
　　observation 181–7
　　transcripts 66–76, 182, 183–4,
　　　185–6
cognitive psychology 20
collaborative curriculum development
　　230–44
collaborative learning 65–8
　　reasons for 3
　　versus competitive learning 33–4
　　and achievement 33
collaborative research 40–55, 56–80
collaborative teacher education 8,
　　38–9, 179–91
collaborative teaching
　　concerns 172–3, 225–8
　　reasons for 1
　　phases in 166–72
　　strategies for 174–5
　　study of 6, 120–40
collaborative writing 100–17
communication
　　as negotiation 42
cooperative learning 3–5, 30–6
curriculum development 230–49

deafness education 121–40
educational models 30–1
ethnography 41–55, 56–80
experiential learning 1, 2, 11,
　　14–39

FOCUS observation scheme 180–6

grammar teaching and learning 27–9,
　　68–75

humanistic education 1
humanistic psychology 2, 15

input and interaction 83–5

Koto-ku Project 141–61

language
　　and context 50–2, 81, 100
　　functions 53–5
　　socialisation 52–5, 85–9
learner-centredness 2–3, 32, 37–8
learners as researchers 44–50
learner training
　　see learning-how-to-learn
learning
　　tasks 82–3, 85
　　teams 34–6
learning-how-to-learn 21–9
learning process 2
　　phases in 65–76
literacy
　　development 40–55
　　events 101–2

268

Author index

Index